TRANSC

Transgender Migrations brings together a top-notch collection of emerging and established scholars to examine the way that the term "migration" can be used not only to look at the way trans bodies migrate from one gender to the other, but the way that trans people migrate in the larger geopolitical contexts of immigration reform, the war on terror, the war on drugs, and the increased policing of national borders.

The book centers trans-ing experiences, identities, and politics, and treats these identities as inextricably intertwined with other social identities, institutions, and discourses of sexuality, nationality, race and ethnicity, globalization, colonialism, and terrorism. The chapter authors explore not only the movement of bodies in, through, and across spaces and borders, but also chart the metamorphoses of these bodies in relation to migration and mobility.

Transgender Migrations takes the theory documented in *The Transgender Studies Reader* and blows it up to a global scale. It is the logical next step for scholarship in this dynamic, emerging field.

With contributions by Aren Z. Aizura, Nael Bhanji, Lucas Crawford, Jin Haritaworn, Eva Hayward, Vek Lewis, Quinn Miller, C. Riley Snorton, Don Romesburg.

Trystan T. Cotten is Associate Professor of Ethnic and Ger   nia State University, Stanislaus.

NEW DIRECTIONS IN AMERICAN HISTORY

TRANSGENDER MIGRATIONS

The Bodies, Borders, and Politics of Transition

Edited by Trystan T. Cotten

Routledge
Taylor & Francis Group

NEW YORK AND LONDON

First published 2012
by Routledge
711 Third Avenue, New York, NY 10017

Simultaneously published in the UK
by Routledge
2 Park Square, Milton Park, Abingdon, Oxon OX14 4RN

Routledge is an imprint of the Taylor & Francis Group, an informa business

Library of Congress Cataloging in Publication Data
Transgender migrations : the bodies, borders, and politics of transition / edited
by Trystan Cotten.
p. cm.
Includes bibliographical references and index.
1. Transgenderism. 2. Transgender people. 3. Gay immigrants. I. Cotten,
Trystan T., 1986–
HQ77.9.T71587 2011
306.76'809--dc22
2011003237

ISBN: 978-0-415-88845-5 (hbk)
ISBN: 978-0-415-88846-2 (pbk)
ISBN: 978-0-203-80826-9 (ebk)

Typeset in Bembo
by Taylor & Francis Books

Printed and bound in the United States of America on acid-free paper
by Walsworth Publishing Company, Marceline, MO

SUSTAINABLE
FORESTRY
INITIATIVE

Certified Sourcing
www.sfiprogram.org
SFI-00555
The SFI label applies to the text stock.

For my beloved femme Isabella
A woman of brilliance, beauty, and abundant grace

Contents

FIGURES

ACKNOWLEDGEMENTS

My first extension of gratitude goes to Susan Stryker, whose certainty that this topic would be of interest to other scholars encouraged me to publish the call-for-papers after it sat in my research files for two years. Without her encouragement the call might still be in my files today.

I am also most grateful to the scholars whose work is featured here. Their cutting-edge brilliance, creativity, and professionalism made the writing and editorial process relatively smooth. I also want to acknowledge the productive relationships with several scholars whose work was initially part of the manuscript but are not a part of the final collection. Our dialogues undoubtedly had an impact on my thinking about the intersections between transgender, queer, migration, and diaspora discourses of which I am grateful.

It is important to shore up the unpaid labor and emotional support that (many) partners of academics provide without financial recompense or public recognition. My wife, Isabella Abrahams, has been a tremendous supporter of my research and transition and an important interlocutor on trans and queer issues over the years. Many thanks for her proofing and assistance with preparing this book.

Kimberly Guinta runs a tight ship at Routledge, which makes her and her staff a joy to work with and this project the smoothest of my publishing experiences by far.

I also want to give special thanks to Rebecca Novack and Ulrika Dahl for their invaluable commentary and guidance in the eleventh hour of preparations. Their insight, support, and cheers helped carry this project to the finish line.

INTRODUCTION: MIGRATION AND MORPHING

Trystan T. Cotten

Writing an introduction to this collection is tricky and challenging, for its subject matter not only exceeds efforts to define it within specific disciplinary and discursive parameters. But also because transgender migrations resist the unifying rhetorical function of introductions, pointing to the subject's rich generative potential to open up new critical dialogues and terrains of theorizing in/across migration, diaspora, transgender, and queer studies. So, it is with this understanding of transgender migrations' unruliness that I offer readers a brief, anti-totalizing introduction to the shifting heterotopic terrains of transgender migrations.

Transgender theory has emerged and been spurred in the last decade by queer studies' turn to the global, geographical, and affective in exploring the impact of capitalism's global expansion on LGBT (lesbian, gay, bisexual, and transgender) life and politics, and the roles of gender and sexuality in this expansion. Cross-fertilizations of diaspora and migration studies, social and cultural geography, with queer methods and theory have broadened the analytical scope in each of these fields and generated new critical frameworks and studies focusing on queer diaspora and migration; queer tourism and globalization; homonationalism and homonormativity; the (geo) politics of asylum and citizenship in queer migrations, to name some (Cruz-Malavé and Manalansan 2002; Luibheid and Cantu 2005; Patton and Sanchez-Eppler 2000; Puar 2002, 2007). These disciplinary and discursive integrations and proliferations have shaped and will continue to shape the course of transgender discursive for-mation(s), including the very signifying permutations of trans itself: its critical inquiries and pursuits, analytical objects, and critical modalities.

Transgender Migrations continues this discursive turn toward the geopolitical, spatial, and archival, centering specifically on transgender bodies, movements, and politics in explorations of trans diaspora, subjectification, movement, travel, and migration, conceptions of home, placedness and belonging, and others. We treat the intersections, assemblages, genealogies, and geographies of movement, ranging from bodily biological processes to interlocking mobilities of identity and subjectivity to the geopolitics of transnational migrations. This collection is a rhizome that "ceaselessly establishes connections between semiotic chains, organizations of power, and circumstances relevant to the arts, sciences and social struggles" (Deleuze and Guattari 1987: 7). Jumping off Susan Stryker's query of how we might "critically trans-our world," and "bursting 'trans' wide open," the authors assembled here deploy "trans operations and movements" as a heuristic frame to open up new lines of flight and terrains of critical thought, demarcating new concepts, investigative frontiers, and critical methods (Stryker 2008).

Questions invariably arise. What are transgender migrations? What forms and directions do these movements take? How do they unfold and what bodies, discourses, knowledges, and spatialities do they mobilize, connect, generate, disperse, and disseminate? What new knowledges and critical methods are opened up by a critical focus specifically on transgender migrations? Transgender migrations comprise movements of desire, agency, and generativity without unitary subjects or foundations. They are heterotopic, multidimensional mobilities whose viral flows and circuits resist teleology, linearity, and tidy, discrete borders. Theorizing these movements, we hope to push a broad range of critical discourses—trans, queer, migration, diaspora, feminist, and others—forward to meld, mesh, and birth new concepts that transform thought itself like Eva Hayward's "symbiogenesis," which articulates a trans aesthetics of becoming imperceptible or intense and territorializing towards a post-subject, post-human(ist) landscape. We explore movements and morphings of various kinds involving bodies and spaces in transit(ion) across multiple borders, temporalities, social, and sexual configurations. These geographies and genealogies deontologize space exploring crucial intersections between materiality and movement of bodies, signs, affective structures, and (built) space. We are also cautious not to tie trans to a singular mobility, identity, spatiality, or discipline, and concur with Stryker that trans is more critically productive when it is allowed to roam nomadically across diverse discursive registers, critical intersectionalities, spatialities, and temporalities (Stryker 2008: 12–13).

The first two studies treat assemblage(s) of discursive and non-discursive practices that secure/manage life (bodies) and labor (production) against the backdrop of certain geopolitical shifts and proliferations spurred by the last two decades of global capitalist expansion. These geographies map the intricate processes of (de)territorialization of space inhabited and traversed by bodies marked by complexly constituted intersectional subjectivities. Both explore how discourses of sexual knowledge and affective ascriptions pathologize migrant bodies in contests of (ownership of) public space whose discursive effects produce deserving subjects, token objects, and extinguishable abjects with significant consequences of citizenship for each. They open up how trans and queer are used heuristically in critical discourse, moreover, by analyzing bodies undergoing transit/ions other than gender—national, cultural economic, and geographical migrations—as they interact with bodies transing gender (and other) borders and spaces.

In chapter one, Jin Haritaworn charts the dialogics of (white) queer and trans ascension to disembodied possession through a racial logics of embodied dispossession of Turkish migrants in the Kreuzberg ghetto of Berlin, examining how the exceptionalist discourses enable and obscure these oppositional movements of dis/enfranchisements. Haritaworn builds on the work of Sarah Ahmed and Jasbir Puar with a critical study of queer/transgender necropolitics, affective orientations, and sexual exceptionalism in broader transnational context. He asks how have some formerly closeted, criminalized and pathologized queer intimacies become acceptable today, signifying signs of love, care, freedom and free choice and orienting us (in both memory and forgetfulness) differently towards different queer times and places, from the concentration camp, prison, asylum and "ghetto" to those of national socialism, the AIDS crisis, neoliberalism, and military occupations of the Middle East? Haritaworn goes on to show how these ascensions of white/queer/trans-ness depend on and require Oriental constructions of Turkish migrants as hateful and regressive obstacles to change (defined as neoliberal), whose movement through these same spaces follows a related but deferred time line. These necropolitical conversions translate into social, political and economic gains—queer/transgender enfranchisement through gentrification, legislative and policing protections, and state funding for cultural production and development—for queer and transgender bodies that can access and perform neoliberal scripts of citizenship. In doing so, Haritaworn also rethinks the marginality of transgender bodies and practices in queer movements and spaces.

Chapter two examines political, affective, and discursive developments that converge in the making of Tecate, Baja California's (ironically anti-queer/transgender) "queer" turn against the national tide in Mexican enfranchisement of queer and transgender. Vek Lewis explores an assemblage of legislation, media discourses, local political cultures, town geographies, and moral genealogies in the Northern border towns of Mexico to explain this peculiar emergence of municipal codes prohibiting cross-dressing in public aimed at *travesti* bodies in 2002. But this code, Lewis argues, was not about identity (*travesti*) per se, but about the control of movement in and through space of certain nonconforming gender bodies. Rather, a series of national, political, social and economic forces coalesce to create conditions in which certain notions of contamination and risk came to stick to *travesti* bodies in similar ways that hate and envy were ascribed to Turkish migrants in Haritaworn's study. In doing so, Lewis raises important questions about the "liberatory presumptions of borderzones as depicted in much cultural theory," supported by empirical evidence of how sexual/gender, geographical, and spatial borderlands evolve, in certain developmental conditions, into zones of contradiction and intolerance. His work encourages a rethinking of liberal strategies of representative democracy and distributive justice used historically to counter these developments in light of contemporary geopolitical developments.

The next three chapters treat the ways in which space shapes movements of various kinds—from the biological and sensorial-corporeal to the social, cultural and political—and how bodies in transit(ion) shape, expand, and trans (and queer) space and spatiality. Eva Hayward and Lucas Crawford explore the generative relations between movement and materiality: how embodiment unfolds in continuous dialogical exchanges between biological and chemical processes within the body and the discourses, institutions and social systems of its subjectification. Crawford and Quinn Miller extend the critical scope of Jack Halberstam's transgender aesthetics, moreover, beyond fleshy bodies and representation to explorations of (built) space, architectural practices, and their disciplinary effects and transformative possibilities (Halberstam 2005).

In a clever and rather witty genealogy of hygiene mapping the birth of the modern washroom, Crawford suggests that gender-neutral bathrooms may not be the best strategy to alleviate transgender dilemmas with public washrooms, because they do not disrupt its disciplinary practices of managing bodies, populations, and their movements, but merely continue the regulation of bodies in binary gender codes. He asks how might washroom architecture be transed to disrupt and reconfigure these spatial landscapes and discursive practices, and what shapes would their features take? How would they foreground and make more explicit certain fictions of inviolable subjects and gender linearity and naturalization underlying them? Crawford presents several examples of trans publics that artfully shore up their architectural and historical contingencies and counter modernist imperatives of timelessness, linearity, and order. In doing so, they also produce a counter ethics to modernism, one of "dynamic materiality" that reminds that "material 'in transition' need not move swiftly, linearly, or with a mind to erase all remainders and excesses."

While Crawford argues for counterpublics that dismantle the closet's regulatory structure, Quinn Miller explores how their aesthetics served to mobilize trans queer desire (bodies) and expand queer space(s) for trans queer eroticism, self-expression and cultural expansion. Building on Halberstam's transgender aesthetics and queer temporalities, Miller mines the archives of mid-century queer visual culture to (re) read 1960s and 1970s storefronts, "queer exteriors," and print ads for their *transgressive* aesthetic of fluidity, performativity, and mobility. Evidencing a "legacy of trans participation in lesbian and gay formations," these aesthetics complicated distinctions between the abstract and figural and conveyed important intangibles about the sexual and gender practices of a particular location while simultaneously mobilizing queer and trans bodies. Miller enables an historical understanding of queer counterpublics and temporalities, reminding us that radical, disruptive cultural practices did not just emerge with Stonewall or postmodernity, but have been a part of our queer past long before.

The next chapter points to fruitful theoretical connections between transgender discourses, animal studies, and nomadology. Continuing her project of autoethnographic theorizing, Eva Hayward challenges tropes of corporeal lack and entrapment in transsexual discourses with an arachnotropic rhizome of transpositioning that (re)articulates the boundaries and relations between humans, animals, technology, and (urban) space(s). She moves critical dialogue of the transitioning subject beyond the textual confines of Prosser's theory of trans narrativity and out into its intensifying intertextualities of becoming (a symbiogenesis) with/other animate and inanimate matter, environments and architectures. Linear teleologies and their promise of final arrival in much transsexual autobiography shatter and disperse in infinite fractals of continuing generativity and connectivity across cityscapes, architectural and molecular structures, biogenetic processes, social pulses, and techno-linguistic vibrations that pull this trans special be(com)ing *"back through itself* in order to feel mending." Hayward's transposition, centering the isomorphic corporeality of spiders, horses, trans women and their habitats, opens up new lines of flight in post/ humanist discourse and seduces us to becoming-woman, opening outwardly to meld and mesh with other intensities in transforming ourselves and world.

The next two chapters theorize movement(s) of modernist subjects of transgender yearnings who, coming from meager social origins in an era obsessed with racial, national, sexual, and gender hierarchies, learned strategically how to cross many borders and ride their liminality to continually reinvent themselves. Both chapters underscore the difficult paradoxes of transcendence and immanence of these multiple migrations.

In chapter six, C. Riley Snorton maps the shifting terrain and consolidating movements of gender and racial identification in James Weldon Johnson's *The Autobiography of an Ex-Colored Man*. He traces aesthetics of transgender yearning in the text's complex imbrications of racial and gender identification and critique of Afromodernist conceptions of gender, sexuality, and race. Snorton combines (seemingly) oppositional theories of queer performativity and trans materiality to trans this (already quared) text to show how it is as much about achieving a stable (racialized) gender identity, as inhabiting a racial subjectivity. Significantly, Snorton's (re)reading of *Autobiography* transes the text's normative gender identity formation, which has been taken for granted in previous criticism, denaturalizing its origins and stability, to reveal its psychosexual fragilities as shaped by the projects of African American modernism. In doing so, he highlights the absence of critical intersectional analysis in trans autobiography criticism and the necessity of theorizing textual nuances of gender as both separate and relative to sexual identity in African American literary criticism.

Trans queer female impersonator Rae Bourbon moved through life with vivacity and flare, and, unlike the *travestis* of Lewis's study, managed to turn the paradoxes and contradictions of border crossing into what Don Romesburg describes as a transgender cosmopolitan citizenship to live "beyond the confines of heteronormative fusions of sex/gender/sexuality congruence." Romesburg explicates various components of Bourbon's transgressive aesthetics—transborder discourses, transtextuality, and queer kinship—which Bourbon employed adroitly to navigate the minefields of nationalism, racism, homophobia, and state violence and live a full vivacious life on terms of Bourbon's own making.

The open-ended, multidirectional profusions and intensities of transgender migrations requires a similar anti-totalizing gesture of ending with two inquiries that critique tropes of movement and arrival in (some) transgender discourses and point to further exploratory directions of theorizing in trans, queer, migration, and diaspora studies. Both chapters extend Jay Prosser's work on transgender tropes of travel in important new directions, exploring how their discursive elisions and erasures reproduce various normative structures of discipline and domination. Theorizing from an archive of transsexual autobiography, employer resource manuals, and transition roadmaps, Aizura argues that persistent characterizations of transitioning as a journey outward that is (always already) a return home domesticates transsexuality's potential to disrupt and destabilize binary gender and reifies its normativity by closeting transitioning bodies and gender's indeterminacy to another place (another country, a vacation, etc.) away from public view. These outward returns home also elide the realities of socio-economics, race, ethnicity, nationality, religion, and migrant status that affect transition choices and trajectories, reify a liberal individualist model of transition and meritocracy, and geographically privilege white western middle-class subjectivity.

Nael Bhanji picks up where Aizura leaves off and brings us full circle to considerations of the politics of trans and queer agency and community building initiated by Haritaworn. Reading transgender theory through postcolonial theory and experiences of diaspora and migration, he uncovers the infusion of nationalist, racial, and colonial impulses in certain transgender discourses of homecoming that sentimentalize spaces of normative (nationalist, gendered, racial/ethnic, class, and sexual) belonging. Bhanji identifies the yearning for home and rhetorical sleights-of-hand informing the racial and class politics of queer and trans complicity with normative and neoliberalism regimes that make space(s) like Kreuzberg and others inhospitable to bodies that do not properly orient themselves to these projects and expand the parameters of citizenship for the former at the expense of the latter. Drawing on Ahmed's work on affects and orientations, he argues for the necessity of theorizing the (dis)embodied dissonances of transing from specifically historical and political frameworks that also interrogate the political ramifications of transgender movements toward home, mapping the permeable interwoven relationality both within transgender communities and its linkages to other bodies (similarly displaced and dislocated) who also migrate and are in transit/ions across numerous borders and spaces shaped by global capitalist expansion.

Finally, the disproportionate representation of male and/or masculine identified authors in this collection requires some explanation. It resulted from a combination of chance, accident, and poor timing. The original line-up was more balanced and included seven female, feminine, and/or femme identified authors. However, four withdrawals (at different stages), insurmountable translation challenges, and reviewer commentaries left Eva Hayward as our sole female author. Finding submissions by women in the eleventh hour (and there was no guarantee) would have held publication back for another six months, maybe longer, as it would have required formulating and distributing another call-for-papers, editing, revising, and submitting to additional reviews. I decided against delaying the book, surmising that the one or two essays that we might (or might not) have received would not have changed the skewed gender ratio enough to balance our line-up any less problematic. Bear in mind, however, that a number of our trans, male, and/or masculine identified authors were socialized and lived in female bodies at some point earlier in their lives. The traces of their pasts are grafted (and still legible) on their bodies and consciousness, illustrating the destabilizing capacity of transgender migrations to disrupt (simplistic) categorization and critiques and force more complex readings of bodies, borders, and identities.

PART I
Affective Alien(n)ations and Queer (Re)territorializations

1

COLORFUL BODIES IN THE MULTIKULTI METROPOLIS

Vitality, Victimology and Transgressive Citizenship in Berlin

Jin Haritaworn

This chapter positions itself within a growing body of critical feminist, queer and trans writings on racism, militarism, gentrification, and imprisonment.[1] Like others before me, I seek to scandalize the complicity of sexual and gendered politics in state violence and neglect, and the reinvention of practices such as the dismantling of the welfare state, the mass incarceration of the chronically unemployable, and the wars without end as signs of love, care, diversity, and vitality, often in the name of human (including women's, gay and, in a much more complicated way, trans) rights. In this, I am drawing on Jasbir Puar's queer necropolitics[2] to explore how new sexually and gender non-conforming citizenries are invited into life, to leave the realm of death, and of the perverse, to other "populations targeted for segregation, disposal, or death" (Puar 2007: xii). Puar draws our attention to the sexual productiveness of the "war on terror," which enables the U.S. and other "western" nations to invent traditions of gay-friendliness and sexual freedom (despite continuing homophobia) against a common enemy whose monstrosity is fantasized as intimate im/property.

Here, I will extend this critique in two ways. First, how are exceptionalist ideologies and necropolitical techniques globalized? While feminist writers are paying increasing attention to the transnational, critical queer and trans studies tend to perpetuate an ethnocentric U.S. focus, which evades global inequalities and the unequal travel of political agendas around rights, protection and identity across national and continental borders (see Cruz-Malavé and Manalansan 2002). Nevertheless, I argue that examining the geopolitics of gender and sexuality is both necessary and insightful. For example, how do we make sense of the sudden ubiquity of hate crime activism all over the globe? How does this intersect with the globalization of affective regimes of terror, security and militarization, across different scales, of the national, global and local? This chapter will argue that intimate knowledges of race, class and space may work to bring the "war on terror" home, through locally emplotted stories of injured queers, colorful trans people, violent strangers, and the evocative setting of the "revitalizing ghetto." At the same time, in the course of these stories' circulation through transnational feminist, queer and trans counterpublics, wider familial identities of a coherent nation, Europe and West become imaginable through the fantasy of a shared constitutive Other, and boundaries policed by an increasingly diverse array of symbolic border guards.

Second, the relationship of the gender non-conforming subject to what Puar calls homonationalism (the growing convergence and complicity between nationalist and homonormative citizenship agendas) and its transnational variations has so far been acutely neglected.[3] How have genderqueer and trans people been "included" in necropolitical regimes of hate crime and diversity policing, and how have exceptionalist arguments entered and shaped trans and drag spaces? My archive is limited to a series of homophobia and transphobia debates in late 2000s Berlin, which reassigns gender and sexual violence to "migrants."[4] Given the privileged space of Berlin as a global queer Eldorado, the speed with which local narratives of violence travel through transnational queer counterpublics, and the need to examine totalized notions of, on the one hand, queer and trans politics and identities, and on the other, Islam (which in West Europe interpellate the bulk of the racialized), against their local contexts and meanings, my close reading of these events should nevertheless allow some wider insights.

In this, I will both draw on and complicate existing critiques, which have located the trans subject largely at the receiving end of nationalism. For example, trans people have been described as the (unraced and mistaken) victims of counter-terrorist surveillance at airports and other sites of compulsory identification (e.g., Thaemlitz 2007; Wilchins 2003). Other critiques have rightly highlighted the exclusionary workings of a "homonormative" politics of respectability (Duggan 2003) which has employed gender and sexual conformity as key strategies for assimilation, thus leaving behind trans people alongside the movement's other embarrassing margins (e.g., Namaste 1996; Rivera 2002). Efforts to include the trans often remain, in Dean Spade's (n.d.) terms, "LGB-fake-T," and are haunted by a long tradition of sacrificing trans rights and protections for quick legislative gains. While all this is true, I will argue that we need to depart from an essentialist notion of trans suffering, which cannot account for race, class and other power divisions between trans people, and sometimes perpetuates rather than contests the problems associated with assimilationism (see also Lamble 2008). I will suggest instead that white trans and genderqueer people have actively inserted themselves into racialized debates on neighborhood and nation, often by directly mimicking the very gay identity politics which exclude them. Homonationalism, in this, has been an important route to belonging.[5]

This forces us to re-examine trans agency in ways which trouble dichotomies of "assimilated gays" v. "transgressive trans people," and to think through the shifting and unstable relationships between various processes of belonging and abjection around race, class, trans/gender and sexuality. How does exceptionalism justify the state of exception (Puar 2007), where "our freedom" must be protected, if necessary by force, from Others who "hate" it? What are the emotional politics (Ahmed 2004) of sexual and gendered exceptionalism? How do affective readings of "liberated trans people" and "homo/transphobic Muslims" serve to realign bodies and spaces, stitching the enfranchisement of some to the disenfranchisement of others, often within the same citizenship discourse (e.g., around health, security or diversity)? How have trans activists contested, expanded and co-authored ideas about "Islam" as a particularly gender-oppressive "culture"?

In examining trans and genderqueer reworkings of the "Muslim homophobia" discourse, I am especially interested in how this discourse at once circumscribes and enables trans agency. While collapsing trans-ness back into homosexuality, it also labors towards a public that embraces, maybe for the first time, gender diversity as its property, in order to constitute itself as post-phobic and superior to "homophobic and transphobic societies." I describe this public as an intimate one, as it is saturated with and constituted by affect (Ahmed 2004; Berlant 2008; Cvetkovich 2003). As I will show, different intimacies circulate through it at different volumes and speeds, in spectacles of gender and sexual freedom that invite new performers and audiences to the public stage.

Queer Lovers and Hateful Others: The "Migrant Homophobia" Archive

The hate crime discourse made its entry onto the German scene in 2008. It found its first bodies on the genderqueer scene: In the summer that year, a group of visitors and performers at the Drag Festival Berlin were involved in a violent incident which was quickly attributed to men of Turkish origin, and gave rise to a series of media and policy responses which introduced the term "*Hasskriminalität*" to a wider German public. The privileged place which the gender non-conforming body assumed in the institutionalization of the hate crime framework may at first surprise. Racialized violence discourses were certainly not alien to white-dominated queer and trans scenes, yet the actors who invested in them most systematically followed a homonormative politics. The figure of the victim of transphobia nevertheless became instantly legible as the offspring of an already-existing migrant *homo*phobia script, whose full genealogy must be addressed elsewhere, but whose main landmarks and figurations I will briefly map out.[6]

The homophobic migrant is crafted in the late 1990s, when the big gay organizations turn to "migrants," hitherto marginal to mainstream gay politics, in search of new constituencies, new *raisons d'être*, and an expanded public which will recognize sexual politics as part of a broader, national agenda. Rather than incidental or a natural result of migrant particularity, the racialization of gender and sexuality which constitutes the ground on which the hate crime discourse arrives is the result of performativity, of a labor which, as Sarah Ahmed puts it, conceals itself through repetition and affective proximities (see Ahmed 2004: 91–92). The homophobic migrant fits this family well—he is instantly adopted as a newcomer whose resemblance makes him seem to have been here forever. The ease with which the homophobic migrant becomes common sense in 2000s Germany belies the decade-long efforts which go into crafting this figure: From the simultaneous integration debates and the Europe-wide "crisis in multiculturalism," blown up into a panic big enough to include even gay expertise (an assimilation which occurs by performing an Other as unassimilable); to a domestic violence paradigm which is increasingly Orientalized as a function of "Muslim" cultures and gender relations, thus creating space for new metonymies between Muslim sexism and Muslim homophobia, and women of color and white gay men, who suffer from identical forces; to the so-called "Muslim Test" of German nationality, which attempts to shore up a belatedly reformed law of the blood, or *ius sanguinis*, by enlisting new border guards, and inventing new traditions, or "core values," of women-and-gay friendliness; to the Simon study, a quantitative psychosocial study of homophobic attitudes in "migrant" v. "German" pupils in Berlin, commissioned by the biggest gay organization, funded by the state, and disseminated by the mainstream media, which renders scientific and respectable what by then everybody knows: that "migrants" are *more homophobic* than "Germans," and that the twain, as the unhyphenable categoric opposition under comparison already suggests, shall never meet.

The Simon study (2008) flags the changed terrain of visibility which resulted from this decade of media activism. There is much to say about the research project's flawed methodology: from its reification of *the homosexual* as the undefined and undifferentiated, pre-constituted victim of hateful attitudes, quantifiable through five-point scales and digital values, to its racist categorization, which instructed interviewees they could only be German if they had four German grandparents, and pitted "homosexuals" and "migrants" in a mutually exclusive, competitive stance. Most problematically, the study converts oppression into a "psychological tendency" ("negative affects," "emotions," "cognitions," and "behavioral tendencies") which has nothing to do with the myriad ways in which gender and sexual identities are assigned, produced and policed in everyday as well as institutional encounters of, often, banal violence (Simon 2008: 88). Instead, oppression is re-designed to become a *bad affect* which can be clearly located in bodies already known to be "Muslim." Thus, most of the variables and "items" used for measuring and correlating homophobic attitudes, including religiosity, traditional masculinity, perceptions of racist discrimination, and deficient integration, are recognizable, to both research objects and readers, as crude stereotypes of people of Turkish and Arab origin.[7]

Here, I am especially interested in the visual politics of the study. Several of the newspaper articles reporting on it were accompanied by gay kisses.[8] The images broke with a convention of privatizing, criminalizing and pathologizing same-sex intimacy, and constructed at least *some* queer intimacies (a qualification we will examine) as a pleasant sight. They mediated a new kind of affective knowledge of gay lovers as part of a public willing to protect its minoritized citizens from the hate of Others.[9] Let us take a look at one such kiss, which adorned the aptly-named article "Migrant Kids Against Gays" in the liberal/left-leaning broadsheet *Süddeutsche Zeitung* (Grassmann 2007). (This image can be viewed at the following website: http://www.sueddeutsche.de/panorama/migrantenkinder-gegen-schwule-homophobes-berlin-1.335341.) The two bodies chosen to visually mediate Simon's findings bear a particular "orientation" (Ahmed 2006) towards us. The non-trans men seem incidental to the text, their photo taken maybe from one of the online Pride archives now often circulated. They remain anonymous but nevertheless look comfortably familiar in their gender presentation as well as their whiteness. Their muscle tees hug their gym-built torsos tightly, swelling and folding in just the right places. There is no baggy excess, no angled planes hiding badly-fitting binders. Their hair is short but slick, their 1970s sun shades signify Camp rather than sissy: an aesthetic but virile masculinity that a straight girl might wish for in a boy-friend who could dress a little better.

The bodies of the two kissers claim space, open up towards us. Their kiss takes place in public, on a square maybe. To a queer observer the spectacle might evoke nostalgia, reminding "us" of the kiss-in of the late 1980s (whether or not we are of its time and place), that icon of radical queer history and AIDS activism which, queer historiographers tell us, gave birth to Queer (Seidman 1996). It is the ultimate symbol of transgression, of in-your-face direct action, which claims space in a hostile public that is far from friendly towards queer and trans people and would carelessly watch "us" die (Cvetkovich 2003).[10]

The public kiss in front of our eyes, too, has an audience, but one that is far from hostile. "We" appear to stand close-by, with more witnesses gathered opposite in the background, gathering around the two lovers. As readers and onlookers, we become witnesses to their queer love. Not only do we approve of it, we would protect it even, from Others who lack "our" openness, who are excluded from view.[11] In Puar's terms, the two gay men, formerly marked for death through AIDS, are "folded (back) into life" (Puar 2007: 36). In contrast to the 1980s kiss-in, this performance of queer sexuality draws its spectators in without repelling "us," or repressing "them." The kiss we are watching is not diseased, pornographic or repugnant, but is out in the open. It is drawn out and savored, no quick fumble hidden away in a public toilet, or a closet. It is uncensored; proudly displayed under the rainbow flag.

This imag/ining of sexual liberation as always-already achieved belies, of course, the recency with which full humanity was, formally, extended and is, substantively, still sorely lacking (see Haritaworn 2008). I would argue that the gay kiss, and the new desire to flaunt, sponsor and circulate it, fulfills a specific role in allaying and displacing continuing anxieties around queer intimacies. "We" are able to witness this love communally because of Others who abstain from this communing, who may even need to be kept away, because their intrinsic hatred makes them want to injure this love. Our stance, in contrast, is not necessarily a loving one. Nowhere in the accompanying article are we asked to love queer people (who remain curiously absent from it); rather, we tolerate them as an inevitable byproduct of a free society. Our stance, then, is a protectionist one. "We" can come closer because Others hate them. By positioning its heterosexual audience oppositionally—white bodies that open up intimately, versus brown bodies that shrink back, backwards even—the kiss thus turns us towards a new kind of membership ideology, which enfranchises a new (sexual) subject but in the same breath disenfranchises (racial/religious) Others.

The queer intimacies which become a pleasant sight in the visual field staked out by Simon and his funders, commissioners and mediators differ markedly from the bodies involved in the Drag Festival incident. In its whiteness, its coherence, its liberated desires, and its normative desirability, the innocent victim of "Muslim homophobia" repeats hegemonic values of the neoliberal nation (privacy, respectability, beauty, freedom, choice) in ways which will be complicated for the gender non-conforming subject. Nevertheless, the drama of the queer lover and the hateful Other carves out an affective territory big enough to include bodies and desires which transgress the bounds of respectability. This, as we shall see next, is partly an effect of its setting: "the ghetto," the quintessential scene of crime, danger and sexual violence.

Dysfunctional Ghetto, Diverse Metropolis: Setting the (Hate) Crime Scene

Before turning to the Drag Festival incident and its various mediations, we must attend to its geographical setting, Kreuzberg. The Berlin district has since the 1970s been a predominantly migrant working-class neighborhood, which nevertheless underwent massive changes after German reunification, when it moved from the "shadows of the wall" to the "heart of the city" (MacDougall forthcoming; Petzen 2008). The area was long the quintessential German "ghetto," whose decline is the migrants' own fault, a testimony to their lack of responsibility and integration. The blueprint of this deraced fantasy, as Petzen (2008) and Stehle (2006) show, is notably not Warsaw—but Harlem and, more recently, the Parisian banlieues. From the 1970s onwards, the "Turkish ghetto in Kreuzberg" will provide the natural scene for successive moral panics, both "uncanny microcosm" of what's wrong with society, and "prophetic looking glass" of what's to come if "we" don't put a stop to "this" (MacDougall forthcoming): be it immigration or segregation, crime and disorder, mal-integration and parallel societies, terror and insecurity, or violence against women or queers. It is the natural habitat of an ever-growing array of dangerous and undesirable figures, including gangs, drugs, patriarchs, school dropouts, and women with headscarves, who are later joined by terrorists, honor killers and homophobes. Like other "ghettoes" trans-Atlantically, Kreuzberg thus serves as a depoliticizing figure, which normalizes gender, race and class divisions as a function of "their" inherent deficiencies, and "our" failure to discipline and control them (Lentin and Titley forthcoming).

By the 1990s, this dystopic view becomes overlaid with a utopian one. While "Turkish" Kreuzberg becomes a site of vitality and happy diversity, the "ghetto" moves into "Arab" Neukölln, its poorer neighbor. Jennifer Petzen, in her ethnography of queer migrant spaces organized by people of color with diasporic links to Turkey, traces Kreuzberg's ascent from "*Ausländer Ghetto*" to "*multikulti Kiez*" (hip mixed neighborhood):

> Kreuzberg was both a place to which draft dodgers, queers, squatters and anarchists had flocked, as well as a hip, multicultural neighborhood which became popular with investors, yuppies with young children and students. Social progressives, especially those looking to be on the right side of racism, moved in to prove they wanted to live in a multicultural society.
>
> *(Petzen 2008: 169)*

This intersects with an older transnational imagination of Berlin as sexually exceptional. According to Jen Petzen, the mythical status of Berlin, as a locale that is both "not Germany" and the forerunner of a *more progressive* Germany, also serves to displace the country's image as genocidally racist, ethnically homogenous, and *closed* to the world.[12] Petzen highlights the role of sexual freedom in a collective identity which constructs the Nazi period as an aberration that distracts from the city's "real" genealogy in the Weimar Republic:

> One often hears from proud Berliners that Berlin is not Germany. Berlin has had a reputation since the Weimar Republic for its "anything goes" atmosphere, is known for its erotic and queer cabaret ... and is commonly regarded to be the capital of queer Germany. ... Even guidebooks written for straight audiences talk about Berlin's sexual history and how the city prides itself for being the successor to the wild Berlin of the Weimar Republic.
>
> *(Petzen 2008: 152)*

If earlier generations of queer cosmopolitans have looked to the gayborhood Schöneberg, with its cabaret clubs and gay discotheques, the revitalizing "ghetto," crumbling but painfully, dangerously, and romantically alive, has a particular hold on current queer imaginations.[13] In the last two decades especially, there has been a noticeable flock of queer migrants, both from within Germany and from other parts of Europe, North America and the Global North, into Kreuzberg and Neukölln.

This intersects with changes in urban policy, from a welfare to a revanchist neoliberal model, and with changes in architectural and planning fashions. Carla MacDougall's (forthcoming) history of social protest in Kreuzberg documents these shifts from a social movement perspective. While in the 1970s, the turn-of-the-century buildings seemed destined for large-scale demolition—functionalist planners at the time saw them as backward and decidedly unfashionable—in the 1980s Kreuzberg is declared a "careful urban renewal area." It long remains a cheap area to live, as well as a relatively safe space for queers and people of color alike. In the mid-2000s, however, the 20-year tenancy contracts expire, and more and more houses are sold or upgraded. With its beautiful old buildings (once awaiting demolition, now sites and symbols of vitality), its numerous ethnic eateries and bohemian cafes, and its rebellious counter-cultural flair, the area is becoming ever more popular with newcomers, including race and class-privileged queers, from all over the Global North. Those once confined to the area, on the other hand (who happen to bear the brunt of accelerating restructuring, unemployment and racist and revanchist policing), are less and less able to afford to live in it (see TOPOS 2008). Already, Kreuzberg has the most expensive rents for new tenancies, and is traded as the biggest ascendant on the Berlin property market (GSW 2010: 1; Holm 2010). The district fits the model of the "creative city", popularized by gay planner Richard Florida (2002), whose neoliberal ethos of diversity, vitality, and economic growth very well has space for (some) queers. In this model, queers with race and class privileges, alongside artists, students and other alternative lifestylers, are imagined, in settler colonial manner, as "pioneers" daring to venture into new territories hitherto considered ungentrifiable.[14]

Gender and sexuality have not so far made it into official planning policies in Berlin. In activist communities, too, the role of race and class-privileged queers and trans people as gentrifiers has been neglected and remains unpoliticized outside small informal networks of queer and trans people of color, whose voices are already precarious. Where queers and gentrification have been discussed together, this has often located "queers" at the receiving hand of gentrification by later waves of gentrifiers. In the meantime, it may be insightful that the mayor of Neukölln, known for his brutal policing of the poor, stated in an interview with the Berlin gay magazine that the problem of the district is that it does not attract the right kind of people (*Siegessäule* October 2008). We know from other contexts that the formation of gayborhoods often goes along with the displacement of queer and trans people of color alongside other people of color (Manalansan 2005; Tongson 2007). A well-researched example is the gentrification of Christopher Street in New York City, where the Stonewall riot happened in 1969, now yearly commemorated worldwide as the birth of the LGBT community. As the area is rapidly gaining value, homeless people, many of whom from the very groups involved in the riots (young, gender non-conforming, of color), are being violently displaced by police and private security guards. Many of the gentrifiers are white middle-class gay men who own flats and businesses in the area (*Fierce* 2008; Hanhardt 2008). This brings to the fore how classed, raced and gendered forms of violence come together in the constitution of queer and trans spaces. Above all, it illustrates the powerful effects of economic privilege. Thus, some gay (and presumably trans) subjects now enjoy rights and privileges as consumer citizens who are able to mobilize the state in order to protect their property against racialized and poor Others, both LGBT and non-LGBT.

Such celebrations of the diverse and lively city are also threaded through the Simon study debate. The *Süddeutsche* featuring the gay kiss begins and ends with a description of Berlin as a cosmopolitan city "open to the world," where "a gay politician has been elected mayor twice," and where such findings should be, quoting a local politician, "alarming" and "concerning." This displaces older tropes of difference, which privileged cultural difference, and the multicultural city, as signs of cosmopolitanism, diversity and vitality. The substitution of sexual for cultural diversity also occurs in Simon's (2008) own article, which after celebrating sexual tolerance as a sign of Germany's openness diagnoses people of color as failing this openness through their deficient "integration," which is at once a key variable for their "homophobia":

> The extent of personal integration into German society was captured through five items: "I find it easy to live according to the rules and values of the German culture," "I don't want to live in Germany forever," "I feel part of the German society," "Do you have German friends?" (none, few, some, many, very many) and "How much do you feel connected with Germans?" (not at all, a bit, average, quite a lot).
>
> *(Simon 2008: 91)*

We may speculate that these items would work very differently for people not marked "migrants." In an older liberal multicultural framework especially, a white German desiring to live with a variety of cultures, travel or even live outside of Germany, feel part of other societies, and have "very many" foreign friends, would have passed for the quintessential cosmopolitan. This shows mixing to be a changing and differential sign, which grants some mobility while keeping others stuck, in crumbling houses and neighborhoods, whose spatial and social segregation apparently has nothing to do with race and class oppression, but is an inherent function of bad cultures which *segregate themselves* (see Ahmed 2000). We may thus place different figures of mixing and contact, as well as their Others, in the same plane of analysis: the queer cosmopolitan v. the self-segregating migrant, the queer gentrifier v. the neglectful migrant. We may put the Simon study debate back in conversation with the creative city, by speculating how the discourses on self-segregation, and conversely the "improved social mix" which is needed to "revitalize the ghetto," demand the ghosting of people of color from even these dysfunctional spaces, at the very moment they recover. The study, after all, was designed and written at several mutually constitutive junctures and displacements: Of a liberal multiculturalist discourse, appreciative of cultural difference and cross-ethnic conviviality, by a new assimilationism, deeply distrustful of ethnicity. Of the ghetto as a site of social death and demolition, by the gentrifying inner city. Of a welfare approach to difference, by a neoliberal and penal one, which nevertheless clings to diversity and tolerance for its ego ideal, whose failures become Others' by design.

We can attend to these displacements without succumbing to a nostalgia for earlier times, even if they appear benign against the current context. We may instead revisit the past to understand how we arrived here. I want to suggest a bio- and necropolitical framework for making sense of this highly contradictory place, where scores are sentenced to an unremarkable social death, often in the name of maximizing life, and its neoliberal revanchist idioms of diversity and vitality. The "regenerating neighborhood" is thus figured ambivalently and melancholically, as a site of pleasure and danger where the racialized become toxic remnants whose main use lies in their cheap and exotic labor, products and buildings, repackaged for the symbolic and material service and sustenance of the properly alive.[15]

We shall now examine how race and class-privileged queers, including those whose genders burst the lovely sight of the homonormative kiss, were incited into life in late 2000s Berlin, in the face of huge remaining contradictions around transphobia. I will explore the particular moves and performances which enabled activists to bring the colorful genderqueer body into greater proximity with ideals of diversity and vitality and technologies of protection and punishment, in ways which repeat, diversify and expand the homonationalist drama of queer lovers and hateful Others in the revitalized ghetto, and obscure the homogenizing, gentrifying movement of white middle-class people with alternative genders and sexualities into Kreuzberg.

"In the Most Queer Friendly Street in Berlin": Enter the Gender Non-Conforming Subject

Less than a year after the publication of the Simon study, in June 2008, a moral panic erupted that produced new local knowledges of Kreuzberg as a site of violent homophobia and transphobia. While the incident in question was contested, including between those involved (who variously described the event as a drunken road-rage incident that was neither racialized nor particularly gendered, or as a hate crime committed by members of a Turkish fascist organization), the story that circulated most widely and rapidly was that a group of "lesbians" had been beaten up by a group of "Turks." The event was but the first in an ongoing series of incidents that became rapidly recognizable through the same, increasingly sophisticated, frame of "migrant homophobia."[16]

Ironically, the new sexual episteme on Islam and migration, forged in years of homonormative activism, rendered respectable by the Simon study, and popularized by journalists close to the big gay organizations, found its first real-life "case" in a left-wing gender/queer setting. The scene was the Drag Festival, an alternative event that invited people "from all over Europe and Israel" to come together for four days of performances across the gender binary (Drag Festival 2008a). The characters were a nationally mixed group of performers and visitors, encompassing queer women, drag kings, genderqueers and transgendered people, who on their way home from the closing party at the famous alternative club SO36 got involved in a street altercation which had several of them injured. The backdrop was Kreuzberg, at its most dangerously diverse. In the words of a visiting performer: "I was very surprised that such a thing happened in the most queer friendly street in Berlin" (Zoé 2008a). Both the alternative subcultural setting and its queer and genderqueer inhabitants, then, markedly differed from the assimilationism of professional gay organizing. Nevertheless, and despite the alternative media spaces within which it took place—including left-wing newspapers, indymedia, queer, trans and gender studies e-discussion lists—the debate that ensued followed the well-trodden path mapped out in advance by respectable gender-conforming white gay men.

This may have been because the raced and classed setting of Kreuzberg, and the presence of queers (queers, moreover, participating in an internationally publicized festival), rendered the story instantly familiar. Or it may have been that in order for the incident to become an event, a recognizable narrative of sexual and gender oppression had to be put forth. In fact, the first pieces of information were published by the Drag Festival organizers themselves. In a press release published the next day, which included a call for action, the organizers clearly conceptualized what had happened as *homo*phobia:

> In order to raise awareness of the attack, but also of the increasingly homophobic climate in Kreuzberg, there will be a demonstration on Mariannen Square (the place where the attack happened) on 9 June at 7pm, with the motto "Smash Homophobia!"
>
> *(Drag Festival 2008b)*

The press release and the demonstration were taken up by several newspapers, magazines and internet news sites. All of these represented the event as "homophobic." Many described the people beaten up as "women" or "lesbians" (*tageszeitung* 9/06/2008, *Indymedia* 8/06/2008, *Antifaschistische Linke Berlin* 8/06/2008, *Siegessäule* 07/2008, *Jungle World* 26/06/2008).

Besides performing the bodies and intimacies involved in the attack in a certain way, the debate produced particular ideas about the space of Kreuzberg. It is the "good mix" Kreuzberg that emerges here, a Kreuzberg that is diverse and alternative, and which needs defending. A few weeks after the Drag Festival, this spatial trope is taken up and expanded by the organizers of the next alternative queer event in Berlin, the Kreuzberg Pride ("Transgenial Christopher Street Day" [TCSD]). Starting in Kreuzberg, but spreading in recent years to neighboring Neukölln, where many queers have moved to escape rising rents, this Counter-Pride event is organized yearly as an alternative to the mainstream Pride's assimiliationism and commercialism. The event call protests the "homophobic, transphobic and sexist assaults in Neukölln and Kreuzberg," as well as "fascists" against whom "we" need to unite (TCSD 2008). At the same time, it pronounces itself "against displacement, against discrimination, against commercial shit," as well as against the "gentrification of our neighborhoods," implied to be caused by yuppies. By placing gentrification, violence, Neukölln, Kreuzberg, and fascism side by side—one side, which opposes queers—the authors repeat, and enable, the dominant trope of "the ghetto" as a space of violence and degeneracy in need of intervention. This critique eclipses earlier waves of gentrification and the ongoing displacement of working-class people of color, some of whom are indeed queer, by the market, the police, and the socially and geographically mobile, some of whom are also queer. It leaves no space for people of color, other than as an absent presence in close proximity to the evils against which "we" need to unify. The queer "we" of the Kreuzberg Pride is figured universally, both in its experiences of injury (see Kuntsman 2009), and in its claims to a neighborhood, "our neighborhood," which are both innocent and equally meaningful to all queers. Run over on the intersections are queer and trans people of color, whose safety needs may be quite different, and include both protection from institutionally racist police—for whom sexually and gender non-conforming people of color may be an especially easy target—and a neighborhood which remains a safe and affordable space for queer and racialized people alike. Told as a story of violence, the Kreuzberg Pride call nevertheless drones out the massive, habitual, unspeakable and systematic violence which precedes, enables and follows on from it. It thereby repeats the ambivalent narrative of inner-city regeneration, whose vitality and diversity are embodied by colorful queers threatened by those *who don't like diversity, who hate our lifestyle, who don't like life.*

The alternative queer discourse on violence and gentrification thus repeats the neoliberal and revanchist discourse on diversity in the revitalized inner city. While inserting a certain (white) alternative queerness into the lively neighborhood, it eclipses the political and spatial entitlements of the racialized, and positions them as the enemies of life. This is repeated in media reports of the Drag Festival incident, which described the "perpetrators" as unambiguously Turkish. The Drag Festival press release authors themselves appeared to go out of their way to avoid this racist ascription, naming the "perpetrators" instead as Grey Wolves and fascists:[17] "This is not, however, a 'migrant' problem, as often described by some right-wing German populists" (Drag Festival 2008b). Instead, they highlighted that festival goers had also been harassed by drunken German football fans in the area. While invoking the sign of (Turkish) fascism rather than Turkishness enabled the authors to identify their speech act as anti-racist, this did not prevent readers from recognizing the "fascists" as "Turks."[18] For example, a reporter of the left-wing daily *Tageszeitung*, who had participated in the Festival, described the "perpetrators" as "a few Turks," whom she swiftly linked with the "usual Oriental scene in Berlin-Kreuzberg [which] now seems sinister to me." In the same part, she invoked a "brutal" masculinity and an "aggressiveness in the street which is against everything which cannot be grasped in traditional norms" (Luig 2008). The invocation of fascism did not, therefore, interrupt the circulation of the sexual knowledges popularized by the Simon study, as well as through several years of homonormative activism. It served, rather, to prevent an ascription of racism to the Drag Festival organizers themselves: we did not name the homophobes as "Turks," hence we are not racist. Furthermore, given the significance of fascism to German identities and counter-identities, it served to displace all allegations of oppressiveness onto the Other, who hereby became the origin of not only homo/transphobia but also of racism and fascism. This also served to "politically correct" the actions which followed: a day after the incident, a few thousand mainly white queers marched through, not only Kreuzberg (the "Turkish area"), but also Neukölln (the "Arab area"), thus gluing the "*multi-kulti Kiez*" and the "ghetto" into one "neighborhood" imaginable as Muslim, and demanding similar, albeit unspecified, intervention.[19]

How did the sign "Turkish" and its political euphemism, "Grey Wolf," come to stick, in Sara Ahmed's (2004) terms, to the bodies of "the perpetrators"? Neither their ethnic or political identity seemed clear in the accounts of the "victims" themselves, who did not all position the events in the same way. One person with whom I emailed after the incident, for example, described the perpetrators as conspicuously "blonde." While there is of course no obvious relation between hair color and ethnicity, his choice to describe the perpetrators thus is nevertheless significant given the privileging of hair color in German practices of phenotyping (with "blonde" being an implicitly "white" marker). Even the presence of Grey Wolves was in this narrative largely based on the account by only one of the Drag Festival goers, who according to my informant had provoked the attackers in "a 'game' to see who is more macho, but this game got lots of us beaten up." To cover up their responsibility in escalating the violence, the person then claimed to have seen a Grey Wolves sticker on the car of the attackers, and thereby began a "conspiracy theory" which quickly became the source of new truths about "Kreuzberg" and "migrant homophobia."

Even though the supposed "Turkishness" of the attackers was thus contested, it nonetheless quickly became common knowledge. In Sara Ahmed's terms, affect sticks to certain bodies, is read as residing within them, and emanating from them: Fear, or fearsomeness, is already in the bodies of "Turkish" men, so that the mere mention of gender violence alongside Turkishness (the location of a club, a faint imag/ining of a sticker) is enough to "recognize" the perpetrators as Turkish. This affective reading has nothing to do, it seems, with racist histories, representations and iconographies of violence. As Ahmed explains in her earlier work, the thing about the stranger is that they are not strange at all, "we" always already know them—which is why "we" easily *re*-cognize them (Ahmed 2000).

Unsurprisingly maybe, the wider media cited and repeated these ascriptions. The special issue in the *Jungle World* carried the title "Homophobia among Turks and other Germans." Three years after the "honor killing" debate and one year after the Simon study, the *Jungle World* authors can take for granted the existence of "Turkish homophobia" as an object which can be known, defined, described and acted on. The Turkishness of homophobia is further authenticated in the subtitle "Bissu schwül oder was?"—"You gay or what?"—which is deliberately misspelled, with an additional umlaut on the "schwul" (*gay*), in a mockery of Turkish writing and Turkish-German slang. Not only can homophobes be known at first sight—they are, of course, Turkish, it's in their culture, they cannot even say "gay," and lack a vocabulary for homosexuality. But "we" *know* them intimately. "We" speak their language, while they can only ever mimic "ours."

This cultural imperialism is threaded throughout the issue. The five articles repeat and build on an Orientalist archive of gender and sexuality which should by now be familiar. The main article (Bozic 2008) quotes the Simon study as stating that homophobic attitudes among migrant youth are "significantly more wide-spread," and as citing "religiosity" and the "acceptance of traditional norms of masculinity" as causes of homophobia. Further sources of expert knowledges are the LSVD, Maneo and Café Positiv, all white non-trans gay organizations which have been instrumental in fomenting moral panics over "homophobic migrants," and are again cited as complaining about harassment by "migrants." The only gender non-conforming sources in the article are the press release by the Drag Festival, and statements by Fatma Souad, the organizer of the queer Turkish night *Gay Hane* in SO36. She is paraphrased as saying that "Gay and Transsexual Turks" (cited in the male form, "*Türken*") who "question ideas of masculinity" are treated as "fouling the nest" (p. 3).

While the special issue is described as a response to the Drag Festival incident, the positionalities and visualities that it invites into a sympathetic public are quite different from the injured female-assigned, genderqueer bodies, some of whom were themselves migrants and visitors from abroad. The central actors of the issue are non-trans white gay men, the same gay activists who have long invested in the "migrant homophobia" debate and will benefit from the resulting policy changes. In the lead article, "transphobia" is mentioned only once, but "homophobia" or *Schwulenfeindlichkeit* (hostility towards gay men) 22 times. On the title, there is not a single reference to transphobia. On the contrary, the subtitle announces the forthcoming Pride as "protesting against sexist incidents in Kreuzberg and Neukölln."

Nevertheless, drag is chosen to visually mediate the topic of "Turkish homophobia" on the cover of the special issue. In front of an urban silhouette, "queers" are beating up "Turks," two opposing groups whose stark contrasts are marked through their coloring and shape. While the "queers" are wearing colorful clothes—three wear little dresses, one wears leather—the "Turks" are gray, monochrome, and covered. Several of them are labeled as *Graue Wölfe* ("Grey Wolves," again misspelled with additional umlauts on "gray"). The "queer" diversity of features and hairstyles—long, blond, curly, red, shaved—contrasts with the "Turkish" uniformity of styles and expressions—moustache, short hair, monotonous face. The "queers" are painted in lively, moving swings and strokes—they kick, punch, bite, threaten their adversaries with colorful sex toys. The "Turks," on the other hand, are in straight lines—they are square and rigid, leaning *back*wards, or immobile, fixed; standing still. They look primitive, and this inscription racial: the big noses, bent bodies, long arms, which hang at the level of the genitals, are suggestive of extreme-right iconography, rather than of a left-wing newspaper.

The two groups move in different directions. While the "queers" are moving towards the "Turks" (albeit with force), the latter move backwards. Their homo/transphobia appears to be at the same time a refusal, in Sara Ahmed's (2006) terms, to orient themselves towards the "right" objects. The passivity of the Oriental, who can only be shaken up by force, has of course a long genealogy, from Karl Marx's

(1968) writings on India and China to Raphael Patai, whose anthropological study *The Arab Mind*, published in 1976, recommended anal sex as a torture method for Arab men. According to Patai, being forced into a passive role violated their masculinity and therefore presented the ultimate degrading act.

In fact, the image covering the *Jungle World* uncannily reminds me of Abu Ghraib, the prison torture scandal which was allegedly inspired by Patai's "findings." Jasbir Puar (2007) has, of course, helped us understand Abu Ghraib as a spectacular performance of Orientalism, rather than a mere instance of cultural offensiveness. Abu Ghraib created knowledges of Orientalized sexuality, knowledges which the debate on "migrant homophobia" implicitly cites and repeats: the idea that Muslim men have a particular, "traditional" masculinity, that they are especially homophobic, but also eternally sodomized—there is a trace of the old Orient in here, which was homoerotic rather than homophobic (Massad 2007). At the same time, this racializing performance rests on a certain knowledge of "queer" sex. Anal sex is at once a tool of liberation and indistinguishable from rape (Puar 2007). On the *Jungle World* cover, this double signification is extended to other queer and trans practices and identities: the use of vibrators, BDSM, leather, and drag.

This euphemizing of sexual violence (as freeing rather than violating) is of course enabled by the use of the comic—a *medium* which is by definition funny and over-the-top. The comic allows the event to be staged as a battle which brings the "war on terror" home. While the winners are clearly the queers, the imagery is nevertheless unflattering. The drag queens especially catch our eye with their big build, their bad style, their furry bodies and faces. The drag spectacle highlights the contradictions of the LGBT participation in racism and war. It has little of the normalcy and attractiveness of the gay kiss. It is, on the contrary, a freak show, which amuses, makes us voyeuristic, draws us in, and repels us at the same time (see Ahmed 2004 on disgust). The war is here waged sexually. Its weapons are anal plugs which are still fuming, a rubber baton which is forced into a bottom, high heels which aim between the legs. The most effective weapon (judging by the atypically emotional face of the Turkish "victim") are the protruding genitals of a drag queen or MTF, which are equipped with a big piercing. This transphobic representation—which characteristically aims at the disgust which modified genitals evoke in non-trans people—nevertheless blends seamlessly with the claim of "German" progressiveness and "Turkish" regressiveness.

The ambivalence with which trans and genderqueer narratives of spatialized and ethnocized violence have been incorporated by the *Jungle World* is reflective of the contradictory context of trans citizenship. The prior emergence of a moral panic around "migrant homophobia" has created space for a certain trans and genderqueer voice to enter into the public discourse. However, this narrative foregrounds experiences of injury and violence rather than expressions of gender non-conforming agency that might threaten a gender system which constructs trans bodies as worthless in the first place. Normalized subjects emerge in this narrative as benevolent saviors of injured bodies and identities, whose innocence and deservingness derives from their need for protection from Others who hate them. The injured narrative that is circulated between gender non-conforming people and their audience leaves intact a system of compulsory heterosexuality and forcible gender assignment, which instead becomes imaginable as "tolerant" and "protective" against Others who are converted into the real origins of violence; the constitutive outside to an expanded, inclusive community. Ironically, the limited space generated by this victimology is quickly ceded again to the same homonormative subjects who have traditionally excluded gender non-conforming voices and experiences from their spaces.

Nevertheless, the Drag Festival debate launches the trans subject firmly into the public discourse. Within six months of the Drag Festival, two action plans are brought before the Berlin parliament, both of which mention transphobia alongside homophobia. The first, by the Green Party opposition, for the first time brings the term *"Hasskriminalität"* to a wider public. It explicitly names "migrants" as the root of the problem, which is clearly defined as a *criminal* one whose rightful arenas are the courts and the police (Bündnis 90/Die Grünen 2008).

To the relief of many observers, the Green action plan, which brims with racist interpretations and criminalizing measures, is hijacked by the "red-red" coalition between Social Democrats and the new, more socialist-leaning party The Left (SPD/Die Linke 2009). The red-red motion, which is passed by a huge majority in early 2010, is considerably more progressive, in part as a result of anti-racist queer lobbying. It critiques a narrow penal approach and warns against scapegoating people of color. Instead, it describes heteronormativity as a pervasive problem, and calls for broad anti-homophobic (and, at least nominally, anti-transphobic) interventions in education, youth work, and the civil service. In progressive sexual scenes, the motion has been received with excitement. Nevertheless, it inherits the racialized hate crime framework. The police, described as (in English) "diversity" and "best practice" model for other institutions, are given considerable space. The motion thus cites a globalized neoliberal citizenship paradigm where punitiveness, efficiency, diversity and vitality become synonymous. While rejecting changes in penal law, the red-red motion implicitly follows the example of Britain, where hate crime legislation served to convert the police into the main patron of LGBT community events such as Pride, LGBT History Month and the Trans Community Conference in 2008, at the very same time that racialized populations were experiencing ever-increasing levels of stop and search and other revanchist and anti-"terrorism" measures.[20]

The red-red paper not only fails to interrupt, but actively scripts, the drama of the hateful Other who must be educated into the cosmopolitan community. This drama comes with a particular setting: An exceptional space of diversity, vitality, tolerance, and freedom, where homophobic acts and feelings should be unthinkable. An innocent victim who besides his (*sic*) sexual orientation has done nothing wrong, and clearly deserves "our" protection. A brutal, senseless perpetrator who happens to resemble older targets of law makers, enforcers, journalists, teachers, and youth workers. The red-red motion, like other media, academic and political texts on migrant homophobia, opens with a particular description of Berlin.

> Berlin is a city of diverse cultures [and] lifestyles … Berlin stands up for and declares its belief in ["bekennt sich zu"] cultural diversity and differences in sexual orientation … The openness of the metropolis Berlin has matured in a long process … However, the shocking attacks on lesbians, gay men, transsexuals and transgenders (*sic*) in the past months sadly also show that the acceptance of sexual and gender diversity is not shared by all people in this city.
>
> *(SPD/Die Linke 2009: 1)*

Berlin is here figured as an idyllic space of diversity, openness and tolerance. Like other narratives of tolerance, however, this fantasy also describes its limits (Brown 2005). Not only is homophobic and transphobic intolerance an anomaly that can be located in particular times and bodies, it also marks groups "in this city" whose cultures and lifestyles are *intolerable*. This description of Berlin as exceptionalist, and homophobic violence as exceptional, is nevertheless nostalgic. It requires a declaration of belief, a leap of faith. The fantasy of a diversity-loving Berlin is in stark tension with the pervasive discrimination which the paper documents: the lack of safety for sexually and gender non-conforming people, especially young people, in schools, in their families, and in the streets; the institutional homophobia and transphobia of police and other authorities; the hauntings of a recently de-criminalized past. The comprehensive catalogue of policy measures appears to hurry to fill this gap, to catch up with a collective ego ideal that fantasizes itself as already liberated and friendly towards gays (and, to a lesser extent, trans people). It is pronounced at a volume which drones out the pervasive violence which the paper decries, and which is neither new, nor exceptional, nor locatable with a few rotten apples.

In spring 2010, the red-red plan is translated into a household decision, promising an unprecedented sum of 2.1 million Euro (2.8 million U.S. dollars) to the LGBT non-profit sector. In the non-profit sector, there is a noticeable rush to include new victim groups and cover the intersections: The Lesbian Advice Centre, who have a strong Black and migrant focus, but have resisted trans inclusion in the past, have begun to build a trans focus. Mainly unfunded thus far, trans projects are rumored to become the big winners of the debate, and have already begun to increase their public profile, most recently through a well-visited Transgender Day held in the town hall, Schöneberg (whose gentrified part is the "gayborhood") in November 2009, which reproduced the usual problems of building a mainly white Northern trans community on the graves of those whose deaths sometimes seem more valuable than their lives (see Lamble 2008).[21]

Conclusion

I have highlighted some of the contradictions of the trans citizenship discourses and practices which have emerged from the German "Muslim homo/transphobia" debate. The unprecedented movement of trans voices and experiences into the mainstream appeared to be possible only as a result of embracing narratives of violence and injury, which in turn were intelligible only as *homo*phobia. In this, the prior racialization of this discourse served as a key vehicle for this movement. We may ask ourselves if there would have been a debate at all if the attack had not been strategically presented as the latest case of "migrant homophobia." While inserting themselves into this debate enabled trans and genderqueer actors to achieve considerable visibility, this visibility depended on the leveling of the very differences which they aimed to highlight. It also served to bolster the very homonormative interests which have traditionally excluded trans and genderqueer people.

Nevertheless, there are real symbolic and material gains for trans and gender non-conforming subjects. The genderqueer interlocutors managed to perform membership, or ownership even, over a Kreuzberg which emerges as the home of colorful counter-cultures. In the process, older ideas of diversity which revolved around race are displaced. Migrants, especially straight people of Turkish origin, appear both stuck and out of place in this Kreuzberg. Backward, melancholic, they orient themselves to the wrong objects. They refuse to move on; that is, move towards whiteness/queerness (which becomes one and the same in this exceptionalist logic). When they do so, it is always in a threatening manner. Straight migrants become "affect aliens" in Kreuzberg (Ahmed 2010). This relies on the mobilizing of a highly essentialist notion of affect, as residing in particular bodies: Simon's "Turkish migrant" who is disgusted by homosexuals and therefore needs to attack. By locating homophobic affect firmly elsewhere, in the body of the "Turkish migrant," who in a post-Fordist environment of mass unemployment is ultimately disposable, new publics and counterpublics emerge and perform, which are able to imagine themselves as queer-friendly. By sticking "violence" to "their" bodies, "we" are not only able to negate ours. We are able to re-imagine ourselves as benevolent witnesses and protectors to queer lovers and queer bodies. Because "they" attack, "we" defend. "Homophobic Islam" thus becomes the constitutive outside of a nation which imagines itself as intrinsically friendly towards gays, trans people, even queers, and is willing to keep those constructed as Muslims out quite literally, through regimes of immigration, citizenship law, or criminalization.

The centrality of transgressive bodies, images, and spaces (drag, the kiss-in, the radical queer left) in the "migrant homophobia" debate forces us to move beyond simple dichotomies of gay v. trans, and assimilation v. transgression. Multiple processes of assimilation are intersecting in this renegotiation of national boundaries, which cannot be understood in isolation from each other. There is the forcible assimilation of a population redefined as "Muslim," which is always already unassimilable. Then there is the eager assimilationism of a new gay subject, who attempts to enter into sovereignty (albeit not always successfully) by assuming himself an assimilatory position towards the racial/religious Other. And finally, the membership claims of trans, queer and genderqueer people, who at once critique gay citizenship projects and mimic them. In the place of a simple critique of assimilation, then, we need to be attentive to multiple complicities and exceptionalisms, both of the single-issue, identitarian gay politics which has traditionally been the subject of queer and trans critique, and of more unexpected expressions of sexual and gendered agency. As I have attempted to show in this chapter, this needs to be extended to the very notion of transgression itself.

Notes

1 This chapter has been shaped by many real and imagined conversations and communities. Amongst others, I am indebted to Agathangelou et al. (2008), Bassichis, Lee and Spade (forthcoming), Fekete (2006), Hanhardt (2008), INCITE! (2006), Kuntsman (2009), Petzen (2005) and Puar (2007). The biggest thanks goes to SUSPECT, our queer/trans of color anti-violence group in Berlin which birthed and held so many of the ideas formulated here and has, since I first wrote this chapter, managed to scandalize many of the problems discussed here (see http://nohomonationalism.blogspot.com/).

2 My thoughts on bio- and necropolitics are indebted to Adi Kuntsman and Silvia Posocco, my co-editors on the queer necropolitics project, which we are currently preparing for publication.

3 The tension of trans and genderqueer inclusion in homonormative LGB-fake-T (Spade n.d.) politics will be further explored in the course of this chapter. On homo-neo-colonialism, see Bacchetta and Haritaworn (forthcoming).

4 The term "migrant," once coined in multi-ethnic coalitions which contested *ius sanguinis* notions of Germanness, now euphemizes the racist paradigm it was meant to supplant: the eternal "foreigner" has largely collapsed into "the Turkish migrant," who has more recently become recognizable through globalized notions of "Islam" (see Yıldız 2009). The chapter is based on an (ongoing) media ethnography and analysis of gay, queer, and trans activations of the "migrant homophobia" and hate crime debate in Berlin which has intensified over the course of the 2000s. In this chapter I focus on trans activists' own articulations in press releases, websites and brochures, and trace their circulation in the broader media, including gender studies e-lists, indymedia and other alternative news websites, as well as the national press. I also draw on my own participant observation in queer and trans communities in Berlin, where I regularly spend time as a visiting trans of color researcher and activist. Since writing this text, the migrant homo/transphobia archive has further mushroomed, resulting in a series of policy measures and political activities which while relevant must remain outside its remit.

5 A further interesting case study is Britain, where the belated extension of rights to subjects recognizable as transsexual under the Gender Recognition Act 2004 coincided with the "war on terror." New Labour policies of diversity and equality ushered in a new class of professionalized trans consultants and community representatives who perform citizenship through voluntary acts of "consultation and participation." Here, too, the hate crime discourse was a central route for bringing transphobia onto the social map alongside homophobia, and the police, alongside the National Health Service, have been a key site of trans citizenship. Meanwhile, stop-and-search and other harassment techniques against non-white people in Britain are on the rise, and "anti-terrorism" legislation has given police unprecedented powers to criminalize racialized communities.

6 See Haritaworn and Petzen (forthcoming) for a closer reading of the history of German homonationalism.

7 See Haritaworn (2010) for a more detailed analysis of the study's findings and methods. The Simon study is also interesting as an illustration of the rise of "psy" discourses

(Rose 1989), including pedagogy, psychology, gender and masculinities studies, social and youth work, in the construction of racialized youth, whose prior "dysfunctional" status is increasingly converted into "criminality." Thus, media and legal discourses on youth criminality are now peopled by hateful young men of color whose bad cultures, families and experiences have rendered them incapable of empathizing with their victims, to the point where incarceration becomes the only effective pedagogy, and therapy (Haritaworn forthcoming).

8 These kisses in turn overlap with an ever-growing queer archive which includes state-sponsored poster, advertising and kiss-in campaigns by the big gay organizations, which are often staged in both gentrifying and neglected "problem neighborhoods" (see Haritaworn forthcoming).

9 Besides the *Süddeutsche* article examined here, the left-wing *tageszeitung*, too, chose an image of gay male intimacy, the hugging protagonists of *Brokeback Mountain*. See Martin Manalansan's (2007) and Heather Love's (2008) analyses of the film (whose globalized intimate public would deserve an analysis in its own right) as homo-normative and metronormative. While I lack the space to elaborate on this here, it is important to note that the proliferation of gay kisses examined in this section is not singular but part of an ongoing publicity and visibility campaign by the big gay organizations which closely repeats national and neoliberal ideals of privacy, respectability, choice and freedom, and more often than not draws on an explicitly racialized iconography and vocabulary (see Haritaworn forthcoming).

10 It is instructive that around the same time, the homonationalist organizations began to stage kiss-ins and kiss poster campaigns in racialized and working-class neighborhoods, thus marking these as homophobic and in need of education and intervention (see Haritaworn forthcoming).

11 Sara Ahmed (2006) argues that politics involve orientation: Which way do we turn? Which kinds of bodies do we identify as part of "our community"? She thus reclaims a non-ontological, phenomenological concept of sexual "orientation" for a critical queer project.

12 Besides the Holocaust, the sharp increase in racist murders and arson attacks on asylum seekers' homes and migrant businesses in the early 1990s was a subject of international attention (e.g., Campt 2002).

13 At the time of editing this essay, I am exploring this with regard to a transnationally produced and cast film set in Berlin, the queer zombie porn *Otto, or Up with Dead People* by Canadian gay filmmaker Bruce LaBruce. Set in a crumbling, graffitied, mortally alive Berlin, the film in fact follows the hate crime script loyally, up to its racialized conclusion.

14 Richard Florida's work has been influential in Europe as well. His creativity index correlates the number of gay people in an area with its economic success, whilst celebrating this as a sign of diversity: "homosexuality represents the last frontier (*sic*) of diversity in our society, and thus a place that welcomes the gay community welcomes all kinds of people" (Florida 2002: 56). Such celebrations of gay gentrification, while increasingly mainstream, are of course not new. See Castells' (1983) early account of gay men as model regenerators of the Castro district in San Francisco. Critical queer discussions of Berlin are missing so far, but see Smith, Sambale, and Eick (2007) on alternative gentrification and Neukölln.

15 See El-Tayeb (forthcoming) for a similar account of race and class in the West European inner city.

16 The political actions in the wake of the Drag Festival were followed by several other actions and media debates, including a kiss-in in front of an Iranian-owned falafel shop whose owner was alleged to be homophobic in summer 2009 (see Haritaworn and Petzen forthcoming).

17 The special issue which the left-wing weekly *Jungle World* dedicated to the incident was far less ambivalent. The author of the lead article actively critiqued the Drag

Festival organizers for awkwardly evading the "perpetrators'" ethnicity. The title of the article: "Homophobic Turkish Youth and the Fear of Racism Allegations" (Bozic 2008).

18 We can explore the Orientalization of fascism in German debates alongside the Orientalization of sexism, homophobia and transphobia (Cengiz Barskanmaz 2009, personal communication).

19 The Drag Festival organizers distanced themselves from this reading: "The cue that the perpetrators may have been members of the Grey Wolves (sticker on car) points to an organized, right-wing group and not to 'the Turks in Kreuzberg'. There is a difference" (my translation, cited in Bozic 2008: 3). They add that "Careful language is important in order to avoid falling into the simplistic 'It's their fault' logic of the racist everyday which surrounds us all." In the July 2008 issue of the *Siegessäule*, the organizers are praised for "managing the tightrope of not allowing the demo to be determined by racisms." But even after the racist media debate erupted, the story was not revisited. In the post-festival brochure, the attack is again ascribed to the Grey Wolves, an ascription which is again followed by an anti-racist caveat (Thilmann 2008: 30). The alternative witness accounts that contested the Turkishness or even Grey Wolfness of the attackers, on the other hand, find no mention. The brochure further contains two interviews with visiting performers from Israel and Poland, one of whom is quoted as saying: "It's not that shocking for us to hear that something like this happened, especially it is not that shocking because it was a turkish extremist organization" (Zoé 2008b). The preface to the brochure is written by Claudia Roth, the leader of the Green Party, who funded the festival. Celebrating drag people's agency in subverting the gender binary, Roth confirms that "Drag is political" and argues that: "Artists from Italy, where Drag Kings are still largely unknown, will report about their experiences as well as artists from Poland and Israel" (Roth 2008: 1). The Drag Festival could thus also be examined as a transnational space where multiple exceptionalisms are at work.

20 While more analysis is needed into the bio- and necropolitical intersection of diversity policing and more traditional kinds of punitive and revanchist policing and militarism (e.g., through the wars on immigration, poverty, drugs and terror), we may note that the homo/transphobic hate crime discourse has already resulted in increased police deployment in migrant neighbourhoods, with the expressed goal of protecting queers, trans people and sex workers. In February 2010, the biggest gay organization opens its new project, the "Rainbow Protection Circle." Held in the city hall of Schöneberg, the district whose nicer part is known as the gayborhood, it is introduced by the district mayor, who greets us with the words "discrimination and intolerance do not belong in a modern community. They belong sanctioned." Praising measures which the city has already taken in order to address what by now everyone knows to be an increase in homophobic violence in Schöneberg, he highlights the establishment of a "safety forum" in order to ensure a "safe living environment"—first and foremost through an increase in police patrols, which have already been sent to the area. Sitting close to the speaker's desk is the lesbian half of the "Contact partner for same-sex lifestyles."

21 In this, trans activists are fast catching up with their homonationalist predecessors. When in summer 2009, migrant trans sex workers are attacked in one of the poorest areas in Berlin, close to the gayborhood in Schöneberg, the event turns instantly into a single-issue transgender topic which has little to do with racism, poverty, or violence against sex workers. One of the organizers brings a placard whose racial/religious target and racialized outlook is quite clear: "Transphobic People Go To Hell!" While I lack the space to discuss this here, we can examine this move from the ghetto into the gayborhood, and the erasure of multiply minoritized trans bodies which accompanies it, in terms of a similar necropolitical conversion. Thus, the reason why TDOR was held in the prestigious town hall, Schöneberg was that these attacks had happened in Schöneberg.

2

FORGING "MORAL GEOGRAPHIES"

Law, Sexual Minorities and Internal Tensions in
Northern Mexico Border Towns

Vek Lewis

Introduction

In 2002, ordinances in the name of "good conduct" were formulated and passed in
Tecate, Baja California, Mexico, as part of the revised Police and Good Governance
Code. The ordinance against youths present in public spaces between 10:30pm and
5:00am was promulgated in May of that year in the name of public peace. The one
pertaining to the presence of "men dressed as women" in public spaces was coded
in terms of infractions against morality and passed in November of the same year.
Those who voted on these new laws—which went counter to federal law in the
Mexican Republic that prohibits discrimination on the basis of gender, ethnicity
and sexual preference—included people from all over the political spectrum: the
Institutional Revolutionary Party (PRI), the National Action Party (PAN) and the
Democratic Revolutionary Party (PRD).

While moral codes against scandal and ordinances against youths in public
have, lamentably, been relatively common across the Republic at different times,
this was the first and only place in Mexico that had specifically encoded in law—
and in recent times—a prohibition against cross-dressing or cross-living at federal,
state or municipal levels. Where gender, sexuality and the processes of legal regulation are concerned, work to date looks principally at federal and state law.
Taking the form of very ambiguous codes against infractions of moral conduct,
most legal frameworks that affect sexual and other minorities in the Mexican
republic obtain, however, at municipal levels, and are understudied as to their
effects and their interactions with local political cultures.[1] Although the Tecate case
garnered a lot of attention from international media and human rights groups, the
actual formation and passing of its anti-cross-dressing code has not been examined
in these terms.

The present chapter aims to address this gap, both in reference to the Tecate case and municipal law and political cultures more generally. Where journalists and activists from the United States reflect on such cases and make reference to homophobia and machismo, understanding Mexico as a place where sexism and the hatred of difference is endemic, they reduce legal discrimination or persecution to a question of culture.[2] I remained cautious of such essentialism, knowing also the diversity of Mexico, especially in its celebrated border contact zones. This is what motivated my research there and my fundamental questions remain: Why did such regressive laws—the one against young people in public after hours, but, for the limits of this chapter, against "men dressed as women"—get proposed and passed in Tecate in 2002? How is it that, especially in the Northern border states, they are either being invoked or tabled on the agenda in some places?[3] What is particular to the Northern states that means that, in spite of the everyday transformation of social and economic relations still in process, gains for sexual minorities that have begun to be secured in Mexico City (such as civil unions and gender recognition) do not obtain in Baja California, Sonora, Tamaulipas, Coahuila, Chihuahua and Nuevo Laredo, for example?[4] Does not this contradict, in some degree, some of the liberatory assertions made in cultural studies about border zones and cultures?

In order to answer these questions considerable data on context is required. It is all too common that people generalize, not only about homophobia or machismo in Mexico, but also about that theoretical field nominated "borderlands." To provide context, I address this problem first, thereby situating my study, its theoretical commitments and orientation. Some critical theoretical approaches to the sociology of the law and the legal discourse are outlined to further define my central assumptions. Then I break down some essential aspects of Mexican law that highlight the discursive lineage that has evolved to criminalize so-called "morally dissident" subjects (González Pérez 2003). Morality is an important concept to unpack and explore, and as such I will pay due attention to its critical role in the social discourses of the time, such as those found in the media; I will also take into account institutional practices that structure the lives of sexual minorities, especially the most visible and vulnerable, here, *travestis*, an identity term in Mexico that intertwines a (homo)sexual subjectivity among subjects birth assigned as male with a feminine presentation. Some *travestis* live in many ways socially as women. Such a definition is provisional and does not pretend to be complete; what is most apparent is that *travesti* oftentimes traverses the Anglo-American divide of gendered identities and sexual ones, and hence does not translate easily to "transgender," a term not always familiar to self-describing gays and transvestites in Northern Mexico.[5]

Having said this, the present chapter isn't particularly concerned with identity claims or disputes.[6] Instead, it is concerned with the making and re-making of the terms of morality in cultural and legal systems, whence said terms arise and how they both assert and insert themselves in the social text. Put simply, what was at issue in the Tecate legislation and the agenda that it established around order and morality was not identity per se, but, rather, the regulation of socially sanctioned forms of public conduct and presence in/movement through space.

Mapping Borders and Border Lives

There are many myths about the borderlands and border people just as there are many myths about "trans" and other sexually diverse people. All have been made into metaphors that do little to throw light on the shifting realities of the borders of everyday life in these contexts (Namaste 2000; Vila 2000b). In the case of all these subjects, the concern is often situated on the moment of crossing. But what of those who have stayed put in the borderlands? What of those who have stayed put or grown up in these sites and are also trans? Such questions are very rarely raised in scholarship that goes under the name "border studies" in the Anglo-American academy. In this regard, Pablo Vila (2000b) notes a misalignment between *teoría y estudios de la frontera* elaborated from the Mexican side and Border Theory/Studies from the U.S. A vision of the border dweller and the border crosser, emerging from Chicano Studies and taken up by cultural studies generally, begins to prevail in the 1980s, and the move from empirically based work to literary and cultural theory is marked. In this formation the "border crosser"—in a problematic use of the singular—is the privileged subject. This work, while rich, has tended to forgo a consideration of differences within border environments themselves. The present study, in contrast, is cognizant of the fact that there is no one Mexico–US borderland, but rather, to quote Vila:

> at least four different border environments: Tijuana-San Diego-Los Angeles, the Sonora-Arizona border, Juárez-El Paso, Lower Rio Grande-Tamaulipas. Each is the locus of very different processes of internal and international migration, ethnic composition, and political identities on both sides of the border.
>
> *(Vila 2000a: 6–7)*

The work of Vila (2000a, 2000b) and also that of Óscar Martínez, *Border People* (1994) is attuned to these particularities within different border spaces. For both scholars, the nation-state, though the dominant influence, is not the only reinforcer of borders; so too are many border people themselves. A reassertion of nationalism and/or regionalism can be found there, which can be expressed as an intolerance for hybridity.[7] This is important to the context under examination in this chapter.

This chapter is hence more informed by anthropologies of space and social relations than border theory. But since the project is also based on interviews with subjects from towns in the region, some of whom were directly affected by the law, I also construct findings based on my own data. The issue of the relation of moral visions to the law also guides the kinds of questions I ask. To begin exploring these dimensions I draw not only on theories of the working and reworking of moral spaces, but also on socio-legal studies and discourse analysis. A central element of the present chapter is the analysis of the law itself and discourse surrounding it. No view of the discursive power of law and legal discourse in Mexico as a whole or in the specific instance of Tecate, however, is even possible without first making plain the critical framework through which I subsequently conduct my analysis. The following section provides a review of chief critical views of the law in order to accomplish this.

Sociologies of Law and Legal Discourse Analysis

Modern and contemporary critical social theorists unanimously view the law as an instrument of power; they differ in regard to its systematicity and organization. In this way they make a key break from functionalist views and question the law's status as autonomous and objective, taking an external view and underlining how and why law comes into being, what are its bases and chief claims, and the varied interests to which it may respond. A Marxist view would hold that juridical forms exist to protect State property interests (Marx 1867; Marx and Engels 1846). Other thinkers part ways with Marx with a view of power relations and the law that encompasses functions beyond the economic: the integration of society, with aspects both repressive and restitutive (Durkheim 1893); as a highly rationalized but permeated system (Weber [1924] 1958); as a setting of communicative action that negotiates the terms of common interests and values in a society (Habermas 1984, 1996), thereby establishing its authority. In a somewhat different vein, Foucault (1975, 1978) connects law and power with the discipline of bodies and behaviors achieved in and through institutional practices and knowledge formations; further, people become subjects of the law via the kind of classificatory individuation at the heart of normalization regimes that aggregate behaviors to certain truths about persons and subjectivity, an effect that congeals over time, subsequent to the set of processes that a law enables. While it is true that Foucault's later work on security, population and governmentality (Foucault 1991, 2007) both supplements and exceeds this account of law and normalization, what is common to most prominent engagements with the force of legal discourse per se is a concern with norms, the establishment of truths, facts, socially produced and enacted meanings and forms of authority and legitimization of certain actors and world views.

The tension between the "normative" and the "factual" is one not deeply examined as Niemi-Kiesiläinen, Päivi Honkatukia and Minna Ruuskanen note (2007: 73); since legal "facts" are not simply "out there" but are constructed through social and linguistic processes, close attention to legal language (as well as social settings in which values attain the status of truths) would appear of great import. To take our cue from Mariana Valverde and her study on English Canadian municipal vice laws (2003) some chief questions might be: If laws emerge from and reflect value systems where do these value systems come from? What do they reference? How do they achieve their power/legitimacy? In the instance of penal law, how are the terms of vice and virtue established, for example? When a judge references community standards, to what facts and truths does s/he appeal, and how are these established? What evidence is drawn upon in claiming the existence of urban ills? If we see that at heart they are moral claims, how are they seen as rational, valid, and acceptable? How do they accrue legitimacy? Have do they have authority as facts or truths?

Valverde underlines the hybrid nature of the knowledges law draws upon. So-called "low-status knowledges" inform the construction of law and its central concepts and assumptions (2003: 2). Says Valverde, "non-expert knowledges of right and wrong, order and disorder, vice and virtue" are present in legal language and decisions (2). The terms of reference that produce understandings of vice and virtue are not empirically based, as her study shows. Framing legal language and action in terms of discursive processes and formation, as Valverde does, is useful; in these terms, law is but one discursive field among others, which interrelate in a dialogic way.

The understanding of discourse I employ here encompasses the level of the formation—which puts limits on what is thinkable about a phenomenon and structures perception around it, in this case, cross-dressing in public—but it also entails, in a way that facilitates my methodology, the level of the *utterance* itself. This is a level that is much easier to isolate and analyze concretely. A critical discourse analysis approach (Fairclough 1995; Van Dijk 2003) will also allow for the minute analysis of the very language employed in the specific case of the Tecate laws, the genres they draw upon, and the formats, models and schemata (normativizing assumptions) traceable in the legislation, especially as these connect to those that circulate in prominent domains such as the media. The media, I hold, constitutes precisely the kind of supposedly "external" social discourse that permeates the law—existing in a dialogic relation with respect to its construction of truths and norms. In the next section I offer some background on the historical textures of the formation of legal truths and norms in Mexico, with particular attention given to the disciplinary domain of (sexual) morality.

Mexican Systems of Law and Normativity

To furnish a better grasp of the setting and frameworks in which legal knowledge and power in its general instance can have any application or authority in the Mexican context, some clarification of the particular way in which legal formations have been shaped in the Republic is in order.

The legal framework for a modern Mexico was forged in the era of positivism by elite members of an old oligarchic sector, during the 30-year reign (1876–80; 1884–1910) of Porfirio Díaz (an era known as the "Porfiriato") and during the intervening period of the *Maximilianato* under French rule, both of which preceded Mexico's revolution. Given these beginnings, the norms expressed in law are deeply classed, embodying a ruling capitalist elite's morality. Indeed, the order of laws that form the historical legal backdrop for the kind promulgated in Tecate in 2002 are expressive of this kind of bourgeois *habitus*, to invoke Pierre Bourdieu, especially those that pertain at Federal and State level in the name of *buenas costumbres* (good custom).[8]

Although many laws that impact on the sexually different were founded during the liberal, secular state of the Porfiriato, their premises are based on religious ones, namely, the spirit of canonic law that sanctions against the expression of forms of lust, which is in effect any form of sexual activity outside the institution of marriage (Castañeda 1998). Since independence in 1821, Mexico followed the French tradition of the Napoleonic Code, that is, anything done sexually in private between adults isn't a crime. And yet regulations around disturbance of public order, causing "spectacles" and "scandals" are another matter. Laws against public disturbance and offences against "good custom" have existed since this time.

That public behavior and the notion of custom (what is normal, what is usual and expected) are the grounds for legal inscription and prohibition clearly takes us away from identity, and into a realm of social appearances. *Costumbres* in Spanish language terms are habitual modes of functioning and acting, as established by tradition, and achieved via repetition to the extent that their force as a basic property or precept becomes beyond question. A performance, of sorts, in Butlerian terms. *Costumbre*/custom suggests something that is done commonly, a group of attributes or characteristics that can be associated with a person or nation. Those said to be against good customs are against the norm, the observance of tradition, and possibly do not qualify as an identifiable part of the social collective that retains/reproduces this tradition. Linked to manners and decorum and their possible lack, bad custom—conduct unbecoming—might undo one's status in society and as a bearer of subjecthood.

Scholars such as Josefina Fernández argue that laws that invoke *buenas costumbres* and *la moral pública* (public morality), established in the nineteenth century, essentially respond to the perceived danger (that may be read in different ways by different social players) of so-called unruly and immoral bodies, and propose the reformation of manners via the universalization of bourgeois norms of public conduct (Fernández 2004: 25).

Such a framework shares much in common with the historical lineage set forth by Foucault (1991) in his account of evolving techniques of security over populations in the context of European capital cities. Such cities acted as centers with economic, moral and administrative functions. The main rationale of techniques of security was to regulate the circulation of "men and things," and thereby ensure the maximization of the common good and the health of the public sphere. Potential dangers or risks to these were to be identified via the determination of whatever stood out statistically as "abnormal": whether that was plague or deviation from a determined normality. Such a vision of the conjunction of the economic and moral and the control and quarantine of threat is supported by the work of Jorge Salessi (2000), who examines the objectification and regulation of populations and the creation of ethnic and sexual others in the context of late nineteenth century Buenos Aires. Salessi's genealogy of the construction of the medico-legal gaze and perceived dangers to Argentinian society takes its lead from Foucault's own framework on security, law, territory and governmentality.[9] While hardly the only "dissident" behavior that would transgress these universalized norms of public conduct, cross-dressing has been "read" juridically as threatening in many places throughout the Republic, even if law has not always singled it out in explicit terms, but instead subsumed it conceptually under regulations of sexual display and morality.

Ivonne Szasz looks at the Mexican legal/penal system in reference to sexual behaviors and norms. All discourses about sex and sexuality are concerned with values, she notes (Szasz 2007: 61). The Mexican legal system, which mixes traditions from both Christian and secular state formation, is bound up with normativity. "To the extent to which juridical norms are articulated in language," Szasz argues, "the examination of legal texts helps clarify the complexity of the links between power and meanings found in the formulation of norms making specific reference to sexuality" (61). Statements such as Szasz's justify my approach here.

Because of Mexico's cultural inheritance, the distinction between moral and juridical norms is especially fuzzy in the country (62). Indeed, it was not until the nominal separation of Church and State (after the Revolution's 1917 constitution) that the move from conceptualizing difference in sexual norms and conduct in moral terms to the terms of identity was even possible, and this has occurred in uneven ways through the Republic, with many jurisdictions retaining a vision of conduct and manners and their moral force. This is important to bear in mind in the context of Mexico, especially in regard to much its theorized cultural, political and economic "hybridity" (see Canclini 1989). Legal and moral determinations are no exception. The section that follows pursues in greater detail competing notions of morality and how these play out in the social domain in the Mexican border towns in question.

Morality: Different Spaces, Different Spatialities

The concept of morality has been subject to diverse elaborations, from those who hold a view that what is moral is a reflection of eternal values of innate goodness, to sociological and Marxist perspectives that explain the origin of morals within society, from which moral systems spring and feed through to individuals, organizing their relations and perceptions. A Marxist view sees morality as the values of the dominant class that extends its particular ideas and beliefs to other groups in the name of social control (ideology). For Bourdieu, morality might be seen as connected to class, but not a form of false consciousness. It might be understood in connection to his notions of doxa and habitus (as previously cited): commonly held but unquestioned assumptions and dispositions, mental schemes and beliefs that explain the world through which an individual moves, but which are subjective as well as unconscious.[10] The outward expressions of these dispositions, beliefs and schemes are thrown into relief when there is a conflict of moralities, assuming that the reigning moral order makes alternative moralities and world views at all visible. The status of a master morality might be explained by virtue of its extension and embodiment in a range of cultural sites, attitudes and spaces.

Morality, which is not solely what people believe but also what motivates their actions, not just a point of view, but something to which all points of view must answer, is lived and imagined differently in different times and places (Smith 2000: 11). According to Chris Philo, cited by Smith, the assumptions and arguments that underlie moral codes "vary considerably from one nation to the next, one community to the next, from one street to the next" (Philo 1991: 16). Smith, drawing on the work of a range of scholars, among them Robert Sack, points to the "moral force of a place [...] its capacity to tie together the particular virtues of truth, justice and the natural, which exist in changing mixtures in different places" (Smith 2000: 9). Although frequently lacking in empirical work on moral discourse, anthropologists have long theorized about its locationality, in reference to the life worlds and folkways of people, Smith observes (16). They have divided their analysis of moral codes and their prevalence and openness to transformation in terms of the "thick," a type which maintains an intact loyalty to local meanings and symbolic networks, resisting what comes from "outside" and the "thin," another type which is porous and permeable to meanings from elsewhere (17).

On interview, many of my respondents—both *travesti* and non-*travesti*—immediately expressed a contrast between Tijuana and Tecate in these terms. Most famous for its beer factory, Tecate is a town roughly 1 to 1.5 hours east of Tijuana by road. In a way similar to other border cities, it is multi-ethnic and displays mixed social composition. At least half of Tecate's present-day population of 91,000 people originally hails from elsewhere. In the midst of a migrational corridor placed at a juncture between border towns and set against a national, geopolitical division with the U.S., Tecate is nothing like its much larger and livelier big sister city, Tijuana, nor Mexicali, to the east. While respondents viewed Tijuana was a place where "anything goes," a place of both freedoms and dangers, they saw Tecate as "staid" and resistant to change, "closed." This can be accounted for, in part, by its different placement in transmigrational flows. Tecate, although it has a border crossing, has never experienced the volume of movement and traffic that Tijuana (and other gateways such as Ciudad Juárez, Chihuahua) is famous for. Neither does it have the immense sprawl that Tijuana or even Mexicali has. It is also a younger town, having been founded as the railway system made its way through what is today's border, into the interior. In Tijuana, one can easily blend in among the many different people that find their way there—as tourists, migrants or transmigrants. There is a certain anonymity of the type found in any big city with a geographical spread. The main choice of transit is car or taxi; the way people move in public spaces is different. Public space is also differently organized. In contrast, in Tecate, walks through the center are a pastime as in many regional cities of the interior. The city occupies a smaller space. If you ask for directions, people query after the family you are looking for. People know each other on this basis, and tend to know what is going on in other people's lives.

In the late 1960s, decades prior to the influx of "elements" from Tijuana, notably brought about by the drug trade in the mid- to late 1990s, one study recorded that 50 percent of residents spoke of the advantages of Tecate as being "the town's character," that it was "peaceful," "small," "quiet," exhibited a "lack of crime," and "high morality" (Price 1967: 15). The same study—now 44 years old—notes in rather pejorative terms:

> Religiosity, while not necessarily centering in church dogma, becomes manifest in the "high moral tone" of the town. The moral orientation of the city can be affirmed by its deviation from the social norms of neighboring towns. Both Tijuana and Mexicali, located within a hundred mile distance of Tecate, have a great part of their economy built around prostitution. People can be seen in these places openly inebriated or lying on the ground drunk from the effects of too much liquor. Both towns have an abundance of policemen patroling their streets. In Tecate, prostitution is absent. Beer is the only alcohol consumed frequently and this is usually taken in moderation. It is difficult to find a policeman here.
>
> *(Price 1967: 16)*

Things have changed, of course, in all three named towns; they have complexified. Notably, apart from working in hairdressing salons, some of the *travestis* affected by the 2002 anti-cross-dressing law were working in commercial sexual exchange in Tecate. And yet, according to one of my informants, a feminist organizer who works in Tijuana but has lived in Tecate all her life, the values articulated by Price are still expressed as reasons to remain in Tecate, which has been less developed economically; in the last decade and a half, however, it is often lamented that Tecate is losing both its traditions and its highly prized sense of order.

Tecate, unlike Tijuana, has never had a tolerance zone for those who work as sex workers in the street. Tijuana's *Zona Norte*, of course, is well-known, and a whole history, spanning more than a century and a half, precedes it. However, in Tecate such spaces do not exist, and the little sex trade that exists occurs in "locales" (private rooms). According to this informant 80–85 percent of the population profess to be "believers"; the majority are from the popular classes—the working poor. Being a small town, the sense of *vigilancia* by your neighbors is a constant. In Tijuana, women, particularly, experience greater freedom and are not simply "watched" for being in public spaces. Indeed, many women secure work increasingly outside of Tecate, and find Tijuana liberating—creating possibilities of independence and self-realization not so possible in Tecate, with its emphasis on family and, according to my feminist informant, stricter gender roles. In reference to different notions of gender and sexual morality, several other informants, resident in Tijuana, composed the following formula: Tecate is *la Virgen Pura* (the Pure Virgin); Tijuana, *la Puta* (the Prostitute); Mexicali, *la Prima Lejana* (the Distant Cousin). One should be careful, of course, not to simply reify such formulations. Tijuana, especially from the northern side of the border, has for a long time been viewed as a source of vice and iniquity, even lawlessness. However, these are not just "northern" impressions; how border cities view each other is also of import.

In the year in which the public order and morality laws were revised, concerns over public security were at an all-time high. José Ramos García and Vicente Sánchez Munguía note that cases of vandalism and drug addiction were prominent at the time, as were the activities of gangs, reputedly brought about from the force-back of internal migrants who had attempted to pass through Tijuana to the United States but found themselves increasingly in Tecate (Ramos García and Sánchez Munguía 2002: 54–56). In other towns like Mexicali, this was and continues to be true; indeed, waves of unorganized and organized crime have spiraled in Baja California Norte, after a chain of developments which will be explored in greater depth further on. The all-too-familiar public posters that cry "ALTO A LA DELINCUENCIA" (end to criminality) in towns like Tecate or Mexicali, splashed alongside in the middle-class sections of town with pro-life posters, demonstrate that public anxiety is something not disconnected from a sense of the risk of invasion of property, body and very embodied moralities.

The physical differences in the cities I have mentioned are also important. As has been observed by Lawrence Herzog, spatialization and socio-economic hierarchization in Mexican cities generally follows the Spanish colonial blueprint— forming a grid work where power emanates from the center square and weakens at the peripheries (Herzog 1990: 72–74). This certainly informs the moral geographies of many towns that have been built along different lines than the urban sprawl of US city design. Tijuana and Mexicali themselves have developed in this US direction; Tecate, meanwhile, has preserved a more characteristic colonial Spanish blueprint. The institutions of that power, local government and the police, lie at the heart of the more elite and "functionary" points of the area surrounding the square. These elements and their spatial placement recall those described by Foucault's work on European cities (1991).

Those poor and outside the main network of economic provision and connection are also spatially plotted as satellite zones. The municipality of Tecate, though demographically small, is made up of such fringe communities spread out over a wider area than Tijuana the municipality. Tijuana city space is more extensive but its municipality is more reduced. When differently spatialized groups within a city municipality cross, for example, from *zonas populares* in a municipality like Tecate to the center of town, their difference can become visible and marked in the elite moral code of the city that regulates and orders flows. *Travestis* typically come from such areas.[11]

Morality and its (Dis)contents: The Legislation and Discourse Around It

It is in this differently plotted moral space that the conservative PRI local government of 2002 announced the revision of its Police and Good Governance Code to add the anti-youth curfew law and the prohibition against cross-dressing in public spaces. The Police and Good Governance Code, which every municipality in Mexico has, centers on public regulation by police to (a) enforce the law, (b) to engender a state of order and legality, (c) to protect property and the public good, (d) to ensure social harmony, health and ecological balance. In the Tecate version, the document's preamble makes reference to these things, adjudicating to police the role as "agents of legality," "arbiters of morality and order," who protect the "integrity of persons in their security, tranquility and enjoyment of goods," as well as ensuring "the moral integrity of the individual and of the family" (Bando de Policía y Gobierno 2002: 1–3). This, the document says, is in the interests of society and "social defence," guaranteeing, via the police and their operations, effective governance (1–3).[12] The role and purpose of police as ascribed here compellingly summons to mind the functions of state reason and governmentality as revealed by Foucault (1991, 2007): to maintain the good of the public order.

In the first chapter of the code, disturbances of the culture of legality and order are manifest in forms of public quarrel, noise, commerce, fairs, rites, diversions, entertainment or ceremonies. Reference is made to maldoers, vagabonds, and the need to remove mad people and children from public view and into protection. Also marked as an offence is the writing of slogans on walls and park benches, especially those in the name of drug consumption or inciting against public morality or the destruction of private property. In this chapter there are also references to public health and the risks of transmission, especially sexual transmission, and then prohibitions against the dumping of rubbish and contamination of public spaces.

Following the first chapter are the articles that contain infractions that refer to the presence of minors after hours and cross-dressing in public spaces (in Articles 31 and 34 respectively). Although the curfew is an important antecedent, having been established prior to the anti-cross-dressing law, looking at the entirety of Article 34 to uncover in what context cross-dressing as an infraction against morality is viewed is especially revealing:

The following are infractions against morality:

* The production and distribution of pornography
* Public nudity and exhibitionism
* Spectacles or numbers in places without a license
* Presence of minors in places for adults
* Alcohol sale to minors
* Betting and gambling
* Carrying out acts inciting prostitution
* Lack of respect toward women, the elderly, disabled and minors

* Being in public under the influence
* Drinking in public, in abandoned buildings or while driving
* Pissing or defecating in public
* Mistreating family
* Carrying out sex acts in public view
* Selling solvents to youngsters
* The male who dresses as a woman and circulates in public view causing social disturbance. (11–16)

The notion of social disturbance loosely connects these numerous and varied infractions. How these have been selected and who may be disturbed by the behaviors mentioned is less than clear. Some of the listed infractions derive from much earlier versions of the code; the "male who dresses as a woman ... in public view" infraction was the most recent addition and is still on the code. Certainly one finds that in the discourse around the addition of this infraction we see traces of the coding of the others of the same article: "men dressing as women" are spoken of in the same breath as exhibitionism, or risk to family and minors. Additionally elements of the first chapter are echoed: risks to sexual health and the reference to contamination of public spaces.

Some of my online research of articles from mainly sympathetic left-wing national papers reported comments from the then mayor who passed the law, Juan Vargas Rodríguez, as to its purpose, motivation and support. Under the title comment "I just want to clean up the city," Vargas Rodríguez remarks on the need to upgrade Tecate's image, protect the natural harmony, order, and mutual respect in the town, and not allow children to see "men dressed as women" and thereby assume that it is correct public behavior, approved of by society (Méndez 2002).

The mayor claimed the support of the majority of townsfolk, and, in other articles, his views were seconded by officials from the Town Hall. Quoted by the BBC online, council advisor José Luis Rojo claims *travestis* disturb public peace and "take advantage of children." Cozme Casares, a senior councilman explains: "The majority of votes for this was to avoid AIDS and prostitution if possible" and for "health reasons" (*BBC News Americas* 2002).

Some 25 years into the HIV/AIDS pandemic, it is accurate to assert that both homosexuals and *travestis*, especially those working in public sex work, have become intensely associated with fears of contamination (as the section on media will show), even if they were not a century ago.[13] HIV/AIDS is a significant factor in profiling how the threat that *travestis* are imagined to present is articulated in culture, and also what motivates and lies behind laws around morality and public order, especially in the area of regulating prostitution.[14]

The statements about protecting children, families, and health help to link the legal force of the Police and Good Governance Code's article's inscription of imputed acts, behaviors, tendencies to stigma and space. Embedded here is the notion that the State incarnates and has ownership over the public spaces and interests. Cross-dressing is an incursion into these spaces and interests. In general, the "public" is associated with that which is of common use or utility for a collectivity; authority over the use of this space is where the matter turns political.

"Public space" in male-dominant bourgeois/capitalist contexts is defined as male. The notion of "male space," that the public belongs to men, has been valuably interrogated by feminists, in connection to things as diverse as labor, social recognition and contesting sexual violence. While those who are unequivocally "men" according to cultural standards can come and go as they please and occupy space as they choose, the movement of anyone who is not considered part of this group, that is, women and gender-non-normative peoples of all kinds, is contingent and provisional: based on rules set down by those who control space. Here I am talking both in a symbolic and literal sense: those who control public space, and who maintain the distinctions of public/private and who "should" be where, in what company and at what times. (The restriction on minors unaccompanied by adults in the curfew code is a good example of this.)

While the framework that understands the gendering of public spaces might go some way to account for the prohibition against "males who dress as women … in public spaces," it is does not necessarily capture what are its chief elements. Although the modern bourgeois construction of public/private based on the (gendered) division of labor and reproduction has been thoroughly questioned (see Bolos 2008), in the political culture of Tecate's then municipal council, this divide is re-installed. It is a divide that concerns sexuality and its expression (not simply gender), relegating it to the private—recalling the tradition of Napoleonic law—especially a sexuality whose expression is deemed negatively productive, with difference a sign for risk to "normal" relations as they are morally imagined. The reference to "prostitution" points up the foreseen need to control both perverse and unruly productivity. The reference to disease impinging on a "natural" harmony coupled with the threat to children imagines cross-dressing as a corruption of a bodily order (degradation/disease) and the corruption of future development in the sanctity of family life.

This notion of social harmony, prominent in the political discourse, has another side that is important to address. Social harmony is often legally articulated in the Mexican context as "*convivencia*." This concept relates to being able to live together in a collective sense. As one writer puts it, showing the relation between this legal ideal and morality/custom laws: "Principles of 'moral pública' and 'buenas costumbres' point to nothing else if not the elaboration of a group of customary norms around collective coexistence" (Millán Dena 2005: 29–35). This certainly obtains a hegemonic character, but it tellingly also potentially unites somewhat disparate groups around certain nodal points that morality names as "national tradition" or heritage. Although government officials and lawmakers will not necessarily invoke morality in the way that Catholic and evangelical groups might, for instance, and may have very different rationales, the invocation of morality often produces uncommon alliances.[15]

Subsequent to the passing and implementation of the anti-cross-dressing code, the mayor who was the law's chief instigator, Juan Vargas Rodríguez, spoke of having fulfilled the public's will. "We have a government that is close to the People," he declaimed (Páez Cárdenas 2002: 5A). The curfew stipulated in the public order article, he said, was to prevent young people from becoming victims of crime (given reports of gang activity) and to remind and educate parents about the importance of the nuclear family. This was passed unanimously, unlike the anti-cross-dressing code, which, although it obtained a majority, met with some opposition. Questioned on this opposition, Vargas Rodríguez assured readers of the newspaper *El mexicano* that, while this was a sign of a healthy democracy, minorities do not rule, majorities do. Further he stated "when minorities, apart from being minorities, incur in behavior sanctioned against by society, they must comply with the norm" (Páez Cárdenas 2002: 5A). Of course, such a statement gives no grounds to a more apparent argument: that his new code in fact creates a norm that forces people to comply in terms of their "public" behavior, or face the consequences.

Again the sense of conduct is underlined, not identity. Indeed, Vargas Rodríguez does not appear opposed to recognizing that minority sectors exist nor does he question their existence. It is when they do not behave in certain expected ways, and when the law and its premises in a shared moral view of acceptable behavior judges this to be so, that said groups fall into the purview of authorities. The degree to which usurpation of normativity is made public, as Mexican sociologist Guillermo Núñez Noriega aptly reminds us, is perhaps more crucial than whether discrete identities are adjudicated as acceptable or unacceptable (Núñez Noriega 1999: 243).[16]

Media and Mediation

In what ways can the statement about "men dressed as women ... who cause social disturbance"—even given law's common claim to truth—make sense? What made this statement effective as a recognizable norm that could be enforced? What I mean is, what sources authorized the notion that cross-dressing, in this instance, causes "social disturbance," and, taking into account the motives given by the town council for the code, that it constitutes, implicitly or explicitly, a threat to order, morality, harmony, mutual respect and, finally, children? And then there are the other two implicit structuring assumptions which point to a typology concerned not just with regulating space, but with registering stigma: the threat of HIV/AIDS and sexual health is arrogated to sex work, and these dangers, in turn, are arrogated to "men dressed as women" in "public spaces." How do these become frames of reference, beyond the "cover-all" explanation of homophobia or fear of difference?

Critical analysts of legal texts and discourse negate the claim to law's autonomy. Law's claims to truth—for instance, that *travestis* simply do disturb public order and go against custom and standards, as often invoked in police and good governance codes throughout Mexico—do not have any kind of empirical basis, but are informed by assumptions about what "community standards" are; the questions raised by Valverde in her study are useful to the Tecate case: What is "good" and "right"? Who gets to represent community concerns, indeed, which community? The critical analyst of legal texts endeavors to make visible the underlying values that structure and authorize these assumptions in a given context, their moral authority. But the analyst who understands the common intertextuality of discourses, like those found in legal texts, looks to other prominent venues for the generation and debate of such values and assumptions in communicative action. To me, the media, as a place of the negotiation of meanings, and one with considerable corporate clout and prevalence all over Mexico, seemed the logical place to go looking for the source of these values.

Travestis emerge as one more suspect manifestation of urban criminality in many Mexican newspapers. They form part of a gallery of *"maleantes"* (miscreants) who present risks to the public. Although also reported on as "victims" of public insecurity, the violence they experience is commonly described as a consequence of their lifestyles and the worlds they inhabit. Victim or victimizer, they present risks to "normal" society, and are associated with theft, drugs, HIV, sex work, as well as intrigue, trickery and duplicity. Headlines are deliberately scandalous: *travestis* are marked for their deviant behavior; their cross-gendered presentation indexes this. It is not granted the status of identity, which is undermined by references in reports to "male" names of arrested subjects. As I have demonstrated in previous research, such representations are by no means confined to print media, and indeed recur throughout television programming (see Lewis 2008).

Looking through local newspapers from the time, such as *La crónica*, *La voz de la frontera*, and *El mexicano*, the one constant across these dailies that emerges is that both the register and topics of reference in the majority of articles generate a multi-voiced narrative centered on values and their everyday transgression. From the high corruption of police and politicians, to the everyday but no less intractable transgressions of public and private, bodily life, the borders of the illicit and the sacred, readers are interpellated in ways that call on their sense of morality, whether that be social, political or sexual. While the line trod around morality and values is by no means uniform, and spaces are made for denunciations and exposés that in varied contexts might be taken as "progressive," nevertheless, the sum effect is one that points to techniques of normativization. There may be contradictions from one article to the next; for instance, on the one hand, politicians are upbraided for their dipping into public funds, a pall thus cast over the trustworthiness of the political system, then one sees editorials on the importance of citizens observing laws. The line of normativity may be moveable; yet there is always a normativizing tendency, and a relationship established between reporters and readers on this basis.

Never is this truer than in the case of sexual morality and values around the family and children. Youth become metaphors of vulnerability and risk. In July, after the passing of the curfew law, *La voz de la frontera* featured an article titled "The family: basis for transformations in Mexico," noting that the country is in the grip of profound changes of all kinds, and drawing attention to parental roles and responsibilities (Jiménez Vega 2002: 7A). Reports on pederasts and young women entering into prostitution are also featured. The importance of upholding the law, and reports on zero tolerance in municipal policy-making are reiterated ("to end anarchy, arrogance, and abuses and to implant a civic and ethical culture of order") (Álvarez 2002: 9A). This article makes use of the phrase "good citizens," remarking, "no-one is above the law."

In reports like these and others from the period, the morally questionable and criminal is thrown into relief. Mixing genres, articles engage their readers in negotiations over moral meanings for acts, behaviors and the occupation of public space. In the period under question, text on the importance of protecting children from hidden dangers, of protecting children from themselves, abound. Indeed, before the proposal and establishment of the anti-youth law we see several examples of a direct engagement with the theme of youth and delinquency, ranging from special feature articles by experts in crime, to notes found in the *policiaca*, the scandal section of each paper that chronicles misdemeanors of every ilk, violence and trespass. Time and again, the age of perpetrators is emphasized: "minor," "youth," "young man with an anti-social aspect," to give just a few examples.

Finding such pieces was not such a surprise, given the way in which research shows just how involved the public is in the production of news in Mexico (Martín-Barbero 1987; Orozco Gómez 1996). However, perhaps in contradiction to the media antecedents found around the "problem of youth" prior to the anti-youth law, very little text directly linking sexual minorities to the register of perversion or criminality was in evidence in the period immediately before the anti-*travesti* law. This is not to underemphasize the importance of the long history of social representations about *travestis* that I have previously highlighted (Lewis 2008). Certainly references to the law, when it was passed, emerge. While they do not attain a criminalizing tone, some are implicitly pejorative, making light of the public fracas of Vargas Rodríguez and what some commentators see as a strange agenda on behalf of the politician (these are Tijuana-based papers). *Travestis* are not referenced as any kind of identity, however; when they are referred to, words like "lifestyle" and reference to their behavior abound ("Homosexuals disguised as women," *El mexicano*, Nov. 7, 2002: 6A).

What was noticeable in the newspapers in the period was the spotlight on HIV/AIDS. "Baja California: Number One for AIDS Deaths," reported an October headline from *La crónica* (Blake 2002: 9A). Four articles in one month (Oct. 28, 29, 31, and Nov. 3) on the topic from this paper connected the phenomenon to migrational patterns, noting that infection rates were also on the increase. In *El mexicano*, the language of epidemia is linked to loitering in public spaces, as the newspaper reports on municipal street sweep campaigns by police. The paper also speculates on massage parlors as a source of HIV (Nov. 8, 2002).

There is no doubt that in the period leading up to 2002 internal migration flows and population growth were at an all-time high. Added to this, as cited in a 2002 Quality of Life in Tecate study, the public demonstrated concerns in that town specifically over the economy, which was experiencing a downturn, and health, as well as public safety. Some concern with crime was noted, with 39 percent claiming it was moderate and 23 percent severe. People said they generally felt safe by day, but not at night in the streets. They were dissatisfied with the number of police (Ganster 2002: 113). Ganster mentions in the same study that Gudelia Rangel, a scholar who works in the area of health and anti-violence campaigns for sexual minorities (including trans women), concluded that few cases of AIDS were actually reported in Tecate in 2002 (114). This breach between empirical reality and what was highlighted in the media as a state-wide problem (AIDS) may be seen as a key piece of data to argue that mediated representations, more than everyday realities, accrued a kind of authority which made any closer analysis obsolete. With the climate of fear around delinquency, organized crime, public safety and risk at its tipping point, the media became an arena for the playing out of a drama without definition or certainty, but with much normative and moral value. In this way they can be seen as forming part of the backdrop to the promulgation of the laws. Although local papers did not always explicitly zero in on gender crossing at the time, the various reports and their logics as outlined above can be seen as providing a sense-making framework through which subjective values and impressions take on the status of the real, and norms become facts. How one makes use of these resources in the name of a moral hegemony—remapping the landscape and populating it with figures of fear—is a matter that speaks to the play-offs in political culture, which the next section explores.

Political Culture and the Forging of Border Moralities

Although, as Roderic Ai Camp points out, "[a] political culture is partially a product of its general culture," the two are not identical (Camp 2007: 56). Culture can encompass beliefs, values, practices, processes and systems of relations that are historically specific to certain groups; political culture is more specific, as it forms at the interface between state and subject. It is influenced by historically specific beliefs, practices, processes and relations but also shapes and reshapes them. Political culture is manifest in the attitudes, orientations and loyalties that people exhibit towards the running of institutions of power in a given society. Political culture is that web of intellectual, affective and evaluative elements which, whether in tune with collective behavior or not, belongs to a particular social group with its own identity. The fruit of everyday experience, secular or religious, the combination of these elements impact on the operation of political systems, and put limits on their success or failure, as Antioko Pérez de la Madrid (2008) argues.

In a culture as ethnically and linguistically diverse as Mexico, while it is difficult to reliably determine characteristics of everyday life that might explain a convergence of life-worlds and world views, for much of the twentieth century, born out of nationalism and hegemony, the country's political culture accrued features that have been well established by scholars. Inheriting the post-revolutionary landscape of the first three decades of the twentieth century, the Institutional Revolutionary Party (PRI) was once the epicenter of national political culture, setting its terms for nearly 70 years until its electoral hegemony was broken at the federal level two years before the Tecate laws were brought in. This had reverberations throughout Mexico, as most of the country had known nothing else but hierarchical, president-centered rule where the difference between the state and the political party was merely a turn of phrase. PRI had garnered at all levels a culture of corporatism—whereby civil society groups were entirely co-opted within the state/party system, and true political plurality was shut off in favor of clientelism, and an executive power that dominated both the judicial and legislative arms of government (Vanden and Prevost 2005).

Although the idea of the state standing in for the people (with all the symbolic gestures) was given its first real shake-up with the famous 1968 Tlatelolco massacre,[17] the major decisive break with the party that foisted a political culture of imposition actually first occurred in Baja California, presaging what would happen nationally in 2000. Enduring losses in 1982, the centralist party finally gave way in 1989 to free elections in that state in which the National Action Party (PAN) gained space, coming to power three terms over the next 11 years (Cleary and Stokes 2006: 22). PAN vowed to eliminate the old politics of populism and presidentialism, looking to make the country "legal," "secure" and "democratic" for investment. This was to be the battle cry of PAN's Vicente Fox, who ushered in the first change of party in nearly a century at the federal level.

The way things have occurred at the subnational and local levels suggests that the populist authoritarianism of the last century is not completely finished, however. Although PAN has increasingly taken over at many levels, PRI still holds 54 percent of all electoral offices, and the transformation of political culture has proven not simply to be a question of change of parties or freer elections. Although Baja California's political landscape demonstrates a mixture of imposition and participation, suggesting that the move to PAN has brought in changes, true involvement of civil society—and a deeper transformation of the state–citizen relationship—is still lacking (Espinoza Valle 2000: 12). This was no truer than in Tecate in 2002.

One of my respondents contrasted Tecate to Tijuana politically, saying that, unlike the latter, Tecate had a political climate that was authoritarian and did not seek to advance juridically. The elite ruling sector was made up of land-owning families that had known each other since the town itself became a town. Tecate had entered into a period of chaos in 2000 when Juan Vargas Rodríguez became mayor of the municipality, the only PRI politician at any level in a state now dominated by PAN and a country led by the same party. The situation on his coming to power was volatile in the town. After some six years of intensified border security following the 1994 establishment by US President Clinton of Operation Gatekeeper, the accompanying dispersal of failed border crossers combined with a depressed local economy created a scenario of mistrust and conflict.[18] Familial-like social relations, mentioned previously, were increasingly diluted. So, too, the ruling political culture of public order, wherein the government was like a stern but protective father and the citizens children, was increasingly complicated in a climate riven by a loss of faith in institutions such as political parties and the police (Brown et al. 2006). Even as of 2002, some 34 percent of Tecate's population had never even crossed the border (Ganster 2002: 124); Tijuana, represented as a space of constant traffic and movement, whose flows now were said to swamp Tecate, was held as the culprit.

If political culture in Mexico has varied since PAN's inception, ranging freely from civic participation to localist and parochial politics depending on the setting (Pérez de la Madrid 2008), Vargas Rodríguez's term represented the reinforcement of the latter, drawing on the over-half-a-century tradition of his party's centralism, and the tendency among people in Tecate to defer to their government on all matters, without actively engaging in the system's functioning. In spite of its reputation as a country where law is not observed, the ideal of legality is something to which a vast majority in Mexico subscribes (Moloeznik 2003: 12–14). In the context of social and economic stability, *tecatenses* responded to the call for more laws and order in a positive sense, seeing the government's role as that of the "protector" of their town and its traditions. In turn, Vargas Rodríguez proposed measures that would increase the surveillance of public space and "suspect" populations and not engage the population in any significant debate or involvement in seeking solutions to both the real and imagined problems that beleaguered the municipality.

Nationally, Vicente Fox promised to eradicate corruption, organized crime and the drug trade, stepping up the militarization of key areas where cartels were in operation; Baja California crossing points were the site of this dramatic escalation. Public insecurity in the state had peaked. This insecurity had both objective and subjective elements. On the objective side, figures from 2001 show that in Baja California 38.57 violent crimes per every 1000 persons were committed, outstripping other states such as Chihuahua, Sonora, Nuevo León, Coahuila, Tamaulipas, and the national average of 12.57 per 1000 persons (Ramos García 2005: 225). The way in which such security is managed has repeatedly been marked by grand gestures, however, pointing to a subjective social construction of fear that preyed on people's prejudices towards groups seen as troublesome or divested of rights.

José Arce Aguilar talks of the use of the question of "public insecurity" as the elaboration of a new electoral merchandise, created by politicians who promise swift measures of legal change to pursue the *males* (ills) that perpetually haunt the landscape (Arce Aguilar 2007: 42–43). In the case of the anti-cross-dressing law in Tecate, *travestis* became such a usable commodity; and in more ways than one. The *travestis* I spoke to threw some light on this juncture. With so many problems beleaguering the municipality, having only just won his recent election and alone in the state as the last PRI mayor, Vargas Rodríguez exploited *travestis* to attract the *morbo* of the public and to distract attention from the real issues. "*Morbo*" is hard to translate into English; but it refers to an excessive interest in "the prurient." *Travestis,* for my informants, pique the interest of the town but mostly for abject reasons. Their utilization, through the tint of morality, could rally people and make the mayor popular. Thanks to their efforts, this tactic of manipulation largely failed; and yet it was predicated on the kind of moral tales told about gays and trans in Mexican sense-making communication forms.

The charge that the law came about as the result of widespread homophobia—and not specifically as a result of a manipulation of a crisis via the use of a moral imaginary—was also cast in doubt by these respondents. I asked a chief informant, Pepa, about what life was like before the code was passed and if they truly noticed any sudden changes subsequent to its enshrinement in the police laws. Pepa's friends—Patricio, Lucho and Gabriela—all gathered round to contribute to the discussion.[19] What were relations with the cops like before the law?

Some of them had *maridos* (husbands or boyfriends) in the force. If they got in trouble, they could worm their way out of things with their connections. This was also true subsequent to the law, but now there was an official code criminalizing public cross-dressing/living. Although none of those present said that they'd been arrested (Had there been any actual arrests? I asked. Yes, they replied, but most of the girls who had been arrested were now living elsewhere or had sought asylum in the U.S.), open harassment by police increased dramatically with the law's founding. Gabriela was pulled out of the doorway of a pool hall by her hair. She wasn't even in the street. Accusations about soliciting abounded, even for those who went to the corner shop to buy milk. The police used this power—the threat of arrest—to secure money or sexual favors from *travestis*. Although prior to the law they had noted some verbal harassment from members of the public, this was not especially pronounced, they said.

Hence, Tecate was not seen—even by those who bore the brunt of the new anti-cross-dressing law—as being especially intolerant, something to which the gays and *travestis* I spoke to there testified. The well-known gay activist Max Mejía explained:

> these days they don't target the gays; years of gay male activism have secured a place in the discourse of human rights that would make references to same sex activity in a hypothetical prohibition impossible. Now, however, the most visible among the sexually diverse—the *travestis*—are targeted.
>
> *(Personal communication with author)*

As *travestismo* is still to gain space as a political identity on the *frontera*, and is articulated foremost as a question of behavior and transgression of morality, it provided in the context of economic and political crisis an untapped reserve to facilitate the social construction of insecurity, made up of the subjective and normativizing imagery familiar in the media. Crisis has not infrequently been translated as a troubling of the two institutions that Mexicans most often cite as their most trusted: the church and the family, both representing the reproduction of the social order and its continuance. In this sense, the state of local political culture, the construction of insecurity and the use of subjective perceptions around moral and even bodily risk (remembering the cited link to HIV) together provided the framework for an attempt at forging a moral and social consensus to control public space and shore up the political dominance of Vargas Rodríguez's increasingly isolated party.

Conclusions

This chapter has offered a reading of the anti-cross-dressing law established in Tecate, Baja California, in 2002 and the context from which it emerged. It has examined the text of the article of the Police and Good Governance Code, reflecting on the conceptual schemata that lie at the heart of the language expressed therein, and the discourse surrounding its production, most notably, in the political setting of the local government that proposed the additional infraction, and the media representations from the time. Further, it has contextualized the bases of these discursive features in terms of the traditions of Mexican law and law's moral commitments. The analysis has also included considerations of the greater social and geopolitical spaces in which morality and moral "truths" are articulated and negotiated, with specific reference to the tensions exhibited at time between Tecate and Tijuana and within the smaller city perimeter of Tecate itself. These tensions were the product of a socially constructed insecurity around the spike in the volume of internal migration and failed transmigration flowing to Tecate from Tijuana, the fortification of the US–Mexico border on which the town is situated, and the intensification of cartel activity, and organized crime, made more prominent due to the militarization of border spaces in the two towns under question. This intensification of violence, conflict and militarization has extended through the greater part of the Northern border and North-eastern gulf states and presents a scenario in which Aguilar's aforementioned political exploitation of public insecurity plays out. Tecate and its anti-cross-dressing law are but one manifestation of that. Cross-dressing was inscribed by the law and talk around it as one more "socially undesirable" expression of risk and transgression that partook of the problems foregrounded in the town at the time. Moreover, the moral interpretation of this purported "behavior," embedded in perceptions of an "other" associated with Tijuana, especially *sex-working* Tijuana, provided material to work with in the punitive politics underway, not just in Tecate, but in other locales exposed to the subjective construction of risk, in its many versions.

My conclusions here point to the above features as possessive of an explicatory power as to why the anti-cross-dressing law was proposed that considerations from border theory, especially in its Anglophone incarnation, cannot bring readily to light. The assumption in much work that goes under that name is that in the borderlands—conceived as a separate "Third" space—cultural and social forms take on a transcendent quality that bedevils binaries and offers spaces of possibility for a range of subjects, typified in the image of the border crosser. Drawing on the more empirical work of scholars of border realities (Martínez 1994; Vila 2000b), one is confronted with a different perspective and forced to reexamine the liberatory pre-sumptions of border zones as depicted in much cultural theory. Indeed, Tecate offers an instance of a border town where narratives of "tradition" and "the people" are actually retooled to serve the ends of social control, to define who, on the basis of a logic of social appearances, belongs to this border society, and who does not. While the notion of cultural purity was mobilized in the Tecate case to clearly ideological ends, pitting an image of national/regional authenticity against the neighbor-doppelganger town of Tijuana, whose most accentuated features are its mixity, "postmodern" heterogeneity, and its moral "looseness," it is not sufficient to simply deconstruct the narrative of Tecate, marking it as an exception. Clearly narratives of custom and manners, in all their moral force, provide a resource that is renewable and far from disappearance in Mexico, particularly in the North.

That decency and public morality laws form part of a Mexican tradition is beyond doubt. However, the Tecate case is also of import for the new-ness of the law in question and the specificity of its terms. In the spirit of Friedrich Nietzsche, the historical origins of laws and institutions do not explain why they still exist. They emerge from conflicting and divergent sites that may temporarily con-verge. Tecate is a case in point, and for this reason it is necessary to attend to the particularities of the moment of the law, its moral values, the political culture that made it possible and the translocal border insecurities and pressures that form the setting from which it emerged—and may emerge elsewhere. Given that Mexican political cultures continue to exhibit uneven mixtures of participation and imposition, and also negotiate a scenario of escalating social conflict and risk, especially, but not merely, in the Northern states, this dynamic requires further attention. Such critical attention, I hold, is necessary not only for sexual minorities in neighboring jurisdictions, but also for a range of other populations who are targeted for "conduct unbecoming" and whose bodies and movements are subject to the redrawing of social, moral and geopolitical spaces in many contemporary border sites.

Acknowledgements

I would like to thank the following people from Tijuana, Mexicali and Tecate who helped me with this study in one way or another: Raúl Ramírez Baena, Laura Gutiérrez, Max Mejía, Víctor Clark Álfaro and Raúl Balbuena. Thanks also to my "border friends" Gaby and Jenny, who drove me around Tijuana and made life fun there; Rodrigo, Carlos, Sergio and Natalia in Mexico City, who set me on the right track and continue to inspire me; and also Erin Taylor in Sydney, Australia, who helped me think morality in a new light.

Notes

1 Mexico is a country made up of 31 states. These states together divide into some 2438 municipalities. Federal, state and municipal laws exist and work together, but also

sometimes against each other. Each state's laws are autonomous of the federal law, but shouldn't be in contradiction to the Constitution. Very often federal and state authorities aren't even aware of discriminatory laws existing at the municipal level.

2 The late Mexican-American Lionel Cantú (1997) importantly notes that the idea of Mexico as the quintessential "land of the macho" also permeates reports made by international LGBT solidarity groups and finds its way into legal cases related to asylum claims lodged by LGBT people of Mexican origin. Although the realities of persecution of gays, lesbians and trans people in several parts of Mexico cannot be denied, the explanations of the same too frequently hinge on reductive arguments that homogenize Mexico as "other" to a "civilized" and "progressive" United States. Mexico thus represents, in such discourse, a backward place, immersed in its oppressive traditions, timeless and unable to change. Gender norms are posited as one arena in which such traditional modes are expressed. This view ignores the major socio-economic transformations that Mexico has undergone in the last few decades and understands culture and gender relations as something static and unified.

3 The more I looked at the municipal level, especially in the North, the more data came to light: Matamoros, Coahuila, 2006: municipal authorities threaten subjects they term "men dressed as women" with legal sanctions, citing a link between their imputed activity in sex work and incidences of sexually transmissible infection (STI) in the town (González Roldán 2006). The municipal health authority says that local law prohibits such subjects from conducting sex work and/or dressing as women, and such is also the case in Torreón, Coahuila. It seems that pre-existent codes around scandal and public disturbance, previously applied to a range of "moral dissidents" in the public eye, are not enough in these legal jurisdictions, just as they were deemed not to be in Tecate.

4 Although the border began to be industrialized and populated with *maquiladoras* (assembly line factories) from the 1960s, after the signing in 1994 of the North American Free Trade Agreement (NAFTA) between the US, Mexico, and Canada, the realities of Mexican labor and economy were subject to radical new conditions, resulting in the undercutting of traditional agriculture, for instance, in the southern states as indigenous farmers lost their livelihood based on the cultivation of corn when US corn products flooded the market at a 40 percent lower price, and mass displacements in search of work, to the border and beyond, resulted. The social, political and economic effects of NAFTA for Mexico have been almost incalculable; transformations in gender and class relations are especially tangible, however, as well as ironic openings into diversified forms of unofficial trade and labor, including drug production and smuggling.

5 What has become historically differentiated out as "transgender" in other (notably US) spaces is often visualized as part of "the homosexual" in Latin American cultures. This compares well to the work of David Valentine (2007), which, although it looks at African American and Latino/a communities of the sexually diverse in New York, manifestly resonates with the kinds of multiple identifications shown among *travestis* in Latin America.

6 This informs my de-privileging of a gender identity lens, which is often the focus in accounts that explain forms of violence and discrimination against trans people as principally gender-based. In the view of much activism and scholarship that analyzes and contests "transphobia," the violation of sex/gender norms is understood as the principal motivator of violence or harassment experienced by trans people. And yet this results from the prioritization of gender as the analytic lens. On closer inspection of many "anti-trans" violence cases, murders of transsexual women can be shown as having more in common the fact that such people have become victims of anti-sex worker attacks, as Viviane Namaste and Mirha-Soleil Ross have argued (see Namaste 2005). Being involved in street sex work produces a condition of visibility that not all trans women are necessarily implicated in, and explanations that connect to sexual

morality and ideologies related to purity would seem to have more substance (due to the widespread stigmatization of sex work historically and in the present day in much of the globe), especially in reference to the Tecate case this chapter examines.

7 Anxieties and conflict are not just produced on the US side with its "Hispanic panic." These city complexes are also crossed and double-crossed—by internal migration and returning transnational migration, periodic daily crossing for commerce, as well as the presence of US-origin people, including North Americans and Chicanos, for trade and tourism. While the borderlands have been held up as a place of seepage of two worlds "bleeding into each other," following Gloria Anzaldúa (1987)—as if all border towns obeyed this logic—I was much more interested in getting on the ground level to view the vagaries in the micro realities of the shaping of moralities, especially around the question of the movement of "moral dissidents" in public space.

8 Bourdieu refers to the *habitus* in *Logic of Practice* as composed of the "common schemes of perception, conception and action" belonging to and expressed by a particular group or social class (Bourdieu 1990: 60). It is made up of "durable, transposable dispositions" that are shaped by and shape the possibilities of being in the social world, one's mobility, values and aspirations (53).

9 This framework is a key supplement to the normativizing features of legal discourse alluded to earlier. However, its focus on processes and practices and not just laws provides a perspective that sheds light on the interaction of the law and state agents that the Tecate case also demonstrates. Foucault's account of the apparatus of governmentality takes the concern off the normalization of individual behaviors via techniques of the discipline of the self secured in regimes of sexuality and gender, for example, and moves to the question of the state that has "the population as its target, political economy as its major form of knowledge, and apparatuses of security as its essential technical instrument" (Foucault 2007: 108). I would concur with Dean Spade's recent urging (2010) to bring in this dimension into trans political activism and inquiry, whereby the center of attention would not be restricted to the terms of (gender) identity and its regulation, but also security, borders and space. The Tecate study forms part of a much wider project I am currently undertaking on internal migrations and the management in laws and by state authorities of transsexuals and *travestis* in other parts of the Mexican nation.

10 Doxa refers specifically to the statements or value expressions that people make that remain unquestioned and taken-for-granted. They depend, however, on specific world views and orthodox assumptions that are particular to one's social and material conditions of existence (Bourdieu 1991: 55–56).

11 Moralities, holds Smith, are what people practice and are "embedded with specific sets of social and physical relationships manifest in geographical space" (Smith 2000: 18). The forces by which one morality becomes dominant, and exercises itself as the view to which all others must answer, emanate from the institutions of power: the courtroom, the police station, the town hall and council chambers of local government. In this way, moralities and their articulation can be understood as the struggle over which set of values and world views are taken as true and representative of a certain people and place, emerging out of the context of competing visions of the same. The struggle to establish the dominant version may construct itself around a certain issue, yet the "universalization" of the morality of a particular social group is never final, and is subject to re-working and contestation from different sites of discursive power.

12 The translation of the text of the code, and that of any other materials originally in Spanish that are cited directly from here on, is mine.

13 As Jeffrey Weeks (1981) notes of England, control of prostitution has historically been enacted through hygiene laws (contagious diseases acts). Certainly in Mexico, as well, many public "modesty" laws and laws around scandal were first generated in an effort to control and monitor sex work, which is not in *sensu stricto* "illegal" in the country.

14 Much good and effective work has been done in Mexico around HIV/AIDS over the years. From the beginning of the advent of the epidemic in Mexico, there has been much organizing both at state and community levels (largely under the jurisdiction of The National Center for the Prevention and Control of HIV/AIDS or CENSIDA). However, the greatest concentration of care and support was limited to five major regions. Outlying regions did not get the same centralized support. Added to this, stigma persists. As Aggleton, Parker, and Maluwa observe: 'All over the world, and especially in Latin America and the Caribbean, [HIV/AIDS] has systematically played to, and reinforced, existing prejudices and anxieties—about homo- and bisexuality, about prostitution and sex work, and about injecting drug use" (2002: 3).

15 It is difficult to say to what extent religious views permeated the construction of morality in the Tecate case. Respondents underlined to me that the religiosity famous in other parts of Mexico, such as in Oaxaca, Chiapas or Puebla, is tempered by an ethics of work and pragmatism that *bajacalifornianos* are known for. Tecate might be viewed as less influenced by this culture of pragmatism at the time, to be sure, due to the "thick" nature of its moral geographies. While the Archbishop publicly supported the anti-youth curfew law, moreover, he did not make any statements in the media about the cross-dressing code.

16 "Effeminate" homosexuals and *travestis*, notes Núñez Noriega, are said to have "costumbres raras": their transgression of what are simultaneously gendered, sexual and moral norms is what makes them suspect in this formulation. Individuals, respectful citizens—who show mutual respect—are exhorted to play down the public show of such "strange" behaviors, which represent "escándalo" (Núñez Noriega 1999: 97). For Núñez Noriega, it is not transgression that is questioned as such; rather, the form in which one exhibits this transgression, when, where and how much matters more (243).

17 The Tlatelolco massacre was a crackdown ordered by President Díaz Ordaz on October 2, 1968, to violently put down the student-led protests against the holding of the Olympics in Mexico City. Over 300 were killed and the event has left an indelible mark on Mexican consciousness.

18 Operation Gatekeeper was a security operation designed to seal crossing points along the border via more patrols, infrared detection technology and fortification of the wall. Claimed a success by the Democrats at the time, it has resulted in ever-more-perilous forms of crossing (and a pushback into the border on the Mexican side), whose most graphic outcome has been the nearly 4000 registered deaths since the Operation's inception. During George W. Bush's administration, there were calls for further fortification post-9/11. Indeed I was in Mexico at this time and recall the panic with the immediate crackdown on flows of Mexican migrants over the border, which Bush secured just days after the attacks on the World Trade Center.

19 The names of the gays and *travestis* I interviewed have been changed to protect their anonymity.

PART II

Trans Aesthetics, Counterpublics and Spatiality

3

TRANSGENDER MOVEMENT(S) AND BEATING THE STRAIGHT FLUSH

Building an Art of Trans Washrooms

Lucas Crawford

A train arrives at a station. A little boy and a little girl, brother and sister, are seated in a compartment face to face next to the window through which the buildings along the station platform can be seen passing as the train pulls to a stop. "Look," says the brother, "We're at Ladies!" "Idiot!" replies his sister, "Can't you see we're at Gentlemen?"

(Lacan 2001: 115)

Introduction

Many bodies and bodies of thought commonly called "trans" make material precisely what is laughable in Lacan's anecdote: swapping the false universal model of gender for the particularity of place and body. As do some trans theorists, this ostensibly juvenile "mistake" configures genders as equally situated, historical, and communal as any town: Susan Stryker, for instance, regards bodies as "mobile architectures" (Stryker 2008: 45) that are built and moved in concert according to the materials, conventions, and collaborations available. However, this queer rejection of universal gender and genre has yet to reach precisely the place to which Lacan and many trans activist campaigns return compulsively: "the washroom." In this homogenizing formulation, "the washroom" is taken for granted as a stable setting rather than as a particular and variable genre of built space that may be a category every bit as gender-charged as male and female. If campaigns for "gender-neutral" washrooms run the risk of foreclosing the matter of washrooms plumb at Lacan's point of focus—the doors—they trust not only the efficiency of a simple change in signage but they also accept as a hermeneutic exactly what Freud is so thrilled to discover when he too interprets trains (in Dora's second dream): a "symbolic geography of sex!" (Freud 1905/1957: 122). When we treat washrooms as monolithic symbols in the geography of transgender, that is, "the washroom" becomes a taken-for-granted genre, one that seems to merely set the stage for pre-existing subjects rather than intervene in their production. While the former is likely the phenomenological experience of many trans people—especially as we travel—are there more nuanced ways in which gender and genre shuttle between subjects and spaces? Or are signs on doors the sole structural elements of washrooms that generate problematic practices of embodiment?

Many queer-savvy architectural theorists question not only this false divide between building and user but also the very possibility that there could ever be such a thing as gender-free architecture to which sexist ideas may then, afterwards, be applied. In Mark Wigley's estimation, for instance, feminist theory too often neglects the role of houses in its repudiation of compulsory domesticity. Despite the concurrent spatial and gendered division of public and private that the family dwelling inaugurates, he argues, we too often forget that "the physical house is the possibility of the patriarchal order that appears to be applied to it" (Wigley 1992: 336). Following Wigley's insistence that the materiality of architecture is moved by conventions of gender every bit as much as our bodies, this chapter asks: What do the lives of transgender have to gain by *not* forgetting washroom architecture in our hopes and campaigns to gain access to these places we need to use when we and our bowels are on the move? While short-term solutions are obviously crucial for those of us whose bodies and diets are quite fluid, will the most basic and necessary way to enrich trans life (or just make it liveable) always be an officially "gender-neutral" washroom?

Taking for granted that trans quality of life must be sought in many ways that exceed the possibilities of laws and regulations, this chapter asks one overarching question: What built features might characterize a trans washroom? In using "trans" to describe a register of affect that is not that of the individual subject (but that nonetheless affects that subject deeply) this chapter neither elides nor champions trans people's accounts about washroom experience. As Stryker, Currah, and Moore describe in their introduction to the "Trans-" issue of *WSQ*, "neither 'gender' nor any of the other suffixes of 'trans-' can be understood in isolation … the lines implied by the very concept of 'trans-' are moving targets, simultaneously composed of multiple determinants" (Stryker, Currah, and Moore 2008: 12). In their account, the action suggested by "trans," which they employ as a verb, is clearly spatial: "transing," they write, "is a practice that takes place within, as well as across or between, gendered spaces" (12). While "trans" here is concerned with transgender proper, then, it is also an operation that works (like "queer") against the very imperative to maintain strict propriety in relation to the identity categories, bodies, lives, and movements that gather around the concepts of gender and sexuality. In pursuit of these goals, this chapter proposes three characteristics of trans-washrooms. Each draws out the stakes of different material experiments upon which users and designers might embark—in ways (and with results) that cannot be prescribed or gauged in advance. If, in Stryker's account, "gender is a percussive symphony of automatisms, reverberating through the space of our bodies" (Stryker 2008: 42), then the trans washrooms this chapter incites will be those that seem to offer a chance to stall these automatic feelings and acts, giving us even just one suspended moment to orient to/with our space and the space of our bodies anew— even while undertaking all of those bodily projects we pursue so automatically that they truly do feel like a "call of nature."

Trans Washrooms Generate and Express Different Publics

Across the street from the Tate Britain, Monica Bonvicini's fully functional art installation drew public curiosity on the former grounds of the Millbank Penitentiary in 2004 (and in Basel in 2003). From the outside, the installation looks like a mysterious box made of mirrors. Inside, visitors find a washroom. Those who enter also realize that the walls are in fact two-way mirrors, which allows users to see through to the outside. From the position of the toilet then, users become the indirect object of the panoptic gaze, as quizzical passers-by approach and inspect the curious mirrored box. This design offers not only a nod to this architectural history with a stainless steel toilet and sink but also the possibility to experience a seeming reversal of Foucault's description of our "carceral" (Foucault 1975: 301) surveillance culture, a theory he extrapolated from precisely such prisons. While the subject of Bentham's panopticon "is seen, but he does not see" (ibid.: 200), the user of '*Don't Miss a Sec.*' occupies the ostensibly enviable position of the guard, he or she who sees all and can never be seen. Counter to the supposedly powerful position the user holds in the visual economy of this space, having a relaxing bowel movement in such a washroom might prove quite difficult (or at least titillating). How appropriate, then, that the user of this washroom is literally boxed in by an image of the public sphere that the washroom itself creates. In one sense, Bonvicini turns the washroom inside-out: she replaces the usually mundane washroom exterior with the very self-appraising and cosmetic technology—the mirror—that often stands in as a symbol for the bodily "maintenance" we pursue in domestic washrooms. By evincing just how profoundly our orderings of space and orderings of affect are mutually reinforcing, Bonvicini's piece confronts the user with a felt lesson about how bodies have *already* absorbed some operations of the public sphere into even their most "natural" (and "naturally" private) functions.

In so doing, '*Don't Miss a Sec.*' generates in the "general public" a series of questions all too familiar to those genderqueer people who may or may not pass: why is everyone looking at me; why is nobody looking at me; and even, can they see my "private" parts?[1] This feeling of fraught privacy-in-public is due partly to a learned knowledge that, in most locales, while trans people are not imagined as part of the public, we variously become public property when others' discomfort is aroused. Like the user hidden in the mirrored box, gender-ambiguous bodies appear in public *as* a kind of secrecy—bodies that, unlike more normative ones, do not feign full disclosure or consent to the social contracts that make us feel safe and unaffected when surrounded by so many (so-called) strangers. Regardless of whether users have any knowledge of trans life, they are given—even if briefly—an affective lesson in the fragility of privacy, visuality, and exposure. Simply put, Bonvicini's piece reminds us that to alter the functions of publicity and privacy is also to change our definitions of *what* we feel comfortable doing *where* and around *whom*—precisely the kind of social change that might make gender-neutral washrooms far less threatening and far more interesting.

With just such a moving washroom in mind, how might a transpublic go far beyond welcoming trans people thought to be constructed elsewhere (in the private home or private psyche) to actually destabilize habits of the body through reconfigurations of space? With histories of cruising, politicking, parading, anal proclivities, flaunting it, coming out, and non-familial structures of affiliation, it seems that the theoretical and subjective figure of the queer seems poised to lead this disruptive charge down the line of private and public.[2] However, while it's easy to imagine some ways in which a public washroom might be "queered" with cruising and the socialities that attend it, it's less obvious how these queer tactics of appropriation could operate to trans the affective habits that shore up our sense of ourselves and our genders as sovereign, unaffected, and generally unmoved by others. While it's been duly noted that the privatization of sex has an obviously anti-queer bent,[3] how does the privatization of more quotidian (or hourly?) bodily acts such as shitting and pissing affect the privatization of the trans/gendered body?

In *Gender Outlaw: On Men, Women, and the Rest of Us*, Kate Bornstein prefaces a chapter with a question she was once asked on the Geraldo Rivera show, followed by her response. When an audience member ask, "Can you orgasm with that vagina?" (Bornstein 1995: 31), Bornstein responds with a quip: "Yah, the plumbing works and so does the electricity" (31). While this configuration of her body as a home sets up a good joke and a fine answer, there is something more subtle at stake in this specific metaphor of "plumbing" (31), a word commonly used by trans people (sometimes jokingly) to not only refer to the nitty-gritty functions of piss and shit, but moreover, to hold these ostensibly purely functional acts quite aside from the sexual and gendered meanings we attribute to genitals. But plumbing, as it turns out, contains its own interesting narrative of bodily management and spatial hygiene. Ellen Lupton and J. Abbott Miller draw a chronology of this very history in *The Bathroom and the Kitchen and the Aesthetics of Waste: A Process of Elimination*, which brings together a great number of historical statistics that—if nothing else— remind us that the advent of modern plumbing is both recent and (understandably) urban-centric: "[In] 1901, New York's Model Tenement House Reform Law requires water to be provided on each floor of new buildings"; "In 1940, 93.5 % of the dwellings in the urban US have running water"; and, "of the more than 40% of Americans living in rural areas, 17.8% have running water in their homes" (Lupton and Miller 1992: 23). Despite the fact that these new technologies were clearly not evenly distributed, the technological advances that allowed for more widespread running water and sewage systems have their crucial and undoubted benefits (including, for instance, "decreased typhoid mortality rates" [23]).

Be that as it may, the conditions in which ubiquitous modern plumbing became imaginable and possible generate (and were generated by) major changes in how the individual could think of him or herself, especially in relation to his or her spaces. One of the main cultural conditions that quickly motivated the imperative for modern plumbing was the common acceptance of the germ theory of disease, which holds "that certain diseases are caused by the invasion of the body by microorganisms, organisms too small to be seen except through a microscope" (*Encyclopedia Britannica Online* 2009). In distinction to its immediate precursor (the model of spontaneous generation), the germ theory pinpointed the body and contact with other bodies as the site of the spread of illness. That is, this new association between the hygienic care of the body with the spread of illness changed both the stakes and the methods of washing oneself. As Georges Teyssot points out in "Cleanliness Takes Command," our definition of cleanliness changes according to public hygiene concerns of the time, "like the plague" (Teyssot 2004: 75):

> In Europe during the sixteenth and seventeenth centuries, people stopped taking baths and cleaned themselves by rubbing their body with fresh and dry linen … Since it was deemed dangerous, all social intercourse which opened up the body to infected air, especially bathing, was prohibited. Doctors asked everybody to get out of bathtubs.
>
> *(Teyssot 2004: 75)*

While this kind of "infected air" kept people away from public bathing facilities, the confirmation of the germ theory changed the space of illness from the "air" of the public sphere to the human body itself, any one of which could now potentially be a carrier of disease. If, in Teyssot's example, the subject appearing in public puts himself at risk, the germ theory of disease changes this: one's entrance into the public sphere may also be an act of putting others at risk, such that the care of one's body becomes a matter of public concern in a new way. Together, such conceptions of the individual and the risk of disease required new ways to attain and rehearse cleanliness, which was accomplished precisely through a fevered desire for plumbing. As Lupton and Miller report, "the discovery that many diseases are waterborne encourages the campaign for clean water, sewer construction, and water and sewer filtration" (Lupton and Miller 1992: 23). Likewise, Nancy Tomes makes it clear that the acceptance of germ theory is one of the major pivot-points in the history of the hygiene industry: even though "sewer traps, toilet designs, window ventilators, and water filtration systems … began to proliferate in the 1870s," it was with "the popularization of the germ theory [that] their numbers showed an explosive increase in the 1880s and 1890s" (Tomes 1997: 517).

In terms of architectural design, the quick spread of plumbing that followed (and reified) the convergence of these new hygienic demands and this version of the individual had one major effect: as William W. Braham describes it, "the regular and abundant presence of water within the household demanded new habits of use and new configurations for its accommodation" (Braham 1997: 214). Whether it's a matter of coincidence and practicality or not, these new spatial arrangements shore up precisely the new kind of privately hygienic subject imagined alongside the germ theory; in the following, Lupton and Miller describe precisely what kinds of hygienic spaces and subjects are thereby reified:

> With the introduction of plumbing to the nineteenth-century household, formerly portable body appliances—bathtubs, wash stands, and chamber pots—assumed a fixed position in the home, tied to water supply and waste disposal pipes. [Siegfried] Giedion has described this as a shift from "nomadic" to "stable" conditions ... By the 1880s, water-supplied appliances were called "set" or "stationary" to distinguish them from the movable devices that preceded them.
>
> *(Lupton and Miller 1992: 27)*

In this quotation, the stakes of this historical narrative for trans embodiment become more explicit: as the implements with which one cares for his or her body become fixed, so, obviously, do both the manner and places in which one does so. The care of the body becomes a private routine fixed in time and space, a medically scientific project rather than an "ars erotica" (Foucault 1978: 59), and a program to follow rather than a great horizon of bodily possibilities. In addition to locking practices into places, the grouping of the toilet, wash stand, and bathtub into one area has created a link between these practices that could have developed otherwise. While the gender-honing practices undertaken in front of the washroom sink and mirror might seem hygienically inappropriate next to the kitchen sink, there was no small amount of resistance to the idea that bathing and defecating ought to happen in the same room either. Lupton and Miller note that "sanitarians were critical of the increasing trend towards including the toilet alongside the lavatory and bathtub. Health critics felt it was not hygienic to mingle functions" (Lupton and Miller 1992: 36). In any case, *that* the cosmetic practices of doing make-up, plucking, moisturizing, hairstyling, and shaving eventually take up residence near one water center and not the other links these gender-managing practices with both cleanliness and repudiation of waste. Just as Foucault laments the consolidating process by which previously diffuse acts were turned into the symptomology of "the homosexual" as "a species" (Foucault 1978: 43), here is an architectural development that binds previously mobile and variously shared acts into a fixed and private room. This "birth of the washroom" would not be possible without (an image of) the public citizen who regards cleanliness as a matter of civic and familial responsibility—far from Warner's hope for "counterpublic" (Warner 2002a: 49) stranger-intimacy, to be sure.

Though he's writing specifically about the relatively recent advent of closets, Wigley's argument that "the emerging ideology of the individual subject depends [on …] the new sense of privacy" (Wigley 1992: 343) is useful in gauging precisely what is at stake for queer and trans embodiment and subjects in the washroom's architectural coding of privacy. In this mutually reinforcing relationship between privacy and the individual, the kind of individual subject for whom the discursive act of "coming out" is imaginable has, that is, not only epistemological but also architectural conditions of possibility. While Sedgwick (1992) has little to say about literal closets in her landmark text,[4] it seems that these body-managing closets are archives of the very versions of selfhood, privacy, and disclosure that have founded the modern queer subject in so many ways. Even this very short story of their development as a genre of room shows what kinds of queer and trans subjects they make possible: ones that must "come out," ones for whom gender is done behind closed doors in literally fixed ways, ones for whom well-managed gender is experienced as a matter of cleanliness, and for whom embodied life is still enmeshed in "the vectors of a disclosure at once compulsory and forbidden" (Sedgwick 1992: 71), be it that "everybody poops" or the knowledge that everyone's washroom is sometimes dirty.[5] With the skeleton of gender rattling in our water closets, might it be far less cynical than it sounds to suggest that gender, and the individual who pursues it fervently, might be better off without a room of its own?

Trans Washrooms Disrupt Routine Hygienic Practices

When a recent spread in *Surface*, a popular men's magazine, gathers a number of cosmetic products, sets them up like pillars against the backdrop of a sunset and open plain, and adds the title "MAN SCAPE," it's clear that representations of hygiene are explicitly "gendered." With the aesthetic and language of the pioneer spirit—not to mention mojito soaps, absinthe creams, and brands such as "Every Man Jack"—products and practices may be easily rebranded as acceptably hetero-masculine and corporations may easily broaden their customer base by writing gender into the incredibly strong imperative most people feel towards being "clean." (This is not to mention "the metrosexual," which is not only a hygienic-sexual term used to quell the homo-anxious fears aroused by an increase in men's cosmetics but also a spatially defined identity that unconvincingly feigns the absence of a relationship between queerness and cosmopolitanism, space and desire, city and sex.) But, this model underestimates the relationship "between" gender and hygiene by configuring gender only as a system of thinking that seems to be applied (after-wards) *to* the ostensibly gender-neutral project of cleanliness and hygiene. If hygiene is thought to innocently pre-exist all gender-charged norms and practices of the body, however, it just may follow the same model of dissimulation that Butler traces in *Bodies that Matter*: it produces the possibility of an un-gendered pre-social "hygiene" in much the same way as the concept of "materiality" (Butler 1993a: ix) allows for a bad-faith concept of "sex" that isn't produced by and through practices of gender. In a note to chapter one, Butler explains this process:

power is established in and through its effects, where these effects are the dissimulated workings of power itself ... this dissimulation operates through the constitution and formation of an epistemic field and set of "knowers"; when this field and these subjects are taken for granted as prediscursive givens, the dissimulating effect of power has succeeded.

(Butler 1993a: 251)

In other words, when hygiene appears (but, moreover, feels) to us to be a gender-neutral project, this might be the moment at which the materializing effects of power are working best. In this model, bodily feelings regarding cleanliness are neither simple results of power nor independent self-determining perpetuators of it: "hygiene" both authorizes and is also the result of the production of (gender-) normative bodies. Reading representations such as "MAN SCAPE" as skewed/ gendered interpretations of an underlying gender-neutral "hygiene," then, misses the bigger picture: it is by marketing and producing new "gendered" practices straight into the ostensibly innocent discourse of hygiene that the daily acts of gender-production that occur in most washrooms are able to appear benign and un-invested. "Hygiene," like "sex," may then be "retroactively installed" (5) as a series of gender-neutral health-oriented regimes. Although quality of life can certainly be improved greatly with plumbing and other hygienic developments, if the case of post-1880s washroom design is any indication, it is worth asking the general question: Is it the supposed neutrality of "cleanliness" that allows the concept of hygiene to dissimulate the power it wields in other matters of the body—such as gender? Specifically, what practices of gender are enabled (invisibly) by this positing of an a priori "hygiene" that comes before all cosmetics and gender?[6]

In the proliferation of hygienic guide books that appear following the confirmation of germ theory, it is the authors' task to convince people (that is, homeowners) to take seriously the new hygienic routines and responsibilities required by this new concept of the human body and home as always-already contagious. Not surprisingly, they often do so by appealing to their readers' desires to be, as one author puts it, "manly" or "womanly" (Frank 1887: 92). In a Boston-published 1887 treatise entitled *Health in our Homes*, the author known only as "Dr. Frank" lays bare the rhetoric that still underlies the (now increasingly capitalist) campaigns to extend the purview of hygiene. As he writes:

A rather unique argument has recently appeared in a popular monthly. It says: Hygiene is manly, and it is also womanly ... A man must live a sanitary life; let him but follow his natural instincts (we say natural, and when we say natural, we do not mean perverted), and he is all right ... To be manly, a man must live as a man, and to live as a man, he must observe the teachings of hygiene; therefore do we come back to the proposition with which we started, that "hygiene is manly."

(Frank 1887: 92)

The tautological quality of this argument is obvious, but perhaps it is actually an accurate description of the way in which hygienic discourse and practices shore up gender norms. In much the same way as Butler describes, hygiene is the "gendered" production that produces itself as pre-existing gender. If it's true that the normative ways in which one comes to feel "clean" in our culture also 1) allow us to feign the day-to-day stability of the body, and 2) so often involve the elimination or modification of bodily features that fall outside our culture's images of normative gender, then perhaps Dr. Frank's tautology is far more telling than it may appear: "hygiene is manly" (Frank 1887: 92) because "man" is not a category or set of bodies possible without the acts and ideas of hygiene, especially its acts of dissimulating its own gender-charged production. While Butler seeks some of the "sex[es] of materiality" (Butler 1993a: 54) rather than the materiality of sex, here we see some of the genders of hygiene rather than ways in which hygiene is "gendered." In the case of Dr. Frank, whose text appears precisely at a time when people must be moved to take on changing definitions of hygiene as an integral part of their sense of self, it was a new version of gender normativity that provided the affective marketing.

The pairing of gender and hygiene obviously has something to do with physically crafting normative bodies; but, how is transgender embodiment circumscribed not only by the hegemony of that system, but by the very ways in which bodily pain, modification, "gendered" selfhood, and hygiene are so tightly wound together? As one such contemporary example of a discourse that seems underpinned by hygienic ideals, I turn to a version of what is probably the most accessible model of transition: the "wrong-body figure" (Prosser 1998: 69) that trans thinkers like Jay Prosser defend. Even in a culture where a multitude of industries (dieting, fitness, cosmetic surgery, anti-aging, hygienic and cosmetic products) can safely take for granted that few if any people feel consistently "right" "in" their bodies, Prosser is correct to see "the wrong body" as a discourse that seems only to adhere to trans people. Arguing against Butler's warning about the heroic use of the concept of materiality, he defends the deployment of this narrative by evincing that "body image ... clearly already has a material force for transsexuals" (69). To illustrate the always-already thoroughly material quality of transsexual body image, Prosser insists that "the ability to give oneself pain ... to harm one's own body, surely depends upon a great degree of bodily alienation" (74). However, the same can surely be said for folks who, in the name of fending off "bodily alienation" and by enduring "pain," pluck their eyebrows one hair at a time, shave their testicles, take steroids, pursue cosmetic surgery, carefully regulate daily muscle injury (what we call weight-lifting), wax their backs, floss their teeth until they bleed, use lasers to remove facial hair, cut themselves, bleach their anuses, wear undergarments with tight wires, use tanning beds, go hungry, and even stand under streams of scalding hot water so often that their skin actually breaks down.[7]

Insofar, then, as *most* people in our culture participate hourly, daily, weekly, and/ or monthly in a number of painful body-modification practices that aim to avoid the alienation that might (for many) accompany various body non-normativities, there is something more than a pre-social feeling residing in trans people that sets us apart. Reviewing the list of body modifications above, it seems that the concepts of hygiene, maintenance, and even cosmetics are the discourses with and through which some bodily traits and practices come to be regarded as keeping a body the way it already was (even though it wasn't) and some traits and practices as making a body radically different (even when they don't). To be absolutely clear: This is not to cast any doubt upon the phenomenological experience of wrong-bodiedness or to equate the scrutiny and struggles of transition with the easier projects named above. Rather, it is to suggest that, while the feelings of "wrong" embodiment are variously ubiquitous, only some folks—good hygienic public citizens—have the privilege (and/or make the choice) to pursue ways of modifying the body that are taught, praised, and made available and enjoyable. Again, to be clear: The point is to see the happy "right" bodies enjoyed by many as not only suspect in their privilege but also as examples of the way in which the materialization of power often feels perfectly fine. Certainly, feeling "right" and comfortable is crucial for anyone's wellbeing; alongside that recognition, this analysis follows Butler in seeing precisely those "right" moments as the most telling, and sometimes, the most dangerous ones (Butler 1993a: 251). One of the tasks of transing "hygiene," then, will be to see the specificity of transgender not as inhering in the bodies or private psyches of trans people, but rather, as produced through discourses whose agents have much to gain in making sure that normative hygienic projects are not seen as comparable to the specificities of culturally abject bodies.

In 2000, the radical New York firm Diller & Scofidio (now Diller Scofidio + Renfro) completed their redesign of Philip Johnson's Brasserie restaurant in the basement of the famous Seagram Building, after the eatery endured a fire in 1995. While the entire restaurant deserves a full-length study of its own, its washrooms are particularly intriguing for their critique of hygienic norms. The sinks in each washroom bear a glowing white message on which to reflect as users wash their hands: in the men's room, "washistopurgeistodenyistowashis" and in the women's, "tocleanistoabsolveistoreformisto."

No one "clean" interpretation may be wrought from the playful texts: where "wash is to purge" becomes "wash is top urge," the usual logic of washroom signs is reversed: the words multiply (interpretations) rather than divide (bodies into rooms). The use of text in single-sex spaces enacts the idea that if a person feels confined to only one room, he or she quite literally only knows half the story (and perhaps not even that much). The space produces what is perhaps a rare feeling: curiosity about the other washroom, which allows washrooms and their differences to easily become a topic of conversation.

Both texts are never-ending, as if to remind us that, owing to the equally never-ending activity of our bodies and the delicate emotional projects we locate there, cleaning is indeed a never-ending cycle. In this sense, Diller & Scofidio suggest that hygiene is always already the project of the incessantly scrubbing Lady Macbeth, even if we invest in cleanliness *happily* rather than with guilt. While it is relatively easy work to point out the ways in which certain bodily acts are treated as shameful, Diller & Scofidio (following Butler's lead) take up the difficult task of questioning the way in which we imbue certain bodily acts with happiness, virtue and self-satisfaction. Washing our hands, that is, for all of its efficiency in slowing the spread of the common cold, functions just as much to allow us to "purge" and "deny" the very uncontrollability of our bodies and to feel the warmth of self-care because of it. The equation of washing with the word "absolve" gets precisely to this point: there is something suspicious about the way in which we use acts of cleanliness to grant ourselves a kind of bodily forgiveness. If our ritualistic hand-washing is indeed a kind of banal mortification of the flesh, the question would be: of what are we trying to be "absolve[d]"?

During plagues such as the Black Death, "large groups of flagellants wandered from town to town scourging themselves in order to save their souls and alleviate the Lord's wrath, believing in the mortification of the flesh as suitable penance for men's sins" (Benedictow 2004: 392). While public hand-washing cannot exactly be equated with "mass flagellation" (392), there is a similar "purg[ing]" and "deny [ing]" of embodiment that underlies our contemporary project of accomplishing emotional work and comfort through the pursuit of cleanliness—the erasure of both messy bodily matter and the culturally unclean notions it represents. How this emotional economy of cleanliness affects transgender is subtle but significant: there is a will here not only to forget the body, but also a desire to be forgiven for even having one. In other words, this emotional pattern in which virtue is accrued through ritual acts of cleansing is neither a new one nor one that espouses a particularly generous view of those who intentionally fixate on embodiment as something to be rethought, reconstructed, and politicized, when the virtuous project is, rather, to cast off the deeds of the body for higher spiritual pursuits as much as possible.

Given the very bold statements emblazoned on the washroom's mirrors, it's no surprise that Diller & Scofidio's sinks also comment on this trend of seeking absolution and purification with cleansing waters. There is only one sink at Brasserie, a long cast resin one that is divided into two parts by the flimsy honeycombed wall between the men's and women's washrooms. Even the choice of materials is telling, as cast resin was also the (highly unusual) material of choice for the restaurant's tables, fixtures we seldom regard as related to the dirtier and less important bottoms of sinks. With no "private" sink for one's own hands, the user takes part in a kind of cleansing that is just slightly more public and communal that we are accustomed to. The soap, rather than affixed to the wall, consists simply in a store-bought plastic container with a pump-top. It sits either in the trough-sink directly or on the small shelf that holds the thick folded paper towels; in the first case, the cleansing agent is not hidden in a dispenser, distributed automatically, or held above the ostensibly dirty sinks. In both cases, soap is neither an element included in the design nor, consequently, a true "fixture" in the room, even if it is always there.

This long sink has one strategically placed drain: exactly in between the two washrooms, which is visible through a gap in the wall. Here, the literal fluidity of personal hygiene runs together, figuring cleanliness as the half-hidden site in which genders don't just meet but mix. If it's around the point of hygiene that gender could actually run together so much more easily—as this section has argued—then Diller & Scofidio's single drain shows us that it's just such material reworkings of the spatiality of hygiene—especially, emphases on gaps and shared messiness rather than on airtight proper places—that are needed for the creation of trans washrooms. We see that our gray water, much like our shit in *every* washroom, all goes to the same place.

Trans Washrooms Foreground Their Own Construction and Mutability

In *The Decorative Art of Today*, one of several manifesto-like collections of essays by the infamous architect Le Corbusier, the modernist imperative to cut off all historical influence is compared gently to a bowel movement: "when we eat," he suggests, "nature knows well how to rid us of what has served its purpose" (Le Corbusier 1987: 189). Tapping into the washroom's status as a relatively new room and modernism's valorization of newness, this scatological metaphor captures the way in which early architectural modernism associated washrooms with an "imagined freedom from the baggage of history" (Lupton and Miller 1992: 25). Lupton and Miller point out that Le Corbusier goes on in *Towards a New Architecture* to define the ideal modern home "as one that adopted the hygienic standards of the bathroom" (26). Washrooms, as "new," small, and oriented towards cleanliness at just a time when "old" came to stand for "dirty," were often figured and built as the vanguard of the new and the modern. As Lupton and Miller summarize it: "while *moderne* and art deco styles 'expressed' modernity, the aesthetic of the bathroom *embodied* it" (26). And for Le Corbusier, apparently, the flush and forget ethic of the washroom was not just a perfect metaphor but also the literal path to making architecture modern.

While this language of newness and novelty sounds promising for the project of changing washrooms or thinking of them as places where embodiment and ideas can change, the "newness" of modern architecture was very carefully couched and practiced so as to control what could be lauded as modern and what was merely a transient (and therefore insignificant) fad. In his readings of attempts by Le Corbusier and Siegfried Giedion to define modern architecture, Wigley shows the underlying conservatism in this seemingly progressive fixation on newness: in Le Corbusier's texts, he argues, "the modern is advertised as the return of ... transcultural and transhistorical truth[s]" (Wigley 1992: 38), while for Giedion, "modern architecture is portrayed as the inevitable product of irreversible psychic forces long at work" (ibid.: 82). Modern architecture, in their accounts, isn't actually new: it merely strips off the falsehoods of ornament and convention that previous styles have accumulated, to reveal the ostensibly pure functionality and cleanliness of modern buildings. Unfortunately, therefore, the newness of the

modern (of which the washroom was a result and a key model) is all too circumscribed: the kind of novelty that could be celebrated was only that which took great
pains to show that it had existed all along, even if in repressed form.

To construct modern style as a transhistorical constant—as existing before and
beyond all styles—its spaces must, then, "somehow exhibit timeless values" (Wigley
1995: 39) even though all spaces are "inevitably time-bound" (39). Washrooms still
(loaded down with the historical baggage of this very attempt to be free from baggage) exhibit this overdetermined aesthetic, be it through the supposedly timeless
and universal gender icons that mark the doors or the "clean" modernist-inspired
blank walls usually found inside. This look of timeless functionality allows a washroom's construction and past to be concealed. As with normative genders, this kind
of dissimulation of material production does much to conceal the possibility that the
body in question could (often quite easily) have become something drastically different, and probably will. In other words, spaces—and probably bodies—that seek
to appear "timeless" (39) do little to foreshadow the possibility of radically different
futures, or of change. Against this modernist imperative, this section analyzes two
washroom renovation projects that refuse to erase their pasts, do not aesthetically
engage with the myth of architectural stability, or feign their own full self-presence.
In revealing their construction and their various incarnations, they not only express
their own contingency and the possibility of future transformations, but they also
offer an ethics of transition that may prove useful to trans people—especially if, in
defending our own changes, we'd like to avoid demonizing other styles (including our
past styles) as "a lie" (Le Corbusier 1987: 87).

In *STUD: Architectures of Masculinity*, editor Joel Sanders offers photographs and
describes two washroom renovations that were undertaken as cost- and space-saving
measures. In Kennedy and Violich Architecture's renovation for the Boston Center
for the Arts, the architects switched the women's room into the former men's room
and vice versa, apparently compelled by "existing plumbing configurations, budget
constraints, and space requirements" (Sanders 1998: 164). Although Kennedy and
Violich remain invested in creating conventional men's and women's rooms (a larger
women's room, and a men's room with urinals), each washroom bears the material
traces of its former existence: urinal fragments have been preserved in plain sight
under the sink in the women's, while "holes of toilet stacks once enclosed in the
women's stalls mark a threshold to the urinal chase in the men's room" (164). These
post-transition washrooms make their own histories readable by refusing to fake a
totally new identity, which would have required erasing the physical marks of the
bodies and practices of its pasts. Obviously, the functionality and viability of these
otherwise conventionally "gendered" washrooms is not compromised for their aesthetic remembrances of their past genders. An ethics of dynamic materiality is
enacted here, one that suggests not only that washrooms can or ought to be
archives of gender but also that material "in transition" need not move swiftly,
linearly, or with a mind to erase all remainders and excesses. By foregrounding its
own past, the washroom configures itself as temporally situated, as vulnerable to the

different needs of different people at different times, and certainly not as sacred single-sex space.

The second washroom renovation documented by Sanders, Sausalito's Headlands Center for the Arts as renovated by the Interim Office of Architecture, also bases its aesthetic sensibility on a refusal to dissimulate pasts and feign timelessness. Housed in a former Army facility, this washroom begins as a men's latrine and moves to a gender-neutral room for the public. Not only does a wall of now-defunct urinals line one wall but also half of the six sinks have no faucets. When Sanders argues that "the dysfunctional remnants of toilet fixtures disturbingly refer to the emasculation of once manly spaces" (Sanders 1998: 165), readers are left to make the obvious but unfortunate interpretive leap between "dysfunctional" and feminized. In Sanders' reading, the washroom is emasculated by either the addition of ostensibly feminine art objects or by the severing of fixtures; either way, there is a link made between passivity, art, castration and femininity. In any case, if something other than "emasculation" has happened with this washroom, perhaps it's a reworking of the very concept of functionality—under the guise of which modernism claimed its timeless style,[8] and, washroom aesthetics and architectures are so often taken-for-granted. Here, supposedly non-functional (or "dysfunctional") fixtures have been deemed important, and in this redefinition of which functions are proper to the washroom, projects like art, thought, documenting pasts, and playfulness are all seen to fit. That this washroom is gender-neutral makes it a particularly fitting one with which to end, if the goals of transing washrooms and campaigning for gender-neutral washrooms are to intimately involve each other. Contrary to Sanders' reading of "emasculation" (165), this washroom shows that the move from single-sex to gender-neutral can—through design as much as signs—add functions rather than mourn the loss of old ones. So-called non-functional bits and pieces cannot be so simply dismissed, as many a trans person could agree. Moreover, this gender-neutral design does not assume or pretend that such a project isn't new or potentially strange; rather, by drawing attention to its own historicity and construction, the design frames the washroom as a mutated and mutable space. In so doing, it offers us the question upon which this chapter as a whole elaborates: why should (and how could) a gender-neutral washroom simply look and feel like most other washrooms?

Conclusion

While the role to be played by officially shared facilities in the project of transing washrooms might be quite significant (as the Sausalito project makes clear), it has become clear that washrooms generate and discipline genders in far more ways than the obvious ones hung on the door. If gender is produced (and dissimulated) partly in front of the mirror, shored up as natural and apolitical through the privacy of the individual that washrooms help afford, and lent an aura of functionality and immutability through the timeless modernist design of these rooms devoted to body devotion (and quickly bracketed off of our living space), then perhaps the very phrase "gender-neutral washroom" names not only an impossible goal but at the same time an insufficiently ambitious one. If, as Butler claims, "there may not be a materiality of sex that is not already burdened by the sex of materiality" (Butler 1993a: 54), so too, as wigley shows there may not be an architecture of hygiene that is not already burdened by the hygienic management of architecture—a cultural cleansing of space that aims to keep everything and everyone in their proper places. Insofar as racism, queerphobia, and classism often appear under the ostensibly apolitical banner of "hygiene" (defenses of gentrification and "cleaning up" cities come quickly to mind), there is much at stake for variously non-normative bodies in questioning the discourses of bodily and cultural hygiene, as well as the fraught link between the two. Given, then, that the washroom's intertwined practices of personal and spatial hygiene participate in the dissimulation of not just normative gender but also the cultural cleansing of the body politic (through categories of ability, size, class, race, and many more) gaining increased access to conventional washrooms may grant trans people no more and no less than fuller participation in a problematic institution that disciplines both bodies and populations.

This chapter offers several ideas about how users, designers, activists, and scholars might variously extend or twist campaigns for gender neutrality into the more indeterminate project of transing washrooms. This orientation to social change is one that belongs (though not exclusively) to aesthetic production and Humanities inquiry: the project of inciting change without ordaining new paths with pre-determined destinations. Not surprisingly, this tension between nuanced aesthetics and the more obvious currency of use value is not at all new to architects, who always face the concurrent tasks of aesthetic production (their own desires) and of designing with certain activities in mind (the needs of users). In the estimation of deconstructivist architect Bernard Tschumi, this relationship between a building's aesthetics and its intended use or "program" must be rethought. Against convention, he argues that a building's design ought not to simply provide an allegory for the activities it is meant to contain; as he writes, "*there must be no identification between architecture and program*" (Tschumi 1996: 204). As a way to rethink functionality, he offers three ways to conceptualize the relationship between program and buildings. Two of these—"crossprogramming" and "transprogramming" (205) might, obviously, provide a literal building ethic and a metaphor for the way in which transgender bodies and studies are planned and built. The former entails "using a spatial configuration for a program not intended for it … a museum inside a car park structure" (205)—a kind of spatial appropriation, architectural drag, or counterpublic use of buildings with which queers may be quite familiar. Tschumi even has this in mind, as he adds this quip to his definition: "reference: crossdressing" (205).

Transprogramming, however, seems far less simplistic than locating a practice in the clothes of a building in which it is not seen to belong: it involves "combining two programs, regardless of their incompatibilities, together with their respective spatial configurations. Reference: planetarium + rollercoaster" (205). Insofar as the washrooms in this chapter are mostly gender-segregated, were produced via unknown conditions of labor, and are likely used in the most normative ways imaginable much of the time, they might best be held up as spaces that are complex, ambivalent, hybrid, and energetically tense with incompatibilities. In other words, they are examples of washrooms that could be productively transprogrammed—by their designers, architects, users, and critical engagements alike. This chapter ends, then, by affirming Tschumi's refusal of conventional programming, where "program" names both the exclusive valorization of officially gender-neutral design plans and also the imperative to politically pre-program transgender or regard explicit rights campaigns as the only kinds of praxis that effect change. Perhaps with these rearrangements of architectural and theoretical fixtures, the perfectly linear paths of tracked trains could be derailed in favour of the more nuanced movements of trans, all by turning one eye awry to the washroom doors that will never swing queerly enough in both ways. From the view of such a rollercoaster, the spaces of our bowel movements may no longer appear so inextricably bound up in convention. Perhaps they are just momentarily stalled.

Notes

1 Jamison Green describes the way that this double-sided crisis of visibility works in *Becoming a Visible Man*. As he writes in regards to transsexual men: "if we are visible we risk being mistreated; if we are invisible, no one will understand what our social or medical needs are. If we are visible, we risk being judged inferior or unreal, inauthentic; if we are invisible, we risk being discovered and cast out, again because no one is educated" (Green 2004: 180).

2 In "Publics and Counterpublics," Michael Warner suggests that queer structures of affiliation have demanded that we think differently about the public and private divide. He seeks, for instance, counterpublics that "try to supply different ways of imagining stranger-sociability and its reflexivity" (Warner 2002a: 88). In a way that speaks to the zone of washrooms, he argues further that "an understanding of queerness has been developing in recent decades that is suited to just this necessity; a culture is developing in which intimate relations and the sexual body can in fact be understood as projects for transformation among strangers" (88). Taking one of the very spaces in which queers, at least historically or stereotypically, form such intimacies, Bonvicini gestures towards a similar reconfiguration of privacy and visuality, offering it via art and affect to the general public.

3 In "Sex in Public," Warner and Berlant critique the way in which homonormative gays, in their estimation, despise the very kind of "flaunting" public sexuality that makes (particular) contemporary queer lives possible: "extinguish ... public sexual culture ... and almost all out gay or queer culture will wither on the vine" (Warner and Berlant 1998: 563). While they seek "sex as it is mediated by publics" (547) and focus on "less obvious scenes of sexuality, like national culture" (547), this chapter adds considerations of gender to their queer-centric analysis. It seeks gender as it is mediated by privacies and less obvious scenes of gender, such as hygienic culture.

4 While Sedgwick (1992) begins *Epistemology of the Closet* with a list of various definitions of the closet—including architectural ones—the text proceeds to emphasize "the closet" primarily as a discursive structure. In "Untitled: the Housing of Gender," Mark

Wigley (1992) shows that the closet cannot be taken for granted as an obvious or ahistorical metaphor as it too shapes the particular version of the individual arising at the time, helping to architecturally create the very kind of subject who could "come out" of a discursive closet. Although his article does not reference Sedgwick, it could easily be read as a companion text, as he traces the development of architectural codes of domestic privacy—an epistemology of the literal closet.

5 As Ilka and Andreas Ruby point out, the washroom—perhaps more than the closet— has its own strange epistemology and economies of open secrecy: "A dirty bathroom harbours the potentially horrifying scenario of discrediting ourselves in front of guests and friends. Such a scenario is particularly embarrassing because the bathroom is the only room in our dwelling in which the visitor is alone ... In the bathroom we are allowed to have secrets, even during the daytime" (Ruby and Ruby 2004: 125). In other words, they are *our* closets that others nonetheless enter and use.

6 Even this divide between cosmetics and hygiene relies on the fraught and ever-changing boundary between what is necessary and what is apparently superfluous or superficial, which seems to rest more often than not on an equally troubling and shifting version of what qualifies as the pursuit of health. In their essay "Medicine or Cosmetics?" in *Bathroom Unplugged*, Ilka and Andreas Ruby show how the washroom is perhaps the key site where this boundary is continually renegotiated. They argue that "in the 20th century the term 'hygiene' underwent ... a functional mutation from medical to cosmetic" (Ruby and Ruby 2004: 119). The history of this shift illustrates the way in which hygiene has as much to do with maintaining a "clean" subject as it does with preventing the spread of illness. But this chapter asks, further, how this history and mutation has imbued our "cosmetic" (which I do not undertake to define in opposition to medical) hygiene with a sense of responsibility, health, and self-care. For an account of the way in which this debate about medical necessity and cosmetics is taken up in conversations about transsexuality, see Cressida J. Heyes' chapter "Feminist Solidarity After Queer Theory: The Case of Transgender" in *Self-Transformations: Foucault, Ethics, and Normalized Bodies* (Heyes 2007).

7 "If we shower every morning, then this is not dictated solely by hygienic necessity; in fact, there is even evidence that our skin may dry out excessively as a result. Yet this malfunction does legitimize a new kind of cosmetic hedonism: after showering we lavishly rub moisturising cream into our thin skin and enjoy the feeling of doing something good to our body (when in fact we are only repairing damage that we have inflicted ourselves)" (Ruby and Ruby 2004: 125).

8 This tendency to justify modernism as functionalism is summarized famously by American architect Louis Sullivan: "form ever follows function" (Sullivan 1896: 4).

4

QUEER EXTERIORS

Transgender Aesthetics in Early Gay and Lesbian Advertising

Quinn Miller

The defining events of my sexual history are often unexpected, involving unpredictable partners in unlikely settings, yet the silent mentor who taught me to cruise and the setting of that fleeting lesson were fitting. Scanning an erotically charged Boystown scene during Chicago's Market Days street fair, I locked into an eyeline match of cinematic proportions with a man I crossed paths with on the sidewalk. The immediate agreement of our looks amplified our uncanny likeness as erotic objects, and the sexual charge between us peaked in the realization that we looked as alike and as dissimilar as any two people in that massive crowd on Halsted Street possibly could. Despite my much longer hair and his height, and the fact that he was self-evidently gay and I was clearly a dyke, we looked strikingly similar, and the sexual charge between us was stunning. Halsted Street's ability to foster such a complex erotics of sameness and difference in a novice fag is hardly surprising. What is surprising, in retrospect, is how this gay tutorial doubled as my initiation into the world of transgender aesthetics, a world Jack Halberstam describes as an "interesting place" where "the abstract and the figural [...] inhabit the same space at the same time" (Halberstam 2005: 124). As I would come to find in the years that followed, self-understanding, sex, and trans aesthetics come together in "queer times and places," which make settings and the people in them more complex. Highlighting the power of a look, whether fleeting or sustained, Sailor Raven explains, "Our vision is transformative" (Raven 2004: 51). Addressing a lover, he writes, "You are new in your own skin because I see you male, something else, something less simple." In some trans contexts, "sex is transformation as we bring each other into the bodies we thought we'd be, how we were meant to exist" (51).

My memorable Market Days encounter, which facilitated new movement across gender through a shared look, is one of many sexual moments that, in shaping

Chicago's geography, remain enshrined by the streetscape of North Halsted. In a very real sense, this expanse helped constitute my trans subjectivity, a formation process that continues to impact the queer space people negotiate in Boystown. The most palpable component of the exchange, besides the visceral feeling of the electric look my cruising mentor and I shared, is a vision of Halsted Street, composed of the businesses I frequented, observed, and cathected on—a landscape marked by a horizon line of building facades stretching from the 7-Eleven to the Chicago Diner, and from the Kit Kat Club to the Abbott Hotel. Gay activist Lou Sullivan's account of his own transformation also hinges on a fleeting encounter. In a letter to a co-worker who saw him as "transparently a heterosexual woman," Sullivan described "finally … beginning to try to reconcile a boy within me" after an "awakening," in which "a beautiful gay came up to me on the street in the fall of '71" (Sullivan [1973] 2006: 164). While the moment was melancholy—Lou was running late and did not speak to the man—the regret that followed fueled his imagination and his transition. He writes, "I knew when I … left that beauty standing there that I'd never stop regretting that moment." The missed opportunity for conversation, camaraderie, and possible sex captures an elusive dimension of Sullivan's transition and a particularly ephemeral element of queer transitions and queer trans culture.

While sex changes are generally registered with respect to the individual, they reverberate through trans people's interpersonal relationships and throughout public culture. Although individual encounters with space are aleatory, practices that create queer space affect the landscape. Even before a gender transition officially begins, and long after it may be more or less complete, one-off encounters produce new kinds of self-perception, gendering habits, erotic imaginaries, and everyday vision. Yet these encounters seem to leave no trace and are absent from most accounts of queer history. In spite of this, trans aesthetics persist, in the living archive of geography around sex and its impact on built environments. While there is little material evidence to marshal in support of such an argument, illustrations of building facades and photographs of cruising spots, which appeared regularly in queer publications from the 1960s into the 1980s, demonstrate the importance of a transgender erotics in gay and lesbian uses of iconic streetscapes. These advertising images produced a powerful aura around "queer exteriors"—representations of places and bodies that endow their surfaces, or their relative absence or ambiguity of identifying marks, with meaning conducive to gender transition and complexity.[1] In this representational system, physical structures like the Kit Kat Club marquee and the Chicago Diner facade, or the buildings lining the streets of Milwaukee, Wisconsin, where Sullivan lived and worked at the time of his letter, carry traces of trans encounters at the level of cultural memory—cultural memory established not only through experience, but also through intertextual networks of media production attuned to sex, transformation, and physical space. Whether queer exteriors are part of public settings generally assumed heteronormative or housed within gay and lesbian commercial districts, they have—as seemingly unremarkable backdrops to trans, and proto-trans, practices—fueled and preserved a diversity of lived histories. In making material an important dynamic between queer space, queer sex, and gender transition, queer exteriors reveal an "erotics of knowledge" tailored to, in the words of Michel de Certeau, "the ecstasy of reading such a cosmos" (de Certeau 1999: 127). During the 1960s and 1970s, advertisements in the gay and lesbian press registered the materiality of transgender experiences, often focalizing themes of queer life through the figure of the building facade. However, assumptions about the closetedness of gay businesses across this period have prevented a more serious study of their aesthetics. Investigating the queer exterior image cycle complicates current understandings of the evolution of LGBT consumer culture and the predominance of the closet prior to mainstream visibility. Its trans aesthetics propel the recovery of diverse histories from within.

The Rise and Fall of the Printed Building Facade

In the U.S., information about gay bars and businesses began circulating internationally, through printed directories as well as word of mouth, at least as early as the 1950s. In the ensuing decades, images of building facades blossomed in the underground and alternative presses. During the 1960s, competing directories emerged, each with extensive domestic and international entries made possible by grassroots participation. After '*Spartacus*' published 3000 entries in its first edition in 1970, it claimed to receive thousands of letters annually, which it used to correct and update its listings. Guides often included a response form for ease of correspondence or a blank page at the back for note taking. *Barfly*, the *Advocate*'s national gay business guide of 1971, called these "trick pages," but notes were expected to include directions to bars off the beaten path and geographical markers for cruising spots, as well as individual phone numbers. As was common, the '*International Guild Guide*' solicited corrections and additions from readers, especially in "states and areas not well represented." The *EOS-Guide 70/71*, published out of Copenhagen, encouraged correspondence with a postcard reply slip. Collaboration lent continuity to the spatial imaginary of the community, as participants prevailed despite hostile owners at many locations and rapid, ongoing change to the overall landscape. Soliciting details for its 1973 issue, the *Incognito Guide* editor wrote, "Tell us the names of the places that you advise to visit in your own country. Our world moves so fast!" In this context, an illustrated ad served as evidence that a bar had stayed in business long enough to warrant publicity. With frequent talk of outdated listings, a picture suggested that the place would be there if and when you showed up. As images of specific locations accumulated across many different publications, the trend came to represent the subcultural commercial infrastructure emerging across the U.S. at this time.[2]

LGBT periodicals of the 1960s and 1970s rarely included pictures of the interiors of the businesses they advertised and reported on. In the early years, these publications were composed mainly of text. Across the 1950s and 1960s, some ads began to include graphics, most of which focused on the place's physical location and exterior appearance, mediating interest about the queer worlds within establishments through the details seen from outside. Building facades, which were rendered more or less obsolete by digital technologies and the rise of mainstream gay consumption across the 1980s and 1990s, were relatively simple drawings and appeared in a range of sizes. In an era before corporate recognition of a gay market, local businesses, which generally stood alone, figured prominently in the domestic and transnational routes of queer travelers. Images of such places were some of the most prominent graphics in gay and lesbian newspapers, pamphlets, magazines, journals, and directories during the early era of gay and lesbian advertising, when people began to use large-scale print production to forge queer connections in public space. As alternative print cultures proliferated across this period, queer publications fostered an intertextual landscape coincident with the local iterations of international commercial networks through graphics that shuttled between figural images—of buildings, bodies, and buildings-as-bodies—and abstract representations—of the imaginative possibilities these buildings and bodies produce, particularly with respect to sexual pleasure.

In queer exteriors, the detailed characteristics of building facades—which served as practical visual cues or functional landmarks—were aestheticized, lending abstract qualities to the apparently figural. These images represented the possibilities of social encounters and sexual exchanges in a manner that circumvented the closet. Specific places were clearly established as queer by their appearance in a lesbian or gay publication, no matter how unmarked their facades appeared. Businesses that may appear to have been hidden, based on their location and lack of signage, were often furtive in a familiar way, with their familiarity hingeing on an apparent secrecy. In the context of a social network of familiarly "furtive" buildings and openly circulated addresses, the nondescript building facade was provocatively emblematic of a set of social relations to which some people were privy and others oblivious. At the time, a building facade with a shadowy entryway in a desolate landscape produced a special sense of mystery about who might congregate inside, how they might be gendered, and what they might want sexually, which made the place more alluring, positioning its interior in a productive and poetic relationship to its exterior. In the broader context of lesbian and gay print culture, this aesthetic associated queer hot spots with mundane buildings, which were common. In line with this aesthetic, queer exteriors in print made imaginative rather than mimetic use of signage. Some ads would enlarge signs, while others would add them. Instead of a direct or predetermined relationship between signage and visibility, their graphics fostered a variety of possible relationships between a building's exterior and what Christopher Reed has called their "look (or antilook)" (Reed 1996: 179).

The mobile culture of gay and lesbian socio-economic networks, which were organized around cruising, community, and a wide range of travel habits, made significant claims on public space. Yet, scholars generally consider bars and other businesses in operation at this time closeted, a classification made without assessing the appearance or social use of specific locations, based on a general consensus about the enforced invisibility of queer life before the ACT UP era. In comparison with constructions of gay visibility in the present, the "shuttered and camouflaged street facades, mazelike entryways, and intimidating signage of gay and lesbian bars" of the past are assumed to correspond with "low imageability," because these markers "do not accommodate the eyes of outsiders" (Usborne 1973: 567). However, contemporary icons like rainbow flags (or rainbow Bud Light signs) are themselves codes that are not universally recognized. The presence of symbols that are now considered evidence of a business's "out" status are often resolutely viewed, in the context of the earlier era of gay and lesbian commerce, as symptomatic of a "closeted economy" (Gluckman and Reed 1997: xv). Within this paradoxical framework, queer exterior images are emblematic of the closeted nature of a subterranean economic network and the secretive social climate it is presumed to have cultivated. Reed, for example, argues that the physical structures of buildings reflected the "secrecy and stigmatization" defining gay life in the 1970s.

Queer establishments' anti-look looks followed from disciplinary measures. However, the anti-look was often concurrently—and sometimes predominantly—a reflection of erotic tastes and sexual scene setting. Patrick Califia (1997) has described this ambiance and facade style as a "token invisibility" required of businesses centered on sex (179). He explains that, within a system of "red light" gentrification that demands sexual commerce remain hidden from respectable classes, specific choices about looks and signage propel queer venues toward a collective aesthetics of mediated visibility, according to which nondescript markers signal, to insiders, an obviously queer facade. "Any time you see a bar called the Eagle," Califia writes, "you know it is a queer leather bar" (190). Throughout this period, an unforthcoming presence contributed to many erotic scenes, and overlaps between queer and straight social spaces were complex. As John Howard (1999) has explained, "Queer locations generated speculation and intrigue. Though purposely removed, they nonetheless fostered curiosity and fascination, for those both likely and unlikely to enter" (96). No matter what kind of clientele a club catered to, the owner could choose to cultivate a clandestine environment, with features like blank brick walls, nearby vacant lots, or boarded-up windows. While gay bars specialized in this kind of decor, they were in many cases no more hidden than straight bars of a similar ilk. In other instances, straight bars with similar looks served as gay meeting places. In yet other instances, the consistently "mixed" character of bars undercut the notion of a closet specific to homosexuality.

The anti-look, which Reed (1996) has argued "characterized not only bars, but the women's bookstores and cafes of the 1970s," circulated widely, disseminating trans aesthetics in relation to—but also apart from—individuals' own night lives and travel plans (190). The typical ad for a range of places—including bookstores, bars, restaurants, sex shops, bathhouses, and hotels—consisted of a sketch of the venue's exterior. A 1982 map of Valencia Street, San Francisco, for example, included renderings of nine notable business locations. The illustration is abstract in that it represents the people of the community with images of something other than themselves, but it is also figural, in that the building facades that stand in for people are rendered in realistic detail, and compose a functional map. Through combinations of figural and abstract aesthetics, queer exteriors conveyed intangible elements about a neighborhood's inhabitants at the same time as the visual information they relayed rendered the community's actual participants accessible in everyday life. The trans aesthetic in queer exteriors worked not only by representing shifts across the abstract and the figural, but also by overlaying the figural and the abstract as one and the same. Queer exteriors produced a transgender aesthetic by complicating distinctions between abstract and figural representations of space in relation to people's bodies and their reception.

In general, transgender forms create mobility between categories of assigned sex and lived gender. Queer exteriors' trans aesthetics projected a space of possibility for the interaction of internal and external manifestations of a place. The abstract dimensions of the graphics' figurative imagery meshed people and places, allowing building facades and bodies to resonate with shifts between the relationship of insides and outsides along a current intertwined with trans identification and practices.

In a mid-1970s ad for the Houston Guest House, a chiseled clone does arm curls with the hotel, suggesting a unique contrast—pictured in the inverse—between the actual place and the action inside (see Figure 4.1). Other illustrations represented spatial mobility alongside the long-standing cross-gender practices of queer cultures, such as in a 1985 ad for the "David Information Network," a service out of San Francisco. The illustration, which referenced *The Wizard of Oz*, featured a young and fragile-looking Dorothy standing nervously at the prominently marked intersection of 18th and Castro Streets as a tornado carries away her rural childhood home ("International"). The ad's depiction of gay migrants through the figure of a young girl and its use of physical structures, street iconography, and the building facade are indicative of a broader connection between gender mobility and transgender aesthetics around space, which were central to the meaning systems of lesbian and gay imagery in pre-1990s print culture, not least in the way their representations of queer gender and specific places coincided across abstract and figurative elements. In positing a new homecoming, for example, the narrative of the "David Information Network" ad pivots on the interior/exterior dynamics it constructs around Dorothy's lost house and the built environment of her new location, as well as on the movement of gender crossing, as related symbols of self-acceptance and collectivity. These ads' use of images of bodies and exteriors suggests an overarching consonance between transgender aesthetics and the vocabulary of lesbian and gay life in the 1960s and 1970s. With the fundamental overlap between the figural and the abstract in the settings they create, a "queer place" emerges where different physiques could be situated in agreement. The dynamics between space, sexual practice, gender, and geography images like this represent the early imaginaries of trans gender that emerged within gay and lesbian social formations.

FIGURE 4.1 The queer exterior as free weight. Charles Deering McCormick Library of Special Collections, Northwestern University Library

This framework allowed queer exterior images and the intertextual network they composed to circumnavigate the social dictum to "closet" sexual difference. Eve Kosofsky Sedgwick (1990) has shown that questions of homo/heterosexual definition take place "in a setting … of urgent homophobic pressure to devalue one of the two nominally symmetrical forms," arguing that an "irresolvably unstable" distinction in sexual classification renders homosexuality "not symmetrical with but subordinated to" heterosexuality (9–10). However, in representing particular places according to a "counterpublic" discourse, queer exteriors designated spaces within which, as Michael Warner puts it, "no one is in the closet" (Warner 2002b: 120). Without appealing to metaphors of the hidden, the invisible, or the underground, these graphics represented a landscape that "suspended" not merely the need to hide but also, more fundamentally, "the presumptive heterosexuality that constitutes the closet for individuals in ordinary speech" (Warner 2002b: 120). Yet, the epistemology of the closet is replicated in studies of LGBT commercial space and its aesthetics, which take the lack of signage, for example, as evidence of a "closet" mentality. In the counterpublic context fostered by queer exteriors, the terms for signifying sex cultures shifted away from the broader discourse privileging heterosexuality.

A late 1970s ad for a San Francisco leather club called Headquarters, for example, described the "hot music," "hot people," and hot food available 24 hours a day, using a sense of disproportion in urban geography and scale to figure the complex dynamics of signage, naming, advertising, and visibility in the world of gay social spaces. Depicting the place as an oasis in a barren landscape along Folsom Street, a district known for its fetish clubs, the illustration showed an empty street scene that doubled as a map. While the image was unpopulated by human figures and evacuated of competing establishments, it invoked the collective social and sexual activity in the surrounding area. As the only physical structure in the graphic, the Headquarters facade is the focus of attention, which directs associations with the general area toward the interior of this particular place, projecting the reputation of Folsom Street and the Country and Western motifs of the image—a rope border, branded "HQ" logo, and saloon-style font—through its exterior. A logo for the New York City leather club 9 Plus makes the figural and abstract aspects of many other architecture- and map-themed graphics apparent. In this 1970 ad, a big black dot offsets a chain of interlocking white ovals that circle the inside of the dark disk, leading to a destination where "x" marks the spot (*Wheels*, January 1969). Together these elements compose a jagged circular shape that suggests machinery, including gears, tires, and the hardware required to work on a vehicle (see Figure 4.2). The graphic both figures and abstracts the physical act of S/M sex, creating an aerial view of Manhattan that synthesizes the erotic imaginary of leather and Levi's fetishes. Overlaying its representation of space onto its representation of sex, it suggests a person could take a number of different routes; start from a variety of initial locations; make some detours along the way; or be deliberately roundabout in the course they charted; and still end up at the club.

FIGURE 4.2 An "x" marks the spot. The aerial exterior as evidence of pleasure. Provided courtesy of Leather Archives & Museum

As the 9 Plus club and Headquarters ads suggest, the powerful dynamics of queer exterior images emerged in the context of multiple continuities and discrepancies in signification across print representations and public space. Intermittent cover illustrations for *The Lesbian Connection* across the late 1970s, which picture the outsides of stores, women's centers, and lesbian couples' houses, demonstrate the various contours of this dynamic. The series of images includes two images focused on individual businesses, a "Womyn's Store" in a decidedly urban area and a "Lesbian Outlet" whose location is less pronounced, as well as a later cover, which represents three uncertainly commercial brownstones set back from the street—a "Lesbian Center," the "Old Dyke's Home" next door, and a building advertising books for sale in its bay window. In some ways, the buildings in the latter image seem less visible as lesbian spaces than the abundantly labeled storefronts represented on the previous covers. At the same time, however, the facades of the less conspicuous buildings seem to say more than their predecessors. While the first two covers are crudely rendered and rely on text to signify lesbian space, the later eschews explanatory signage as the sole condition of visibility, instead using stylized facade detail to represent the exciting possibilities inside the shared world of the structures. This illustration of the space can appear both more closeted and more out, depending on the criteria for visibility and the audience's relationship to queer exteriors.

Complex signifying dynamics are evident in the earliest and most unsophisticated queer exterior images. Through different approaches, extremely simple ads superimposed figural and abstract representation in their interior/exterior dynamics. Many individual ads emphasized unique exteriors by excerpting one element of a structure or framing it within a border. For example, an early 1970s ad for the Café San Marcos, a women's bar in San Francisco's Castro district, provided a partial picture of its baroque exterior against a blank background encompassed by a square shape. Curving the logo of its name to mirror the shape of the arch on its distinctive facade, it uses a minor detail to stand in for the entire structure, which represents its interior permeating the space outside its bounds. In a similar vein, an illustration used to advertise the Academy Hotel on Sunset Boulevard in Hollywood tucked the hotel into the bottom right corner of a larger archway, which lent the small-scale print ad the shape and properties of a keyhole. Like the street map image advertising Headquarters, the arches represent entryways to the world inside. A related movement occurred at the level of the directory. A late 1960s inventory of bars in the state of Illinois included two relatively crudely rendered sketches of building facades alongside a long list of locations for Chicago and Springfield, the smaller state capitol. Due to the page layout, the specific places to which these pictures correspond are unclear, rendering the book itself a passageway into a different world, which is represented by pictures of individual places.

Other ads explored forms of interior/exterior mobility—which resonated with the rendering of building facades in ad illustrations—by uniting sex and space in a wide shot of the landscape that individual cruising spots compose. An illustration for *Vector* magazine conflates the hills of San Francisco with the bulging blue jeans of a reclining man, with the garment's stitching serving as tracks for cable cars and dotted highway lines. An ad for a bar called Cheeks superimposed a man's ass "cheeks" on the downtown Chicago skyline, simultaneously evoking the experience of anal sex and the physical structures that constitute the iconic "Second City." With its visual layout, which offers an abstract portrayal of erotic encounters through the more literal image of penetration by skyscraper, the Cheeks ad creates the kind of "interesting place" to which Halberstam's theory of transgender aesthetics and queer time refers. Covers of the gay leather newsletter *Wheels!* also experimented with different scales and superimpositions, in sketches of men with their motorcycles. An image transposing a biker with his motorcycle merges its representation of the body with the vehicle's machinery to create a phallic kickstand, a protruding tire aligned with the figure's groin, and headlight bulges that both outline muscular shoulders and double as pectoral muscles and protruding nipples (April 1969) (see Figure 4.3).

Another image arranged a set of highway lines around a cyclist. Intersecting in the figure, these roadways represent the erotic and transformative possibilities inherent in the biker's body as he travels, as well as the possible routes he might take. Protruding from him as rays of erotic energy and impending motion, these lines of movement indicate the figure's ability to head in numerous directions. These constructions of space invested in gay iconography around the lure of the road and the topography of the landscape, creating a masculine look through a transgender aesthetic (September 1968).

Gay History and Transgender Aesthetics

The visual discourse of queer exteriors was supported by print texts whose spatial imaginaries conflicted with the closet. The 1969 "Homosexual Intransigent!"

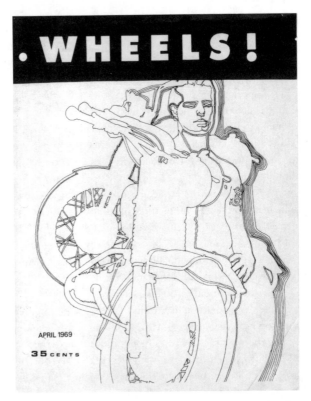

FIGURE 4.3 Interiors, exteriors, and beyond. A topographical study of queer bodies in space. Provided courtesy of Leather Archives & Museum

newsletter *Homosexual Renaissance*, for example, regularly recounted details of gay worlds in New York City and beyond in a column called "Second City." As George Chauncey (1994) has argued, a device like the "second city" metaphor "in effect, reterritorialized the city in order to construct a gay city in the midst of ... the normative city" (23). While significant constraints around access based on class, ability, racism, and racial segregation impacted the publics that formed through queer print media at this time, the mode of address that characterized many gay liberation publications concerned with travel was particularly conducive to the inclusion of a wide range of sexual minorities. The writers of an emblematic magazine called *Ciao!: The World of Gay Travel* (1973–79), a bimonthly color physique journal intended for "gay guys who have no hang ups," generally scripted their columns with an open first person plural voice welcoming to anyone willing to identify with its implicit gay pride rhetoric, unabashed support of pornography and public sex, and interest in travel, beyond the usual urban suspects, to small US towns and a variety of international locations. Likewise, although lesbian social formations were notoriously hostile to transsexual people through the 1970s, queer exteriors such as the *Lesbian Connection* covers and the Valencia map routinely featured trans aesthetics. *Ciao!* in waxing poetic from the perspective of "we" *Ciao!* readers, allowed its public to fill in their own idea of "us" when it made claims, for example, like, "There are a lot of us, and in the bigger cities at least there is no shortage of meeting places; just flipping the pages of the gay travel directory we publish will tell you that much—if you don't already know it" (Nov/Dec 1976).

Across the early period of gay and lesbian advertising, queer commercial networks solidified within the subculture and informal socio-economic structures emerged as an expected and unremarkable aspect of life, creating a sense of ongoing contact with gay and lesbian worlds. The proliferation of queer exterior images made the facades of gay and lesbian businesses a part of readers' visual landscapes, registering the materiality of everyday practices in their aesthetics. *Ciao!* expanded on the entries in gay directories and the illustrations in advertisements by providing details about locations of interest. The magazine's catalog of cruising grounds foregrounded the visual landscape of queer sex cultures by systematically representing these places with photographs of building exteriors. Using the same layout to showcase building exteriors from Baltimore, Maryland and the Italian Riviera, *Ciao!* treated mundane locales as thoroughly and formulaically as the most recognizable international tourist destinations, further emphasizing the potential of the unadorned exterior in the economy of queer visual culture. The building facade was the central element in its exhaustive listings, which ran small black-and-white snapshots alongside text in several of its regular sections, which featured at least five destinations each issue. The sheer quantity of facade photographs in *Ciao!* created an effect similar to the more abstract and stylized queer exterior illustrations. Provoking readers to see the inside of a building without it being shown, these graphics manifested a particular way of relating to space, which fostered transformative modes of communication about gender and sexuality.

At the time, building facades stood as a powerful representation of common everyday practices through which people actively queered space. Queer exterior images emerged in queer print culture as queers began to impact the visual landscape in new ways, and as queer space became a more established part of the built environment. Within the broader context of queer claims on space, printed facades accrued a materiality related to the lived practices of people in these places. These images deployed aesthetic constructions around the question of the closet central to queer representation and the emergence of queer culture across literary, gallery art, and underground film production during the era. The power of individual buildings to evoke a sedimented history that exceeds their location trades on the materiality of transgender aesthetics in early gay and lesbian advertising, and this signifying process corresponds with a legacy of trans participation in lesbian and gay social formations. Photographer Catherine Opie (Reilly 2001) has argued that the social formations of sexual minorities, which thrive at the subcultural level, make an impact on the construction of public space even if dominant culture has no idea they exist, in commentary suggesting that queer and trans genders are crucial to this process. Within Opie's oeuvre, queer people leave their marks on buildings and other physical structures in ways that coincide with how their understandings of themselves mark their own appearance.[3] As Reed explains, although people can constitute queer space, "that doesn't mean it disappears when we leave" (Reed 1996: 123). The landscape, in particular, "is never just a backdrop; it transforms and is in turn transformed ... in the process of its use as a queer site." As Ira Tattelman (1997) argues, the effects of queers in space are long-lasting. New York City's unoccupied old bathhouses, for example, "are not empty of history or meaning" (400). As Tattelman puts it, "The bathhouse still has something valuable to say" (405). Physical structures "have something to say" following from the ephemeral connection between queer experiences and space generally, but also, more specifically, because representations of them spoke volumes in print throughout key decades in queer history.

As the materiality of trans genders and trans movements coincide in sex practices, trans experiences and ethics of perception affect public space. While cruising culture is often reduced to rote anonymous pick-ups, it involves people silently communicating their genders alongside their desires for particular sex acts or sexual scripts. More generally, lesbian and gay culture has circulated important lines of sexual distinction that exceed or displace the "opposite-" or "same-sex" model of sexual identity, most notably in BDSM and fetish cultures. In these ways, some sites of queer erotics have been coextensive with the cultivation of trans erotics. As a result, gay and lesbian sex cultures have been one of the principal settings in which people have elaborated a queer version of what Julia Serano (2007) calls gendering. Trans-positive gendering systems—in which people take cues from gender expression rather than secondary sex characteristics and actively recognizing that the people they encounter in everyday situations may be transsexual or transgender—may seem to have evolved relatively recently, but the groundwork of its aesthetic components were forged earlier, in the broader context of trans aesthetics in a variety of widely circulating queer exteriors.

During the 1960s and 1970s, the terms "gay" and "gay and lesbian" included many gender variant and gender queer people. As Califia writes, "other sexual minorities—lesbians, transvestites and transsexuals, sadomasochists, etc.—tend to make parallel use of any gay male social space when their presence is tolerated" (Califia 1997: 182). Likewise, Howard provides evidence that transgender people participated in these social networks at this historical moment and shows that their experience is a fundamental part of what is known as "gay culture." His study of US Southerners at mid-century includes a trans woman, as well as an intersex man who, after being "labeled female on the birth certificate, lived as a boy, then a gay man, for the rest of his life" (Howard 1999: 123, 122). According to Howard, the "fluid sociability" and the "relative ease" of finding queer sex in a variety of different establishments from the 1950s through the 1970s suggests that, in many regions of America, "conceptions of sexuality that did not privilege sexual object-choice, or the biological sex of one's partner, as a primary technique of categorization" and that queerer approaches coincided with the rigid understandings of homo/heterosexuality, presumed to dominate during the period (99). More specifically, in some places, "queer eroticism was framed not solely as 'orientation'—an essential drive for a partner of a particular ('the same') biological sex—but also as an appetite for a particular gender performance."

Although the idea of travel as a resource for trans people is somewhat counter-intuitive, and severe constraints on transgender people who do not pass or have their papers in order are high, concerns about the limits imposed by discrimination should not overshadow the sense of defiance and self-sufficiency that often marks the personal histories of trans people. The desire to travel can supersede concerns about safety and propel us to circulate in presumably hostile spaces. As Gordon Brent Ingram (1997) writes, "Surviving queer … often requires knowing how to travel across hostile territory—whether it be physical, emotional, cultural, or theoretical" (27). Based on ethnographic research, Howard writes, "Though sometimes subject to intimidation and violence … queer Mississippians proved adept at maneuvering through hostile terrain. They often remade material and ideological spaces and thereby regularly found themselves in the company of like-minded souls" (Howard 1999: xiv). The spatial constructions of media culture and people's identity formations are intertwined, and travel—whether in fantasy or practice—has clearly fueled, inspired, and sustained the lives of queer trans people, who have traveled not only for doctor consultations and operations, but also out of wanderlust and a desire for adventure, sex, self-exploration, and self-reinvention.

The motif of the queer exterior complicates current understandings of LGBT commercial history at the level of material culture and ephemeral experience. Dominant versions of queer history often indicate that, before shifts toward gay and lesbian visibility in the 1990s, bars and the people in them were closeted. Scholars of gay commerce often contrast a "pre-Stonewall 'closet economy,'" of isolated and potentially criminal institutions with the "out" commercial networks of urban gay districts (Gluckman and Reed 1997: xv). Jeffrey Escoffier (1997), for example, describes gay commercial systems prior to the late 1970s as quintessentially closeted in a pre-Stonewall style. In light of more recent developments in gay and lesbian tourism, Jon Binnie and Beverly Skeggs describe the "queer visual statements" of contemporary sites as a product of the "compact visibility" particular to "gay ghettos" or "gay villages" which the authors argue signify in sum, "We're here, we're queer—so get used to it" (Binnie and Skeggs 2006: 230). In spite of the perceived invisibility of early lesbian and gay businesses, and the perceived recent spike in explicitness, however, the closet was not a monolithic force prior to the 1990s (or the 1970s), and it did not prevent businesses from engaging the broader context of the closet in their appearance. As John Grube (1997) shows, "a dichotomy of pre- and post-Stonewall space is too simplistic," and a framework limiting the liberation economy to urban gay neighborhoods is limiting and misleading (127). Yet in the dominant narrative, "out" businesses require straight recognition of a national gay market, an entity Katherine Sender (2004) argues consists of a sanitized demographic of "'respectable' gay consumers" desired by big businesses, ad agencies, and official tourism boards (18).

Representations of the anti-look that many businesses cultivated as part of early lesbian and gay economic networks are not evidence that these places and their patrons were closeted. Queer exteriors indicate what Ingram calls a "well-defined trajectory" toward queer public space that "emerged before the Stonewall riots ... as a key element of cultural expression and community activism" (Ingram 1997: 29). As Sedgwick has established, the epistemology of the closet is an artistic device as well as a regulatory trope. In addition to producing "closeted" and "out" individuals among a homosexual minority, the closet organizes representations of interiors and exteriors, fueling aesthetic explorations—in material and imaginative forms—of the tensions between people's psycho-sexual lives and their interactions with others. The closet is generally seen as an impartial and fully repressive force, and Warner has argued that trans people negotiate a version of the closet, which requires we "come out" about who we are, or are not, as opposed to (or in addition to) coming out about our sexual object choices (Warner 2002b: 53). However, in negotiating sexual encounters in everyday life, the closet is, as a site of productive regulation, also a source of eroticism, gender expression, and self-identification. As Christopher Nealon (2001) points out, postwar physique magazines—typically understood as closeted gay publications passing as straight in a more naïve era—invested in a "delicate" closet, which allowed individual figures to "represent desires" that were "more elusive and more collective than single bodies" (110). In a related alliance of gender, sex, and space, Marcus Rene Van (2004) emphasizes the importance of trans aesthetics and collaborative sexual contexts to the materiality of trans practices. He explains, "Trans sexuality is ... mental and physical pleasure existing in the same space. It's a fragile world, constructed on beliefs and acceptance, and mirrored in a partner's gaze. ... The connection between partners is visceral and real. Our worlds are connected at some place that reaches beneath the surface" (54). Transgender worlds—fragile though they may be—are concretely established through the compatibility of queer gender and sex practices on abstract and figurative registers, in print and practice.

As counterintuitive as it may seem, representations of queer desires—for sex and space—in the early gay and lesbian press pioneered a sophisticated realm of trans aesthetics. In the history of queer representation and its relation to the meanings and use of social space, queer exterior images explored a more complex relationship between places, bodies, perception, and erotics than is typically acknowledged. By representing some of the sexual settings of queer culture in the 1960s and 1970s, while experimenting with relations—and conflations—between the figural and the abstract, the aesthetics of these underground and alternative print cultures helped generate different possible forms of gender and gender transition. The connection between queer and trans representation may appear to be at once highly metaphoric and too literal, yet it is something else altogether, something that captures crucial material aspects of trans history as a long-standing collaborative process that is equally abstract and figural. As a jumble of psycho-sexual sensations, as well as a set of possible medical, legal, and bureaucratic procedures, gender transition is simultaneously figural and abstract, in varying proportions; self-perceptions and physical manifestations of gender shift across surfaces and through spaces. The average illustration of a building facade was a tribute to the built environment and the socio-economic infrastructure that supported everyday experiences of cruising, gender variance, and gender transition. Ads put forth a variety of specific images alongside less tangible ideas about bodies, space, gender, and sex. In generating a complex field of possibilities around the interplay between physical and psychological constructions of interiors and exteriors, these representations register trans people's connections as a primary component within and across different histories of queer culture. Without historiographical insight into the trans aesthetics of gay and lesbian advertising, the material evidence of queer exteriors might be lost amid a more typical history project charting the progress of "same-sex" economic networks, which offer no record of trans people and no place for queers. The trans aesthetics of the queer exterior—which were as conspicuous as the business they pictured—suggests a different history, a system of collective exchange in which the implicit creativity of queer and trans practices are as inseparable as the abstract and figural features of their cultural production.

Notes

Frank Serafino, Russell Maylone, Scott Krafft, Daniel Bao, Rick Storer, Nick Davis, Chuck Kleinhans, Hamid Naficy, and Lynn Spigel assisted in the early phases of this research. I dedicate the chapter to everyone who has ever taken me someplace and to Frank, for introducing me to *Ciao!*

1 I discuss the queer exterior in lesbian and gay publications as a single coherent cycle of representation; however, this trend was staggered over time according to the disparity of wealth between men and women. The types of images I focus on appeared most prominently in gay publications in the 1960s and 1970s and in lesbian newsletters during a later period in the 1970s and 1980s.

2 While issues of privilege and access are crucial to investigations of travel and tourism, participation in queer exterior imagery required less mobility and fewer resources than one might assume.

3 Opie has described her landscape series, which feature building exteriors and strip mall facades, as congruent with her more high-profile portrait series "Being and Having," stating that "the language of the people is embedded in the body of the structures in the same way that the language is embedded on the bodies of my friends and myself as a structure of identity" (Reilly 2001: 93). Addressing a parallel between buildings and human figures, Opie suggests that the relationship between people's identities and their bodies is similar to the relationship between a building and its exterior, arguing that the markings on the facades of buildings and people's modifications of their bodies relate queer/trans histories in public space.

5

SPIDERWOMEN: NOTES ON TRANSPOSITIONS

Eva Hayward

To write this chapter, I took the word "transpositions" for a series of walks through a number of readings, experiences, and streets = the activity of the topic: a mapping through the senses with which one emerges as bodily. To transpose is an act of changing something into another form, or to transfer to a different place or context: transmutations but also translations, alterations in modes of expression. "Transposes" can be perversions or deviations, misdirections that discompose order and arrange-ment. Working through these etymologies of "transpositions," I want to fuse the workings of sex transitions (particularly male-to-female) with forces and excitations of habitat, location, and neighborhood, by which I mean that, for me, transpositions refer to the physical sensation of change, of unprecedented corporeal and sensorial states constituted through transsexual transitions as they are shaped by spatial and environmental orientations. Transpositions are structurally sensuous—sensation is the basic unit of emergence—modalities of simultaneously changing, being, and positioning.

My accounts of male-to-female transsexual transitioning in an urban setting might appear unavoidably as drifts in personal recollection—as in "my story"—but they are meant to suggest, however speculatively, and without aiming toward uni-versalizing, the sensuous transactions between body and environment. It is impos-sible anymore, if even it ever was, to categorically define the ways that transsexuals become trans-sexed. Indeed, attempts to definitively name, chart, and absolutely frame all the matrices of trans-becoming are among the injustices committed against transsexuals (Bailey 2003; Hausman 1995; Jeffreys 2002; Millot 1990; Raymond 1994).

Why? Why this personal approach? The personal is not the same as the individual but an opportunity to see how lived experience is the basis for investigation of more generalizable forms (Sobchack 2006). By redeploying the medicalized legacy of transsexuals self-narrativizing, constructing a diachronic of narrative from a synchronous field of wrong body-ness so that a diagnosis can be given, I use my own carnal knowledge of transsexuality to push back at larger political, historical, and cultural currents. Rather than reading such reflexivity as navel-gazing or as a failure of critical distance, I want to say that transsexuality is necessarily predicated on kinds of self-disclosure and as such the bodily feel of transitioning is unavoidably "personal." Consequently, I offer transpositions not through explanation or definition, but only through description.

> *Tenderloin, tender meat: taken from under the short ribs in the hindquarters, is the loin, animal flesh, or soft underbelly. In common vernacular, a "Tenderloin" is a district of a city where crime and vice are prominent. Perhaps no surprise that hard-boiled detective fiction (Dashiell Hammett lived at 891 Post Street) and film noir (The Maltese Falcon, John Huston, 1941) would emerge from the carnal, wet, and chiaroscuro streets of San Francisco's Tenderloin. My home: 1028 Post Street, San Francisco, part of that Hollywood inspired noir-hood. It is a small studio. A claw-footed bathtub. One view of the neighboring brick building. A fire escape.*
>
> *I am here to "tend my loins," to trans-sex. I am not sure why this neighborhood, but it seems like a return, a need. An act of inverted diaspora? Coming home to a place already made by the labors, deaths, and loves of other trans-women?*

Neighborhood: The *Oxford English Dictionary* tells us that neighborhoods are "a community; a number of people who live close together; a vicinity or surrounding area." They are "the quality, condition, or fact of being situated near to someone or something; nearness, proximity." An urban neighborhood in the U.S.: people moving along streets on foot, or by car or bicycle; cell phones vibrating and ensuing conversations; pigeons sitting on the eaves of buildings; federal and state policies subtending urban plans; a hot day fills alleyways with the stink of urine, rotting food, vomit, and unimaginable things; traffic lights directing movements; city sounds building-out scale and volume; eateries and shops indulging the walker with window scenes. A plenum of gregariousness, a pulse, a conglomerate that constantly respires and excretes, the neighborhood holds ground just as it lurches for new resources. It is a bumptious, lively, coherence of bodies (human and nonhuman), ecosystems, communities, buildings, and sensations. These are not utopic zones of love, though love can be found, neighborhoods are stresses even in apparent moderation, vehemently, intractable.

Out of the midst of this urban verve, gestated by my own *flânerie*, I again wonder: How do transsexuals living in neighborhoods experience the touching nature of these contact zones in relationship to their own sexual transitioning? First, not all transsexuals transition, certainly many do not, and what counts as transitioning varies greatly, but I am specifically interested in those bodies, particularly transwomen or MTFs, who alter themselves through surgeries and hormones to feel themselves as "at home." How might these sensually teeming places come to matter in the changing of one's sex? And, conversely, how do the intensities, energies, and forces that accompany transsexual transitions—radical alterations to bodily sensoriums— shape and reshape a neighborly self? Is there a somatic sociality to trans-becoming? By trans-becoming, I mean simply an emergence of a material, psychical, sensual, and social self through corporeal, spatial, and temporal processes that trans-form the lived body. Rather than accounting for transsexuality as a psychological condition, or a purely sociological production, or as some biological imperative, I offer a supplemental reading that is about the expressiveness of trans-bodies. I'm not proposing that these other registers of interpretation are without merit; however, I wonder what else can be asked about the experience of transitioning. How might transitional bodies be relational, ecological, an expressivity of potentiality?

> *I live directly across from Diva's. Standing outside the bar at all hours, are dazzling women. Their heels cantillate, sounding out the streets. They gather at the entry of the bar, which recedes from the sidewalk just enough to offer shelter and vantage. Their excess, exuberance, is framed by concrete and steel. They are hyper-visual in their shimmer, sparkle, dazzle also resists vision, an excess that confuses eyes; the gilded surface deflects a desire for depth even in its allure.*

There are many peoples and histories—immigration, poverty, gay liberation—at play in San Francisco's Tenderloin (Califia 1997). Significant genealogies of racial politics, struggles for sex-worker justice, immigration rights, gay liberation, and class struggle define the pavement, street corners, community centers, churches and many other structures in this neighborhood. Susan Stryker and Victor Silverman have made a documentary, *Screaming Queens: The Riot at Compton's Cafeteria* (Silverman and Stryker 2005), which depicts transgender political struggles in the Tenderloin, and the unlikely alliances with various social justice movements. They offer an intersectional arrangement of historical legacies and the rekindled activist energies still at work in challenging transphobia, xenophobia, racism, and poverty.

My project is a narrowing, perhaps even a preterition, of these critical efforts by situating the current Diva's bar, 1081 Post Street, San Francisco, as a hub for transwomen activities in this neighborhood. This is arguably an somewhat arbitrary center—though how center are any centers?—but still Diva's is a place of kinds of communion for many transwomen. Some of these women are sex workers, some are not; some women go to the bar seeking community, others pleasure. Some women are simply surviving, while others find that these streets and alleyways are full of consequence. Transwomen of color, poor transwomen, feminine transgenders, immigrants seeking gendered refuge, *fa'afafine*, *kathoey*, *mahu*, and many others also find a sense of belonging among the streets of Post, Geary, Polk, Turk, O'Farrell, and more. Diva's creates its own gravitational drive, an excited charge in the greater pull of the city, a place of coming together (sometimes forced) even if never visited, with many transwomen living in the surrounding area. I am one such woman.

Tergiversation, a politically suspect form of evasion: Some days I try to distance myself from other women working the streets by reading and walking, code switching to shield myself from approach. The performance feels tenuous and necessary, but also ruthless.

I fold myself inward and lower my vision into my feet, my feet "look out" for me. My toes begin to apprehend the crosswalks differently, collaborating my senses into toed-eyed, a planar view that registers beyond the peripheral through reverberation. Often my guise works, but occasionally men slow their cars anyway and signal me for a paid tryst. Depending on my circumstances, I pretend not to notice.

Louise Bourgeois's 'Crouching Spider': on the Embarcadero at Mission Street— Entry Plaza at Pier 14 (see Figure 5.1). Bourgeois's spider is located outside the Tenderloin, but its touch percusses, vibrates, plucks at the streets from the Financial District as far as the Tenderloin, perhaps just as transwomen's heels (for those wearing them) click and clack, resonating far beyond the Tenderloin. It is a sculpture, but also a provocation. How might this spider, and its fleshy referent, elaborate on the relationship between bodies and spaces? After all, a spider's proximity to its web, made of its own secretions, proposes that home and territory are *of* and *with* the body. A spider makes a web to reach out into the upsurge of energies, to eat, to become more than itself.

Bourgeois's sculpture invites me to think about transwomen as spiderwomen, spinsters, over-reaching subjects. Might web building best articulate (with the word's multiple meanings) the act of extending bodily substance through sex transition; that is to ask, do webbing and the capacity to weave remind us that transsexuality is also an expression of the body as an address and habitat? Expressivity of transsexuality is not a trivialization of a very difficult process; on the contrary, transbodily exuberance is an arrangement between sensorial milieu of the self and the profusion of the world. The improvisation is particular, deadly serious, but also always relational.

Crouching Spider: It evokes extreme response; an enormous bronze spider edging water and land. Neither he nor she, it signifies "it." Uncanny; the size is dwarfing. The legs are spindly, poised on sharp tips; even in their stillness they are lively (Bal 2001; Pollock 2005). Its legs are stretched, as if on the move; motion caught in repose. Is it in its territory? Hunting ground? A trope for fear as an emanation of Freud's "phallic mother"? Like its lively counterpart with a cuticle of chitin, this spider's exoskeleton protects it. The networks of nervous and respiratory systems, the hydraulic forces that make other spiders bumptious, are not visible, but this arthropod's segments, its cephalothorax and abdomen are enmeshed and knotted with now cooled, metal joins.

Crouching Spider: The shadow of itself is impossible to ignore, even in fog-heavy San Francisco. Balanced on its own silhouette, a spider in a noir-lit web; it is its *web*. Equally difficult to overlook is the setting. Yes, the city, the Tenderloin neighborhood. Yes, the boundary between ocean and earth. But also, from this angle, the

FIGURE 5.1 *Crouching Spider*. Louise Bourgeois, 2003
Bronze, silver nitrate and polished patina, and stainless steel

Bay Bridge extends it, giving it a capacious outstretch. Though its spinnerets are encased in inorganic hardness, it seems to have spun-out a of filament web made of steel and concrete. The spider metonymizes, generating zones of correlation and correspondence between object and space. It is not an endless reach; all things are not counted equally, though one could go far on these threads. This spider is an urban designer just as it is sculptural, a weaver of cityscapes, concatenating parts of the city into its grasp.

The unfolding scene of Bourgeois's spider stringing out the city from itself recalls Jean-François Lyotard's flaying of the body into what reads like a street map:

> Open the so-called body and spread out all its surfaces: not only the skin with each of its folds, wrinkles, scars, with its great velvety planes, and contiguous to the scalp and its mane of hair, the tender pubic fur, nipples, nails, hard transparent skin under the heel, the light frills of the eyelids, set with lashes … dilate the diafram of the anal sphincter, longitudinally cut and flatten out the black conduit of the rectum, then the colon, then the caecum … armed with scalpels and tweezers, dismantle and lay out the bundles and bodies of the encephalon; and then the whole network of veins and arteries, intact, on an immense mattress, and then the lymphatic network, and the fine bony pieces of the wrist and ankles …
>
> *(Lyotard 1993: 1)*

Lyotard continues: "We must not begin with transgression, we must immediately go to the end of cruelty, construct the anatomy of polymorphous perversion, unfold the immense membrane of the libidinal 'body,' which is quite the inverse of a system of parts" (Lyotard 1993: 2). Lyotard's contiguous membrane is indiscriminate, postmodern, joining diverse elements into irreverent intimacies. He suggests that the liminal body seeks to conserve substances and extend them into ever growing physical and social configurations, while becoming splayed, rendered, eviscerated. Similarly, the webbing from Bourgeois's spider joins, aggregates others with others; sensuality is in the prepositions (Potts 1999).

Silken, spiderlines reference the skeletalization of surface, the web is an extension of the surface affects of the spider; *it feels with its web*. This is not a shallow surface, but a dynamic threshold of sensuality. Likewise, the human body is stretched topographically to affectively and perceptually react through a spatial, temporal, corporeal generativity. Bodies are not ruptured or burst open such that they are boundless. Instead, bodies, like cities and web-builders, are inter- and intra-threadings of many sensuous vectors that relay with the spider in the middle of its web.

Thresholds,: in architectural forms: the sill of doorways, stoops, gates, portals, facades, and kinds of embellishments. But also, interesting nuance: in verb form, thresholding: an intensity that must be exceeded for a reaction to occur. Here in my home, I am freshly aware that my body is a threshold, an entry between rooms, the way the door-frame delimits zones while spiders build tangles across them.

It is not as simple as to say that I am crossing from "man" to "woman." I'm not sure I know what such a claim would mean for me. But, on a scalpel of desire along a hormonal riptide I am crossing the matter of my body on a bridge of sensation. As my body becomes legibly "woman," a white woman, I am aware that the limits of my body are also energized zones. I stay at the threshold, while actively crossing that very threshold; I am caught and yet mobile in a state of articulation as I make myself intelligible enough to myself and to my neighborhood.

In her essay "Dungeon Intimacies: The Poetics of Transsexual Sadomasochism" (2008), Susan Stryker stitches together bodies, places, and histories through the affective and social force of sadomasochism; she is the widow building a web. "I envision my body as a meeting point, a node, where external lines of force and social determination thicken into meat and circulate as movement back into the world" (Stryker 2008: 42). For Stryker, carnal improvisations, pulses, resonances, rhythms "thicken into meat" and bruised tributaries only to flow back out of this subjective reservoir and into political projects and critical interventions.

From Stryker's vantage the cityscape is meshed with *pastpresents* (an always present past in the present) and hauntings such that engaging the space around her is dimensionally extended by "observations into the patterns longer than … lived experience" (37). History is entanglement, knotting, a game of cat's cradle that maps impressions and corporealities through libidinal tracings, erotogenic intensities, and psychical cartographies. The central trope for Stryker's telling is "porosity" as poesis. "Transsexual sadomasochism in dungeon space enacts a *poesis* (an act of artistic creation) that collapses the boundary between the embodied self, its world, and others, allowing one to interpenetrate the others and thereby constitute a specific place" (39). Divides between subjects and objects, selves and others, are ruptured, distorted, generating new subjective configurations, but only through the constraints of an impassioned embodiment. Stryker risks physical integrities—skins welt, shoulders empurple, wrists chafe—to explore the inherent openness or pliability of the body:

> I invent new choreographies of space and time as I dance my whip across the creature's ass. It is not that I somehow internalize as my own the structure or content of the scene in which I participate, receiving its impression the way clay would receive a sculptor's mark. It is rather a proprioceptive awareness, as I flog, of the role of my body as medium in the circuit of transmissions, and of the material efficacy I possess in my subjective ability to choose one thing rather than another or to poetically imagine the shape of a new pattern.
> *(Stryker 2008: 42)*

Just as Stryker recounts her webbed visions of San Francisco places, so her "autoethnographic" (38) accounts of living matter in motion are themselves manifestations of dynamic becoming: the scene of the city cuts through Stryker's body by her acts of "reciprocal vulnerability" (43). Desirous enactments of power and its loss, as Stryker proposes, are "continuous movement in which a force's vector is prolonged and deflected into the movements of living matter"; so too, I want to suggest, is trans-becoming (42).

The transitional self can never risk disembodiment or autogenesis; it is a sensuous self, made such only through the refrain of its sensorium. Senses and their sub-tending registers are reactive to the sensual abundance of the world, but limited by perceptual milieus (i.e., eyes see only so much, ears hear only a fraction of the sounded-out information in an environment). The movement of the sensuous across perceptual registers creates *texture*, which propagates embodiment through the excitation of contingencies and intimacies, leaving marks and traces (Hayward 2010). The passing of sensation through and between perceptual and affective apertures creates remainders of filterings that result in expressiveness. Texture is the unmeta-bolizable *more*, the residue of passing sensation, of animate forces moving across bodies and objects. The emergence of bodiliness is manifested in the iterative and sensuous connectivity through which the limits between self and environment are activated (Grosz 2001; Lingis 2000; Pallasmaa 2005). The transitional body, in this way, is a textural body, generating contractions of the sensorium through the bio-refractions of hormones, surgery, etc.

> At the base of the cliff itself, where it touches the shore, caves have been hewn. … As porous as this stone is the architecture. Building and action interpenetrate in the courtyards, arcades, and stairways. In everything they preserve the scope to become a theater of new, unforeseen, constella-tions. The stamp of the definitive is avoided. No situation appears intended forever, no figure asserts its "thus and not otherwise." This is how architecture, the most binding part of the communal rhythm, comes into being here.
>
> *(Benjamin and Lacis 1978: 165–66)*

Asja Lacis and Walter Benjamin describe an almost erotic interchange between place and flesh; distinctions between body and architecture appear conjugal, loving, enflamed, not unlike Lyotard's libidinal body.

Such structures as bridges, crosswalks, alleys, bus routes, streets are pleats in the city through which bodies pulse. On the SF MUNI, I am hurled through concrete veins and steel arteries, along funiculars and elevators. I hold my body in positions that signify my desire, despite my critical resistance, to "pass." But less obviously, hidden in my interior, estrogens have begun to refigure my olfactory nerves. I'm smelling layers of place, registering different saturations of funk and perfume (Moore, Wisniewski, and Dobs 2003). The interior of the train thickens like a miasmic genealogy, and my altering senses work to make sense of it.

Moving under the city, the train vectors its way toward my endocrinologist and esthetician so that I may undergo something like a second puberty.

> *My body is morphed by a daily dose of 8.5 mg of Premarin, 300 mg of Spironolactone, and regular treatments of laser hair removal. Under the play of bodily forces, my face, breasts, hips, arms, legs, stomach, and shoulders become zones of grumblings, feelings, heavings, pleasures, leakings, and desires.*
>
> *I try scrubbing out the brunt hair follicles on my face and elsewhere from laser hair removal before they grow inflamed, become solfataras, and leave darkened scars. Fat deposits uproot and travel to new sights of colonization: hips widen, breasts grow (and secrete fluid, lactate), face changes from oval to heart-shaped, and musculature softens and dissolves.*

To further illustrate the spatial-sensual-temporal qualities of transposition I offer another example I've written about the "cut" of sex reassignment surgery.

> *The cut is possibility.* For some transsexual women, the cut is not so much an opening of the body, but a generative effort to *pull the body back through itself* in order to feel mending, to feel the growth of new margins. The cut is not just an action; the cut is part of the ongoing materialization by which a transsexual tentatively and mutably becomes. The cut cuts the meat (not primarily a visual operation for the embodied subject, but rather a proprioceptive one), and a space of psychical possibility is thereby created. From the first, a transsexual woman embodiment does not necessarily foreground a wish to "look like" or "look more like a woman" (i.e. passing)—though for some transwomen this may indeed be a wish (fulfilled or not). The point of view of the looker (those who might "read" her) is not the most important feature of trans-subjectivity—the trans-woman wishes to be *of* her body, to "speak" from her body.
>
> *(Hayward 2008: 72)*

This kind of MTF trans-becoming considers how the transsexual emerges through the body's own viscosity, through the energization of corporeal limits. The trans-body is a matrix through which sensations may be drawn back through the body, to make the body familiar. And more so, the affair between the felt-body and the lived-body is also enacted through habitation, the ecosystem of which the self is part. The trans-body, as Lyotard describes of the libidinal body, is threaded through itself, just as it's webbed with its neighborhood (Lyotard 1993). That which prompts a transwoman to transition is also more than her appearance, and her appearance can only ever be understood as metonymic. Her appearance does not make her a woman for she is always already un-male/not-man, but it allows her to become at "home" as a woman, a gendered neighbor, a historical subject (Prosser 1998). Following Lyotard, a transitioning woman is enfleshing elements of her environment within herself and expressing parts of herself back into the environment as part of her transition. The environment, populated with inorganic and organic beings, houses her while she contributes, in real time, to building it. This process serves as the conditions of transpositioning the constitutive activities of sensing and living, and as a generative energy in iterative or "moreover" manifestations. As such, she is a spider in her web, or, more precisely, she is becoming *with* her web, her trap.

> *The sole witness, I spend hours before the refracting reflection of my transmutating body, tending the sensations, newnesses, and curves that I am becoming, manifesting, experiencing. I give my life over to these changes. They exceed beyond what I might have desired. They are unpredictable; they are their own agents (Kirk 1999).*
>
> *Carefully and deliberately I emerge as a transsexual self: my transitioning body and I find, tenderly, a new kind of accommodation, negotiating each other. We create an in-between-ness, a state of process, invention, and sensuous reconstruction.*

A spider, in the corner of my studio, by the window, sits and sits. She is an "American house spider," *Archaearanea tepidariorum*. Her legs are white, and her cephalothorax is brown dusted with black. For now she is alone in her web. She will only live for a little more than a year. If she produces eggs, the spiderlings will float away on their own glossy lines (ballooning). She stays for what seems like days at the center of her web, her touch-world, while the web seems to trap only dust. And then, as if called from across the room, she moves and quickly, even uncannily: there/then not, still/in motion, unsettling/reassuring. This little, air-breathing arthropod, with two body segments, a set of fangs, four pairs of eyes, eight legs, and pairs of movable spinnerets leaves behind a cobweb. Even now after the silvery threads have come to look like unspooled, wooly yarn, the web remains a join, between angles and planes, but without her as the perceiving center it feels ghostly. In contrast, the lived-in web is an optic skin, a resounding connective tissue, building a home that senses in order that the spider might feed, entrap, and make more of herself.

David Quammen counsels that we cannot easily identify with spiders; at best we are curious and at worse we are disturbed (Quammen 1988). It is this abjected nearness that Nina Katchadourian engages in her "Mended Spiderweb" series.[1] With red thread, Katchadourian repairs torn webbing, mixing media to create cross-species rejoinders. Rarely do the spiders accept her interventions, cutting out and discarding her efforts with new silks. The project reminds us of Ludwig Wittgenstein's worry about addressing language problems through language: "We feel as if we had to repair a torn spider's web with our fingers" (Wittgenstein 2001: 39). But there is something about artfulness, inventiveness of the mended webs that speaks to my sense of copresence, to share forms of movement, animation, and percussion. The failure of collaboration, here, doesn't negate the energetic interactions of these species. Error is still expression, an intensity that is engaged by human and spider. Error exposes limits, even the limits of species, which is also a nearness. Spiders build out their worlds, and Katchadourian tunes her art practice to approximate the frequency of spiders' effort. Her red-threaded webs do not look like the spiders', they are always others to each other, but the capacity to create, to syncopate, to improvise, seems a co-reactivity between spiders and peoples. As Alphonso Lingis reminds us, humans are composites of zoo-intensities, animated movements, bio-differentials, making our experience of agency, sexuality, subjectivity less about individuated forms and more about distribution, collection, variation. He asks, "Is not the force of our emotions that of other animals?" (Lingis 2000: 36).

> *After my ordeal with the laser—the post-procedural feel of stung-singed-numbness always reminds me of Blake's "Tyger, tyger, burning bright." I stop by "Olive" (743 Larkin Street). In the windowless lounge, I feel like Alice descending into the rabbit hole, passing from the brightness of "not-passing" (so many staring eyes) to the dim shadows of possibility, of inexpressible hope.*
>
> *As the curvature of my eye lenses changes through estrogen sensitivity, my vision brackets and shuttles between planes of focused activity, so that the variations of shadow in this bar are like scrims, opening up scenes as my eyes shift in their sockets (Krenzer and Dana 2000). I know these perceptual alterations will be assimilated into a bodily norm soon—the body aims for habituation—but in this newness of sensation I delight in how my body feels this familiar place afresh, restored of receivable sensory richness.*

I want to foreground the figure of the "trap" for transsexuals and spiders. First, for transsexuals, rather than emphasizing the feel of "wrong-bodiness" in the now familiar trope, "trapped in the wrong body," what if we highlight other genealogies of the word "trap." Trap is also a mouth, a mode of utterance, the "O" curve of lips and throat that sounds out and names the apprehension of being embodied (Salvaggio 1999). A trap is the wet threshold between tongue and thought. Slang, but like most lustful language longs, cries, erupts. Similarly, in weaving, a trap is a break in the threads of a warp, an unraveling, loosening, unwinding that opens a space in a tapestry. In music, a trap is an ensemble of percussion instruments, drumming out collective arrangements and creative responses. So, the language of being trapped "trapped in a wrong body" must also account for these alternate etymologies of articulation, speaking, oneself into culture and history, but also creating a site, a gap, making room in cultural and political fabrications, and finding a tempo, a beat. In this way, entrapment is always also about thresholds. To be trapped in the body, then, is possibility rather than only confinement, trapped is about building-out, un-knotting so as to rework the territory of embodied self, to speak and receive ranges of sensuous input from one's environment (Hayward 2008; Prosser 1998).

Similarly, the spider's web is a trap, a silk net, a sticky mesh. Created from proteinaceous fibers that are surprisingly light and yet have remarkable tensile strength, this trap is made from the spider; it is an expression of its bodily capacity. The web is a musical improvisation between the spider and its prey, but also between itself and its environment, an expressive extension, a rhythmic prosthesis that defines the limits of spidery sensoriums. As such, webs are predacious selves, augmented parts of the spider and its territory—so entrapment, but also resource and reach. In the speculative spirit of trans-phyla descriptions, it is also this sort of trapping that is at work in the experience of transsexual embodiment.

Exit Theater (156 Eddy Street): Veronica Klaus performs her one-woman show "Family Jewels." In her performance she ponders, "People ask me if I feel like a woman. ... Do I feel like a woman? The truth is, I have no idea whether I feel like any other woman. I have no idea whether I ever felt like any other man. All I know is that I feel like me, Veronica. This person whose existence is partly innate, partly instinct, partly art, the art of creating. ... But I do find as I go through life I become more comfortable asking myself questions like 'Who am I?'" (Klaus 2009).

Might transsexuality be artfulness? If Gilles Deleuze and Félix Guattari read art as not necessarily about aesthetics, but about sensation, about the expressive potential of "cosmological forces" (Deleuze and Guattari 1994), do also the trans-working of flesh, organs, and muscle into new modes of potentiality? Art in verb form is an urge, an incitement, and an induction. By this, I mean something quite serious, not some frivolity of creativity, but art as becoming, of intensifying bodily substance, to resonate. Transsexual embodiment in part is a provocation to live-out, to feel different carnal zones of metamorphosis, transition, and intervention. As such, these provocations are responses to our capacities to resonate (to greater or lesser degrees) with environments, habitats, and spaces.

Transitioning is vibratory; a transitioning woman is, first and importantly, a vibratory being. She is a partly creative response between sensation and environment, and for those who start becoming with Premarin, conjugated from horse urine, this responsiveness begins with animals (even, unfortunately, their brutal instrumentalization). Unavoidably, non-human substances are unleashed into her body, transforming and altering. Through the sexually differentiating forces of horses, the transwoman's body is made emphatically more. And through the provocation of the senses, bodies become threaded through themselves in the act of changing their forms, architectures, ecosystems; an act manifested from drives materialized into exterior potentialities.

We move with the world through the sleeve of senses (touch, sight, smell, taste)—sensitization of the surface. Interiority can only be understood, then, as a sensuous exteriority drawn within the membrane of "self." As Lefebvre writes, that space is "first of all my body, and then it is my body counterpart or 'other,' its mirror-image or shadow: it is the shifting intersection between that which touches, penetrates, threatens or benefits my body on the one hand, and all other bodies on the other" (Lefebvre 1991: 184). And as spiders and webs and some transsexuals are being iteratively reconfigured through sensuous surfaces—threads held together more or less conditionally until they are eaten by the spider who spun them, or swept away in a cleaning frenzy, or reworked after having caught a meal, or simply abandoned for another site.

My body is still my body, but hormones initiate radical relays of transformed bodiliness. I start to wonder if my "conjugated equine estrogens" are reshaping my species— becoming horse—along with my sex. Could mare chemistry be interlacing my own, giving me more of an insight into horse perception than sex perception? I am sure there are no horses in the Tenderloin (although certainly pony/horse play is taking place somewhere in the neighborhood), but as elements of mare urine course through my flesh I am sensitized to how animals and other non-humans are everywhere in the city.

How many transwomen on Post, Larkin, Geary, Jones, O'Farrell, Sutter, Turk, and Taylor are mixing species in their own bodies? How many of us are engaged in some kind of symbiogenetic, transspecies becoming? Transwomen have so often been imagined as porous—the threat of psychosis subtending the transsexual "diagnosis"— literally a sex in pieces. And now I wonder, in this neighborhood, the sphere that my body inhabits, the sphere of the imagination, are our trans-bodies part of the necessary (life's own inventiveness, artfulness; bio-engined investments in variation and potential) knotting of city-selves, a concrescence of contiguity and difference. Could this be transpositioning?

Acknowledgements

I want to thank Katie King, Susan Stryker, Ian Julian Carter, and Lindsay Kelley for reading early drafts of this chapter. Their editorial guidance and advice helped to shape the best parts of this chapter. I also want to thank Jennifer Griggs, who helped me co-organize a panel on "Trans-architecture" at the Translating Identities Conference, University of Vermont, 2008, where I first shared this chapter.

Note

1 To see Nina Katchadourian's work, visit her website: http://www.ninakatchadourian. com/uninvitedcollaborations/spiderwebs.php (Katchadourian 2010).

PART III

Transectionalities: Mapping Multiple Migrations

6

"PASSING FOR WHITE, PASSING FOR MAN"

Johnson's *The Autobiography of an Ex-Colored Man* as Transgender Narrative

C. Riley Snorton

Conventional wisdom suggests that autobiographies tell us three things about its subject: who they are, what they have done, and how that has shaped their outlook on the future. But James Weldon Johnson's *The Autobiography of an Ex-Colored Man* (*Autobiography*) is not an autobiography (Johnson [1912]/1965). As a novel about passing, it inverts the logic of autobiography by providing a narrative that stages the social world personified in the individual rather than an individual's story illuminating larger aspects of society. Its nameless protagonist relates to us a set of cultural logics circulating at the turn of the twentieth century, including pervasive ideologies about race, mobility, industrialization, class, sexuality and gender. *Autobiography*'s reception, popular and critical, contemporaneous and contemporary, reveals the kinds of assumptions its readers make about its protagonist and the text's social contexts. Although numerous scholars (e.g., Goellnicht 1996; Rottenberg 2004; Sheehy 1999) have discussed the complexities of racial, sexual and even generic passing in *Autobiography*, few have attended to the novel's complex renderings of gender and the figurative changes in gender identification that remap the literary terrains traversed in the novel for the unnamed protagonist. Reading *Autobiography* as a text explicitly concerned with the process of gender self-fashioning not only supplements a critical gap in the literature but also provides contemporary theorists an opportunity to think critically through the implications of gender identity in African-American modernist literary traditions.

In her reading of *Autobiography* Heather Andrade (2006) suggests that Johnson's intention in *Autobiography* is to satirize the trope of racial uplift popular among his black male literary contemporaries.[1] She argues that Johnson inverts the black uplift narrative by writing a protagonist that chooses self-interest over self-sacrifice: "as such, while other works reveal the hero's growing racial awareness, Johnson's *Autobiography* plots the anti-hero's movement toward racial disengagement"

(Andrade 2006: 2). Andrade draws on Johnson's autobiography, *Along this Way: The Autobiography of James Weldon Johnson* (Johnson [1933]/2008), to demonstrate how *Autobiography* serves as a narrative of gender passing, i.e., the narrator's anti-hero narrative must be read as troubling contemporaneous ideas about race and gender. Similarly, Martin Summers explains that "Johnson's portrayal of 'passing' is a particularly gendered one and reveals how black middle-class men negotiated their masculine identities within a society and culture dominated by white middle-class males" (Summers 2004: 208). According to Summers, *Autobiography* should also be understood as a narrative that stages the protagonist's move from the raced (as black) space of creative expression to the rational (read: white) space of the marketplace: "By rejecting these cultural and 'racial' characteristics of his African American heritage through his entrance into the rational marketplace, the protagonist is also rejecting his biological and cultural connection to a 'feminine' race" (210).

Summers begins an argument about the relationships among race, biology, gender identity, and passing that requires further interrogation. While Summers focuses on sites of production—creative and industrial—to map out a terrain of shifting dynamics of racialized masculinity in *Autobiography*, I examine key moments of gender crossing in the novel itself. Focusing on depictions of the narrator's site-conditioned sight in *Autobiography*, I argue that the unnamed protagonist not only professes a longing for whiteness but for femininity as well. As such, I am explicitly focusing on the "ex-" prefix in Johnson's title as a generative marker for gender identification as well as race, heightening our attention to the imbrications of these two discursive processes. To be "ex-", I argue, is to understand the experience of being without legible, stable, and coherent racial and gender identities.

In examining what I call "transgender yearnings" in Johnson's *Autobiography*, I draw on Jay Prosser's work on "body narratives," in which he argues that narratives about transsexuality bring the materiality of bodies into view and Judith Butler's work on performativity, which specifically attends to the power of discourse to constitute what it names through citation and repetition, in order to attend to the gendered and racialized subjectivities of the protagonist. I define transgender yearnings as an expressed alignment with another gender or the articulation of "cross-gender" desire. While the literature on *Autobiography* has taken up certain moments in the novel to describe racial ambiguity and instances of same-sex desire (see, e.g., Clarke 1995; Ross 2004; Wallace 1997), little attention is paid to the "transgendered dynamics" of the text. I suggest that these readings of homoeroticism in *Autobiography* are indebted to a modernist analysis, which parallels the erasure of gender non-conformity in the consolidation of the figure of the "homosexual" occurring in sexological literature some 30 years prior to *Autobiography*'s appearance in 1912. Through close readings of the protagonist's moves through geographical sites and spaces of identification, I ultimately suggest that reading *Autobiography* as a transgender narrative allows for a more thorough understanding of the text's critique of Afro-modernist conceptions of gender and sexuality, as well as race.

Like W.E.B. Du Bois's *The Souls of Black Folk* (Du Bois [1903]/1965) and Booker T. Washington's *Up from Slavery* (Washington [1907]/1965), *Autobiography* is a palimpsest of literary forms. As a novel, it relies most heavily on memoir but also draws upon the genres of travel logs, political tracts, and blues historiography. In broad strokes, *Autobiography* explains how its unnamed protagonist chooses to live as an ex-colored man after living as a person of color throughout parts of the United States and Europe. As Richard Kostelanetz explains, "The novel's theme is the many ambiguities of passing—moral, political, emotional; and its predominant action is the narrator's shifting sympathies for white and black identity" (Kostelanetz 1991: 20). As my chapter addresses, the notion of shifting sympathies applies to gender (and sexuality) in addition to race. Following the chronology of the novel, which is to say that the beginning is the end, I chart various instances in which the unnamed narrator describes sites/sights of identification that constitute the narrator's "practical joke on society" and presents a critical terrain for scholars interested in charting the ramifications of gender identity in African-American modernist literature ([1912]/ 1965: 29).

Ex- as Sliding Signifier: Charting Sites of Identification

At the onset of the novel, the protagonist describes suffering from a "vague feeling of unsatisfaction, of regret, of almost remorse, from which I am seeking relief, and of which I shall speak in the last paragraph" ([1912]/1965: 29). The protagonist gives us a roadmap, as it were, for which the pages in between this opening remark and final paragraph are an extended meditation on his choices that ultimately lead the narrator to exclaim that he has sold his birthright for a "mess of pottage" (140). This initial moment gestures toward at least two dimensions of the text, which are critical for understanding gender transgression in the novel. First, the affect-laden bookends of the text that literally structure the narrative signal a sense of loss—of melancholia—which implies certain irreconcilable desires that animate the narrative tension. Secondly (and related), as a bookend narrative, the narrator is an "ex-colored man" at the opening. While many critics have read the succeeding pages as an explanation for how the narrator becomes "ex-colored," we cannot take for granted how the narrator also becomes a "man."

Autobiography begins with faint memories of the narrator's childhood in Georgia. These "dim recollections" brighten considerably as the narrator describes both a love and talent for music and study (30). As the narrator reports, "my school-days ran along very pleasantly," until the narrator realizes through a classroom exercise that the teacher and other classmates do not regard the narrator as white (36). This realization prompts an extended description of the narrator's encounter with a "looking-glass" (37). Often viewed as a pivotal moment for readers attentive to the processes of racialization in the text, *Autobiography*'s "mirror scene" is also evocative of a feminine gender imaginary, which parallels Prosser's argument for how such scenes function in transsexual autobiographies. He contends, " ... mirror scenes in transsexual autobiographies do not merely initiate the plot of transsexuality. Highly staged and self-conscious affairs ... mirror scenes also draw attention to the narrative form [of] the plot, to the surrounding autobiography and its import for transsexuality" (100). The "mirror scene" in Johnson's *Autobiography* demonstrates the import in understanding the novel as a text, which ruminates on the complex imbrications of racial and gender identification. The protagonist relates:

> I rushed up into my own little room, shut the door, and went quickly to where my looking-glass hung on the wall. For an instant I was afraid to look, but when I did, I looked long and earnestly. I had often heard people say to my mother: "What a pretty boy you have!" I was accustomed to hear remarks about my beauty; but now, for the first time I became conscious of it and recognized it. I noticed the ivory whiteness of my skin, the beauty of my mouth, the size and liquid darkness of my eyes, and how the long black lashes that fringed and shaded them produced an effect that was strangely fascinating even to me. I noticed the softness and glossiness of my dark hair that fell in waves over my temples, making my forehead appear whiter than it really was. How long I stood there gazing at my image I do not know.
>
> *(Johnson [1912]/1965: 37)*

This earnest form of looking produces the evidence of the narrator's beauty—which is constituted by the paleness of skin and by the "softness" of the hair, the "beauty of the mouth," and the "long black lashes" that frame the "liquid darkness" of the eyes. The emphasis on feminine attributes in conjunction with the protagonist's whitening gaze recurs throughout the narrative. However, as subsequent descriptions of the protagonist's encounters with racial and gender difference suggest, these articulations are still structured by the logics of white supremacy and heteronormativity. As Catherine Rottenberg explains:

> in heteronormativity, identification with "being a woman" almost always implies (and is inextricably intertwined with) the desire to "be a woman," that is, a desire to live up to the norms of femininity in a particular symbolic order. ... Femininity has thus been posited as desirable, and as something that "women" should approximate.
>
> *(Rottenberg 2004)*

Often *Autobiography*'s protagonist measures himself against other women—most notably his mother. As the action directly following the mirror scene demonstrates, the protagonist must contend with his sense of being more beautiful—a better representation of the feminine ideal—than her. These cross-gender identifications recur throughout the text; frequently the narrator compares himself to women and speculates about how he might be read within a "male gaze." Hence, the narrator's transgender yearnings exist within the framework of heteronormativity. These moments are distinguishable from making recourse to the protagonist's narcissism, which is certainly at play in the narrative, as *Autobiography* stages not only a considerable appreciation of the protagonist's looks but also stages his queer relationships with people of the "same" sex.

Melanie Benson argues that narcissism "becomes the mechanism by which the narrator stills the racial imbalance" (Benson 2003: 76–77). Benson suggests that the mirror scene reflects a particular form of narcissism: "This particular moment of narcissism reveals its own untenability; the mirror reflects an impossible purity, a desire for holism and essentialism rather than true human partiality and hybridity— and so the violent categorizing begins" (ibid.). Benson further argues that, while the surface of the novel demonstrates the narrator's embrace of Blackness (evidenced by a shift in literary heroes[2]), the narrator understands this fact in distinctly mathematical terms: "he speaks incessantly about 'proportions,' 'majorities,' 'minorities,' and 'numbers'; he even describes the white man's pretensions to authority as a 'complex, confusing, and almost contradictory mathematical process'" (166). It is perhaps overstated to characterize the narrator's relationship to racial knowledge as an unproblematic "embrace." Rather, John Sheehy more aptly describes the narrator's racial identity as structured by complex forms of negotiation.[3] Benson's insights on numbers help us to better understand how the novel negotiates popular and social scientific discourse on race and gender. I suggest that we think about the narrator's focus on racial mathematics as a reference to eugenics literature.[4] Siobhan Somerville suggests that, "While gender insubordination offers a powerful explanatory model for the 'invention' of homosexuality, ideologies of gender also, of course, shaped and were shaped by dominant constructions of race" (Somerville 2000: 61). Somerville points to the ways in which "homosexuality"—which during the period of *Autobiography*'s first publication was scientifically understood as discernible on the body—also mirrors the visual logics of race. Her observation is useful in situating the "mirror scene" as a moment that mutually constitutes a racialized, gendered, and sexualized body.

The concluding sentence of the above excerpt from *Autobiography* requires additional attention. The protagonist's voicing of a lack of knowledge with regards to the length of the gaze in the mirror signifies both a trans-like state, while also signaling a sense of irresolvability. Kimberly Benston writes that "such scenes present a simultaneous enactment and theorization of consciousness taking place at key textual moments. Here, African American identity looks on an image of being at once external and internal to itself, an echo or reflection that must revise in order better to see itself" (Benston 1990: 100). Benston's argument works in tandem with Butler's theory of performativity to describe how key textual moments in *Autobiography* also demonstrate how the narrator must bring issues of gender identity into clearer view, as well as various moments throughout the text, in which the protagonist must choose to become a man.

Very shortly after the narrator's racial realization, the protagonist launches into a meditation on ways of seeing and the racial condition. In the discussion, which at various moments reads as innocuous and, at others, pedagogical, the protagonist proclaims:

> And it is this, too, which makes the colored people of this country, in reality a mystery to the whites. It is a difficult thing for a white man to learn what a colored man really thinks; because, generally, with the latter an additional and different light must be brought to bear on what he thinks; and his thoughts are often influenced by considerations so delicate and subtle that it would be impossible for him to confess or explain them to one of the opposite race. This gives to every colored man, in proportion to his intellectuality, a sort of dual personality; there is one phase of him which is disclosed only in the freemasonry of his own race.
>
> *(Johnson [1912]/1965: 39)*

Striking is the construction of race in a vocabulary typically used to describe gender, such as the use of "opposite" race. Maurice Wallace sheds further light on this passage: "the cultural logic of the late nineteenth and early twentieth century supposed that individuals were productively made (like the 'self-made' man) and American-ness was 'artificial and reproducible'" (Wallace 1997: 402–3). Wallace, who is writing about a set of portraits of Prince Hall and Nero Prince, offers a comparison between Grimshaw's 1903 portrait "forgeries" of the masons and a gallery of por-traits represented in *Autobiography*, describing them both as "worthy copies of mas-culine identity." Citing Robert Stepto, Wallace explains that the protagonist's gallery of images "'are valorized as heroic examples that the narrator would do well to emulate'" (ibid.) His comments underscore my reading of *Autobiography* as a text that maps race and gender as projects of self-fashioning, ones that require instruction and are performatively altered through repetition.

These moments of instruction are counterbalanced by moments of slippage in the novel, epitomized in the Atlanta University scene. Donald Goellnicht has suggested that "we underestimate the complexity of the text when we pose the question of the narrator's position as an either/or proposition" (Goellnicht 1996: 17). Goell-nicht proposes that *Autobiography* be read as a text, containing multiple layers of irony in both the narrative and the narrator's voice. Goellnicht then turns to a reading of the narrator's experience at Atlanta University, and, citing the passage below, suggests that the narrator (at odds with the author's beliefs) imposes a white gaze onto the bodies of the students.

> Among the girls especially there were many so fair that it was difficult to believe that they had Negro blood in them. And, too, I could not help noticing that many of the girls, particularly those of the delicate brown shades with black eyes and wavy dark hair, were decidedly pretty. Among the boys

many of the blackest were fine specimens of young manhood, tall, straight, and muscular with magnificent heads; these were the kind of boys who developed into the patriarchal "uncles" of the old slave regime.

(Johnson [1912]/1965: 60)

Goellnicht argues that the narrator "identifies with the girls who are projections of his own self-image, while unwittingly denigrating the 'boys'—a highly loaded epithet—as potential 'Uncle Toms'" (Goellnicht 1996: 20). However, if we are to agree that this passage serves as an example of a white way of seeing, then we must also acknowledge that the narrator's color identification contains a "cross-gender" recognition, i.e., a transgender way of looking. This transgender way of looking can not only be read in the narrator's complimentary way of discussing the young women of "delicate" hues but also in the sexualized way of discussing the black men on campus, as "fine specimens," etc. Prosser argues that the change in the definition of homosexuality required a shift in reading—from reading the texts at face value about gender to reading between the lines to surmise that they were in fact about object choice. Prosser's instructions to read at the surface of a text and body are critical for opening up possibilities of reading this and subsequent scenes for (trans)gender yearnings and identification in *Autobiography*. In this way, critics might view the narrative as an "ironic" reading of race and sexuality—both of which are negotiated in plain sight for their readers in the reflections of the protagonist's gendered musings. The narrator's first meeting of would-be classmates at Atlanta University is one textual example of transgender yearnings—a term constituted as much by identification in ways of seeing as by sites of subjectivity—and demonstrates a subtle and perhaps unwitting earnestness in the narrator's voice.

Melancholia, Hysteria, and the Trauma of Transfixion

While Prosser's ideas assist my reading of the mirror scene in Johnson's *Autobiography*, Butler's theory of "gender melancholia" serve to buttress my argument about the novel's narrative arc, with its various shifts in literary space and identifications. Butler writes that "gender performance allegorizes a loss it cannot grieve, allegorizes the incorporative fantasy of melancholia whereby an object is phatasmatically taken in or on as a way of refusing to let go" (Butler 1993b: 25). Furthermore, drawing on Freud's work on the Oedipal complex, Butler demonstrates how melancholia is constitutive of gender performance within a heterosexual matrix. She explains that the repudiation of the mother becomes the "founding moment ... of gender 'consolidation'": "As the metaphor of consolidation suggests, there are clearly bits and pieces of masculinity to be found within the psychic landscape, dispositions, sexual trends, and aims, but they are diffuse and choice" (Butler 1990: 76). The internalization of the mother marks a rejection of the "heterosexual cathexis" such that the boy "sets up a feminine superego which dissolves and disorganizes masculinity, consolidating feminine libidinal dispositions in its place" (ibid.).

Butler's theory of gender melancholia is premised on the idea that the melancholic figure, based on an original loss of a family relation (symbolic or otherwise), seeks to find symbolic replacements for this loss throughout his or her life. For the unnamed protagonist, the notion of gender melancholia is trenchant. However, *Autobiography* also demonstrates how the ontology of race and the possibility of transgender subjectivity complicate this idea. As I have alluded to earlier, the scene, which directly follows the mirror scene in which the narrator looks critically at his mother, as if for the first time, is a critical moment for understanding an early source of the protagonist's melancholia. He relates: "I had thought of her in a childish way only as the most beautiful woman in the world; now I looked at her searching for defects. I could see that her skin was almost brown, that her hair was not so soft as mine, and that she did differ in some way from the other ladies who came to the house; yet even so, I could see that she was very beautiful" (Johnson [1912]/1965: 37).

While the narrator concludes, "she was very beautiful," the realization of the mother's "almost brown" skin signifies the first loss of the mother, foreshadowing the mother's death, spurring the next phase of the narrator's life and beginning the narrator's nomadic journey. The narrator asks after searching his mother's face for "defects":

> "Well, mother am I white? Are you white?" She answered tremblingly: "No, I am not white, but you—your father is one of the greatest men in the country—the best blood of the South is in you—" This suddenly opened up in my heart a fresh chasm of misgiving and fear, and I almost fiercely demanded: "Who is my father? Where is he?" She stroked my hair and said: "I'll tell you about him some day." I sobbed: "I want to know now." She answered: "No, not now."
>
> *(Johnson [1912]/1965: 37)*

The mother's corporeal difference—both in terms of race and sex—constitutes the epistemological terrain for the narrator's own negotiations of identity. The narrator's mother is both the bearer of difference and knowledge, and as such produces a "hysterical" reaction. Hélène Cixous describes the hysteric as the "one who does not make herself ... she does not make herself but she does make the other. It is said that the hysteric 'makes-believe' the father, plays the father, 'makes-believe' the master" (Bonfen 1998: ix). Understanding the narrator both as hysteric and melancholic resonate in the experiences of the narrator's feeling set apart from a racial identity as well as from a gender identity, and may also explain why the narrator states that when he grew to manhood, he found himself "freer" with elderly white people (Johnson [1912]/1965: 40). These white elderly bodies, we might presume, are read through a distinctly different racial/gendered/sexual lens than the protagonist's own adult ex-colored maleness.

As the narrator is gendered male at the conclusion of the novel, it is imperative for readers to recognize the text as containing transgender possibilities, which do not necessarily map onto the formal characteristics of transsexual narratives. The lynching scene is instrumental to understanding how the narrator, within a matrix of heteronormativity, becomes gendered male.

> There he stood, a man only in form and stature, every sign of degeneracy stamped upon his countenance. His eyes were dull and vacant, indicating not a single ray of thought. Evidently the realization of his fearful fate had robbed him of whatever reasoning power he had ever possessed. He was too stunned and stupefied even to tremble. Fuel was brought from everywhere, oil, the torch: the flames crouched for an instant as though to gather strength, then leaped up as high as their victim's head. He squirmed, he writhed, strained at his chains, then gave out cries and groans that I shall always hear. The cries and groans were choked off by the fire and smoke: but his eyes, bulging from their sockets, rolled from side to side, appealing in vain for help. Some of the crowd yelled and cheered, others seemed appalled at what they had done, and there were those who turned away sickened at the sight. I was fixed to the spot where I stood, powerless to take my eyes from what I did not want to see.
>
> It was over before I realized that time had elapsed. Before I could make myself believe that what I saw was really happening ...
>
> (Johnson [1912]/1965: 127–28)

As in the mirror scene, the protagonist becomes unaware of time, which is perhaps another trope in black modernist literature similar to the spaces that Ralph Ellison's invisible man experiences while listening to music, or the cracks that Violet slips into in Toni Morrison's *Jazz*. However, while the mirror scene, which opens the novel, evokes an irresolvability that structures the action over the course of the book, this lynching scene has the effect of fixing the narrator in the spot where he stood: as ex-colored man. It is significant that this transfixion of identification occurs in a very transient literary space: as our narrator watches the lynching scene as a tableau from his train car window. As Summers explains, "The ever-present threat of lynching and mob violence, which purportedly sought to police an aggressive black male sexuality and often incorporated the horrific act of castration, made any assertion of independence of brazen behavior a potentially perilous action" (Summers 2004: 3). This culture of lynching precipitates the protagonist's response: "I finally made up my mind that I would neither disclaim the black race nor claim the white race; but that I would change my name, raise a moustache, and let the world take me for what it would; that it was not necessary for me to go about with a label of inferiority pasted across my forehead" (Johnson [1912]/1965: 129). Choosing to "pass" for white, changing his name (and therefore severing ties from the father) and donning a moustache, a symbol of masculine maturity evidence a (second?) consolidation of gender in the wake of the gruesome scene/seen of the black lynched body. Ironically, it is his gender that becomes the crowning achievement for the narrator insomuch that it is naturalized even as his racial identity remains precariously "ex-ed."

As mentioned in the proceeding section, *Autobiography* is bookended by an affective meditation on the details of the narrator's life. The narrator concludes:

> My love for my children makes me glad that I am what I am and keeps me from desiring to be otherwise; and yet, when I sometimes open a little box in which I still keep my fast yellowing manuscripts, the only tangible remnants of a varnished dream, a dead ambition, a sacrificed talent, I cannot repress the thought that, after all, I have chosen the lesser part, that I have sold my birthright for a mess of pottage.
>
> *(Johnson [1912]/1965: 140)*

The narrator's children, "a little girl, with hair and eyes dark like mine" and a boy, "who has my temperament, but is fair like his mother, a little golden-headed god" who "occupies an inner sanctuary of [the narrator's] heart," serve to counterbalance the narrator's deep sense of regret (Johnson [1912]/1965: 139). It is in his children that the narrator has truly produced whiteness, and, ironically too, that the narrator has produced his visual likeness within female corporeality and his transsexed sensibilities within an "unambiguous" white male child. Valerie Smith reads *Autobiography* as a tale in which the narrator abandons his racial identity in an effort to accelerate his own upward mobility. She argues that " ... the ex-colored man capitulates whenever obstacles confront him, choosing always material security and personal safety over more precarious and elusive goals" (Smith 1997: 89). Smith ultimately concludes: "The limits of the ex-colored man's autobiography therefore reflect his temperamental shortcomings. He never acquires verbal control over his experience because he cannot manage to look at his life with the necessary steadiness" (ibid.: 89, 100). The unsteadiness of the narrator's gaze, however, presents critics and readers with opportunities to better ascertain the interstitialities of multiple yearnings and identifications that constitute our ever-evolving critical understandings of concepts like "race" and "gender." As Roxanna Pisiak suggests, "The racial themes and subjects of the narrative not only demonstrate the 'slipperiness' of color lines, they also deconstruct the dichotomies of white and black words, and white and black worlds" (Pisiak 1997: 102). So too does *Autobiography* deconstruct gendered knowledges and ways of seeing, while articulating complex expressions of cross-gender desires.

Afromodern Complications

In keeping with its interlocutors, *Autobiography* describes the quotidian and spectacular incidents of a racialized body in space. While there has been much work to understand how Johnson's work intersects with dominant themes of Afromodernism, scholars have yet to look to *Autobiography* as a text that explores the desire for cross-gender identification. Like *Souls of Black Folk* and *Up From Slavery*,

Autobiography's narrator was presumed to provide its readers with invaluable insights on black life in the United States and abroad, a fact Robert Stepto argues is a recurrent theme in Afromodernist texts (Stepto 1991: 164). Stepto suggests that *Autobiography* "is a generic narrative far more than it is a primary or ancillary text in an authenticating construction; indeed, that suggestion is bolstered when we recognize that *The Autobiography* is, like the Washington and Du Bois narratives, a coherent expression of personalized response to systems of signification and symbolic geography occasioned by social structure" (97). *Autobiography*'s symbolic geography also charts out several forms of animating ambivalences, in which the protagonist is somehow colored, heterosexual, and male, and yet he is at various points throughout the narrative either not or more than each of those categories of identification. As Stepto notes, "the grand dialectic in *The Autobiography* binds together multiple expressions of mobility to multiple expressions of confinement" (97). Stepto's offering of a dialectic of mobility and confinement explains the constellation of identifications that occur within the symbolic geography of modernist identity-fashioning and the multiple gendered subjectivities that occur within the course of the narrative.

However, in order to understand how gender works as a dialectic in *Auto-biography*, readers must look to how the protagonist traverses multiple sites of identification through the productive act of passing. As I have discussed elsewhere, "Through the experiences of psychic dissonance, affirmation, disavowal, and recognition, we engage in the process of passing off our daily experiences of embodiment as identifications—creating 'fragile fictions' of personhood" (Snorton 2009: 87). *Autobiography* creates a fragile narrative of racial and gender ambivalence, which subtly but sharply critiques the masculinist impulses of Afromodernity and modernism more generally. To be sure, the narrator is a "self-made man" but not without discernible consternation and painstaking effort. And perhaps, most importantly, not without the lessons learned through travel. The narrative's focus on the protagonist's nomadic living could serve as a literary map for his internal ambivalences about racial and gender identification. My reading of the narrative's transgender yearnings suggests that we might imagine Johnson's *Autobiography* as an important contribution to transgender literature. Situated alongside Ralph Werther's *Autobiography of an Androgyne* (Werther [1918]/2008) and Radclyffe Hall's *The Well of Loneliness* (Hall 1928), the transgender yearnings in *Autobiography* remind of the importance not to assume the constancy of gender or sexual identity in literature dealing explicitly with race matters. Rather, the best critical approaches are those that explore how myriad identities, identifications, and positionalities are mutually constitutive and constantly shifting in and through one another in varying spaces and contexts.

Acknowledgements

I would like to thank Thadious M. Davis, Shana A. Russell, La Marr Jurelle Bruce, Scott Poulson Bryant, Aymar Jean, Sunny Yang, and Mecca Jamilah Sullivan for comments on this chapter.

Notes

1 Johnson is specifically critiquing the racial uplift narratives of W.E.B. Du Bois's *The Souls of Black Folk* and Booker T. Washington's *Up from Slavery*.

2 The narrator proclaims, "My heroes had been King David, then Robert the Bruce; now Frederick Douglass was enshrined in the place of honor" (Johnson [1912]/1965: 417).

3 Sheehy writes, "the boy seeks in this seemingly objective specular image the visible evidence of his identity—a sign or mark which might brand him indisputably as either black or white. He finds instead both 'liquid darkness' and 'ivory whiteness' contraposed, the blackness of his hair falling over his temples, making his forehead seem 'whiter than it really was.' In short, for the boy his mirror image is a doubtful proof of his race, as was his former opinion of himself (as white or, more precisely, as blank or without color), or as are the opinions others will later form of him (as white, black, mulatto, etc.). Barred from what for others seems an objective test of identity, the boy is left in a peculiar position: He may choose his race. This choice, of course, is not an uncomplicated one, entailing as it does either the denial of his own history, on one hand, or the acceptance of an unjustifiable but undeniable economic and social subjugation, on the other" (Sheehy 1999: 401).

4 The text's concern with eugenics becomes more explicit in a later scene between the narrator and a character referred to as the "Texan." While the Texan explicitly espouses the racist overtones of eugenics, with comments such as "no race in the world has ever been able to stand competition with the Anglo–Saxon" (Johnson [1912]/ 1965: 482), the narrator's own calculations might suggest a partial investment in the basic premise of the field, i.e., survival of the fittest.

7

LONGEVITY AND LIMITS IN RAE BOURBON'S LIFE IN MOTION

Don Romesburg

I said I'd never come back ... but here I am ... here I am
I said I'll keep off your track ... but here I am ... here I am
"Here I Am" (1926), performed by Ray Bourbon
at the Folies Bergère in 1936
There is no romance or seduction to living on the borders.
M. Jacqui Alexander's coda for Gloria Anzaldùa
(Alexander 2005: 285)

I have no aversion to the art they term perversion.
I contend that each man's hobby is his own.
You may say that I'm a sissy, in fact an object prissy,
But I've a right to change my mind when I start for home.
(Sometimes I don't get there, but I'll start!)
(Bourbon mid-1940s)

Introduction

What kinds of movement and belonging produce possibilities for a long transgender existence? Comic and female impersonator Rae Bourbon's life, spanning from the end of the nineteenth century into the 1970s, highlights the opportunities and limits of mobility and relationality for material viability and meaningful embodiment on society's margins.

A quick life sketch: Rae had a 60-year career in a profession not known for its longevity. To keep afloat, Bourbon navigated shifting terrains of social attitudes, law enforcement, performance trends, and subcultures. Onstage and off, Rae maneuvered across diverse sexualities, genders, races, and classes. Claiming to be the son of

European royalty and born in 1892 in Chihuahua City, Mexico, young Ramon was raised by a wealthy foster family on a large ranch in Hudspeth County, Texas, as a US citizen. After a supposed move to London for schooling, Bourbon went to Hollywood in the late 1910s. There, the performer played male and female stock parts in movies. Ray (sometimes billed "Rae") hit vaudeville as a drag and/or "pansy" performer across the country in the 1920s, then as a bawdy, tuxedoed comic in Hollywood nightclubs and in drag internationally throughout the 1930s. In the mid-/late 1940s Bourbon toured in Mae West's shows. A purported 1955 sexual reassignment process in Ciudad Juárez, Mexico, led to a formal change in first name from, as the performer sang in one number, "R-A-Y to R-A-E." Rae's gender ambiguity and contradictory documentation leave unclear the motives for claiming to have undergone such a procedure. From the late 1950s on, Bourbon lived and performed within a blend of self-professed public and private male, female, and trans identities. Rae got banned from the nightclubs of Los Angeles, where s/he had been arrested for impersonating a woman, and, in Miami, cops jailed her/him for impersonating a man. By the 1960s, Bourbon enjoyed few privileges of either of the two "legitimate" sexes. Down but not out, in 1966 Rae mounted *Daddy Was a Lady*, an autobiographical musical, in Colorado. Several years later, a Texas jury found the performer guilty of masterminding a murder in which s/he may or may not have been involved. Bourbon died in a small town under confinement, penniless and alone, in 1971 (Bourbon c. late 1960s–1971; Romesburg 2000).

Showcasing how Bourbon managed for so long to pull off such an eccentric, spectacular, and fierce act affirms the creative dignity of the performer's choices and expressions as tactics of possibility within deeply compromised and changing circumstances. It gives all of us strategies and challenges to connect with the negotiations we make in seeking to fashion our existences. Quality of life for all of us gets constrained, somehow, by our not fitting into the world in which we arrive, and in part gets achieved through demanding, by the practice of our own messy lives, something more. Transgender people, in particular, have had to be especially adept at this to simply continue to live.

Rae's life necessitated multiple forms of mobility and migration. These movements were multidirectional, erratic, and eccentric—across national borders and racial, class, sex/gender and sexual subject positions, through diverse US regions and urban and rural locations, within campy performances with multiple and shifting simultaneous meanings, and via overlapping, transient cultures of kinship and allegiance. Rae's oppositional knowledges, forged through exilic living *and* yearnings for belonging, produced new possibilities, or, as Emma Pérez puts it, "new disidentities," at once deeply relational and fiercely independent (Luibhéid 2008; Pérez 2003: 123–24). The same mobilities which facilitated possibility in particular contexts were turned against the performer in others. Appreciating "how trans moves us" in both spatial and affective ways opens up transgender embodiment as a series of multidirectional, productive, and creative practices (Crawford 2008; Sears 2008; Stryker, Currah, and Moore 2008). Those striving to produce livable lives beyond the confines of heteronormative fusions of sex/gender/sexuality congruence need all the tools they can deploy.

This chapter elaborates on mobilities Bourbon pursued to belong meaningfully in the world. It first considers border excursions and exile in Rae's early years, then explores movement enabled by Bourbon's performances of transgender cosmopolitan citizenship. Next, it examines how queer kinships facilitated Rae's transportation. Finally, it argues that Bourbon's self-narrations suggest transgender talents through which Bourbon grasped toward freedom across decades of shifting fortunes. Rae never was granted the rights required to live this life freely, so instead claimed precarious privilege as a flexible tactic and ethic of entitlement. The magnetic effects of innovative agency and immanent foreclosure tell a story of the possibilities and perils of an oppositional citizen-subject on the go.[1]

Borderland Belonging and Exilic Living

Bourbon's birth has at least three or four versions of the truth. Rae claimed to have been born Ramon Icarez, in either in Chihuahua City, Mexico, or "three days out on a ship bound for Vera Cruz," as the illegitimate son of Louisa Bourbon, a Spanish woman, and "Franz Frederick Hapsburg, the grandnephew of the emperor Francis Joseph." Ramon may also have been born on a U.S. ranch near the Mexican border, the child of a mixed Irish- and Mexican-American marriage. Perhaps Rae was born Hal Waddell, son of Frank T. Waddell and "Elizabeth—last name unknown," in Texarkana, Texas. Bourbon's foster parents, also possibly uncle and aunt, also named Waddell, raised Rae as Ramon on a ranch in Hudspeth County below Sierra Blanca, Texas.[2] Bourbon claimed to be unaware until turning 21 that the Waddells were foster parents; it was then that Ramon's foster mother supposedly revealed the blue-blooded borderland ancestry. It came as a shock, and yet, as Rae wrote in the memoir, "I had suspected that something was wrong because I didn't seem to belong to the Family that raised Me." Caught up in this whirl of possibilities were serious challenges for Bourbon regarding race, class, legitimacy, documentation, and allegiance during a period of crucial flux for the Texas–Mexico borderlands. As a queer and transgender exilic traveling subject, Rae grappled from birth to death with an ambivalent relationship to the region, its peoples, and the prospects they all held for personal viability. Ultimately, Bourbon chose to identify with a kind of transnational cosmopolitan citizenship over borderland belonging, but never fully left it behind.

In the borderlands of Bourbon's childhood, racial hierarchies, national boundaries, sexual divisions and gender binaries hardened. Anglo Texans increasingly lumped all Mexicans and Tejanos into the same degraded racial category, reconfiguring "Mexicans" as a "culturally and biologically inferior alien race" (Foley 1997: 45). Still, the Eurocentrism of elites during the rule of Porfirio Diaz (1867–1910) in Mexico pushed against flattening racial claims. In border towns such as El Paso, contests continued for decades around whitening performances of class status,

Spanish bloodline, and European cultural lineage. Some navigated shifting local conditions in an attempt to retain a *blanqueamiento* citizenship encumbered with a "possessive investment in whiteness" (García 1984; Lipsitz 1998; Montejano 1987). Hardening color lines and sharpened anxieties about mestizo sexuality fused with sexological and state constructions of sexual perversion, modern homosexuality, and gender inversion to make the U.S.-Mexico border a "paradigmatic border" symbolically marking differences of global struggle regarding civilization, modernization, capitalism, and American imperialism (Howe, Zaraysky, and Lorentzen 2008; Luibhéid 2008: 178; Pérez 2003: 126). On Texan soil from the 1890s through the 1900s, Bourbon's body (maybe Mexican, certainly same-sex sexually active and gender transgressive) became socially and scientifically more deviant, primitive, even criminal. Ramon may have recognized how identities and social attitudes were mobile and that moving around might be a way to harness rather than be victim to such flux. Bourbon also learned to appeal to different people by performing diverse racial, gender, sexual, and national identities.

Beyond broader structural and sociocultural contexts, dramatic personal events propelled Ramon outward into exilic living. After an idyllic childhood of private tutoring, servants, and days spent roping, riding, and caring for animals, Bourbon, at 11, grew alienated from the ranch once Mrs. Waddell took her second husband. The stepfather hated Ramon's affair with George, a ranch foreman. For the next three years, Ramon and George had a relationship that eventually turned sexual. According to the memoir, one day the two went to the Palace Hotel's bar in nearby Sierra Blanca and, without clear reason, a "Mexican" man shot George dead. In true western novel masculine heroics, Rae describes whipping out a gun and killing the assailant before, in true romance novel feminine hysterics, cradling the dying George and collapsing in shock for four days. To protect Ramon from potential retribution, Mrs. Waddell in 1906 supposedly sent Bourbon, age 14, to a private boarding school in London (Bourbon 1970b).

Off the ranch, a wider world opened up, making possible a life filled for performance, flamboyance, and wit. As a gender transgressive, liminally raced queer, Bourbon was far from dominant Texan codes of masculinity. So Bourbon said, as one later routine went, "To Hell with the Range":

> I don't need the hills and plains and the great wide-open spaces
> I can exercise my bronco in some very narrow places. ...
> I thought a ranch might give me a chance for romance and allure
> But one gets so bucolic when they frolic in manure.
>
> (Bourbon 1956a)

Contrasted with Ramon's teenage relationship with the ranch foreman and Rae's later embrace of big cities and their queer cultures, these characterizations highlight Texan backwardness, repression, tedium, and filth. From an early age Rae yearned for a cosmopolitan world.[3]

Exile, for those expressing what Jay Prosser terms "transgender ambivalence" rather than movement toward gender arrival, is a simultaneously coercive and volitional separation from both origin and settled destination. For transpeople as exilic subjects, traveling is "a strategy for living with the exilic condition" (Basu 2004: 131; Prosser 1998: 177). Home, in this context, might be understood as the place of belonging in which an exile can find refuge and recognition. This "home" directs the strategies of movement, circumstances of displacement, and feelings about them for exilic traveling subjects. For Rae, home was not a space or a consciousness but a profoundly interrelational process of associations with others and access to multiple points of contact and departure. This queer translocal mobility, at once nostalgic and disavowing, required shifting affinities, myriad escape hatches, and capacities for flexibly drawing upon multiple cultural and social resources (La Fountain-Stokes 2008).

Rae did not transcend belonging in or exile from the borderlands. Willfully and inadvertently Bourbon returned to Texas and nearby Mexican towns at crucial life junctures. To renegotiate the terms of the journeys, Rae opted for linguistic, social, and material transborder discourses that blurred the increasingly articulated geopolitical and sociocultural lines between Texas and Mexico. Ramon spoke English and "Mexican Spanish," which, Rae adds in the memoir, was "not unusual because everyone in Texas spoke Mexican Spanish." Healing the wounds of exile involved going back and forth across the border from the 1910s through the 1960s. Rae sometimes referred to Ciudad Juárez as "home" and found it more exciting than other regional towns. Bourbon performed at local clubs such as Hugo's Lobby No. 2, which catered to locals and American tourists with cabaret acts, comics, and striptease. The city also was the site for Rae's purported "sex change operations" and stage performances touting how "She Lost It in Juarez" (Bourbon c. 1969–71, 1970a, 1970b; *El Paso Herald-Post* 1931, 1933; Lomas 2003; Romesburg 2000). Transborder racial and sex/gender performance provided skills of mobility and ambiguity with lifelong utility. Rae appreciated the borderlands multiple languages, word play, and double entendre, and put these into camp action as a comic and female impersonator. They also allowed Rae to evade Texan systems sex/gender, sexuality, race, and nationalism.

Cosmopolitan Citizenship and Transnational Transtextuality

Gender diverse queer migrants must engage in self-authoring to negotiate the multiple relations of power and desire confronting their subjectivities. The challenges and tools at one's disposal differ profoundly for the refugee, transnational laborer, immigrant, tourist, or cosmopolitan citizen (Manalansan 2006). Through literary, interpersonal, and stage performances, Rae reworked the precarious existence of a transnational laborer into a cosmopolitan citizen's grand, gay life.

To distinguish forms of mobility based upon their relationships to capital and labor, Kale Fajardo suggests that we differentiate "travel," which often implies leisure, from "transportation," a disciplined circuit of embodied labor movement between industrialized and consumer spaces. Such circuits, forged in globalization and migration, accommodate alternative queered itineraries and trajectories for those able to navigate its routes (Fajardo 2008). Bourbon found success throughout the first half of the twentieth century along transnational circuits of theater, vaudeville, nightclubs, and movies. Later, circuits became more U.S.-bound, requiring large amounts of transportation to get from one small-town bar to the next big-city female impersonation tourist club. Bourbon navigated shifting laws, policing and immigration bureaucracies regarding cross-dressing, obscenity, and homosexuality, as well as transient profitability. Adept identification of circuits and execution of movement within them made possible the necessary push to get down the road another mile, another year.

Some have articulated the concept of cosmopolitan citizenship in order to underscore statist citizenship's inability to meet the heterogeneous needs of humanity. Others have criticized the elitism bound into cosmopolitanism's claims of virtue. These often support a universalism privileging tourists, intellectuals, tastemakers, industrialists, and artists. Both perspectives emphasize how people's interdependencies exceed the nation-state's capacities to satisfy socio-cultural longings or fulfill economic or political needs (Beck 2004; Linklater 1998). Cosmopolitan citizenship has afforded queer peoples a means to seek affinity beyond state borders and expose the failures of nations to afford viability and respect to sexual- and gender-diverse people. Such queer cosmopolitanism has also reproduced power relations bound into empire, globalization, and transnational consumer capitalism (Burns and Davies 2009; Grewal and Kaplan 2001; Rodriguez 2003). Bourbon's movement shows how, for those able to harness them, these two strains need not be contradictory. Claiming such privilege, however, also does not provide real security.

Through self-narration as a transgender cosmopolitan citizen, Rae lived these tensions. The ideal body of cosmopolitan citizenship is one of privilege, capable of accessing many markets, cultures, and locales while appearing to be self-maintaining in core aspects of being. Queer and gender-transgressive bodies (among many others) get positioned as being overwhelmed by desires and the burdens of embodiment and, thus, undeserving of full citizenship (Canaday 2009; Romesburg 2008). Still, Bourbon managed cosmopolitan citizenship as a tactic and ethic. This required awareness of larger forces, flexible accumulation of risk-mitigation strategies, and performance of belonging and entitlement in multiple environments. Rae accessed transportation along circuits of transnational capital in the entertainment industry. As a cultural producer and worker, Bourbon profited from transgressive cultural mobility. Rae's shows were a commodity that brought urbanity to small-town stages, poked fun at rurality and provincial Americanness in big-city nightclubs, made lowbrow comedy out of the high art of Western civilization, and lampooned peoples from across the globe. Part of the act, onstage and off, was a claim of transtextual privilege in a global network.

Prosser utilizes transtextuality to underscore multiple, overlapping referents in transpeople's self-narration. These shift depending upon the discourses—legal, medical, social, political—a person must access in various moments and locales. To themselves and others, transsexuals (and all people, Prosser suggests) must tell stories about themselves that are not their own in order to more fully realize themselves as viable, recognizable subjects. They also potentially subvert or, at least, make space within these discourses. Film scholar Manthia Diawara refers to transtextuality as "the movement of cultural styles from character to character. … hybridity, multiple subject positions." This contrasts with immanence, or the "trapping of a cultural role in a character" (Diawara and Kolbowski 1998: 51). Combined, these help explain Bourbon's mobility as one exercise of cosmopolitan citizenship. Through both self-narration and performance, Rae flexibly disidentified with myriad subject positions to subversively embrace the marketplace. Because the navigated forces overwhelmed one person's ability to overcome them, the performer always faced threats of immanence. Being read too literally foreclosed upon possibilities and fixed Rae, perilously, into place. Two illustrations of these tensions are Bourbon's self-positioning around imperial privilege and Rae's racial, sexual, and gender mobilities across space and time.

Bourbon flaunted a royal genealogy and showcased regal associations, bragged about substantial wealth, and claimed a liminal Spanishness. In combination, these supported Bourbon's cosmopolitan citizenship. Both blood parents, Rae told everyone from intimate friends to small-town Texan juries, were from noble European lineage and married outside Paris when the mother was pregnant, then she sailed to America. This lineage even ended up on Bourbon's death certificate (Texas Department of Health—Bureau of Vital Statistics 1971). Rae highlights nobility to showcase sophistication and a capacity to rub shoulders comfortably with the powerful. Bourbon supposedly gave special performances before such luminaries as Shanghai's Chow Ling, "Great Grand-Nephew of the Dowager Empress of China" (1930), England's King Edward (1936), and, most implausibly, with Josephine Baker for Spain's Generalissimo Franco and the Duke and Duchess of Alba (1936). The same was claimed of capitalist royalty, such as Cuban sugar king Jorge Sanchez, Al Capone, and Hollywood celebrities. Rae also performed a privilege-laden trickle-down democratics. In Shanghai, Bourbon refers to a servant as "My Mongol," yet tells him to speak to Rae as he would "anyone else" (Bourbon 1956b, c. 1969–71; Romesburg 2000; State of Texas 1971).[4]

Rae self-presented as rich. In the memoir, Bourbon claims that the birth mother had given a staggering $500,000 to the Waddells to raise Ramon. In a story picked up by the *El Paso Herald-Post* at the height of the Great Depression, Bourbon claimed to receive $1.5 million from the Waddell estate (then plugged a show in Ciudad Juárez). At various times Bourbon claimed to have secret European bank accounts and Texan and Mexican land. Rae kept this up until the end, despite being unable to pay for car repairs, housing, pet boarding, or a defense attorney. In practice, Rae was always scheming to make more and was known for haggling ruthlessly with venue owners. Bourbon had high times, yet filed for bankruptcy in 1944 and struggled with poverty throughout the final two decades (Bourbon c. 1969–71; "Juárez Actor," *El Paso Herald-Post* 1931; Romesburg 2000; Wright and Forrest 1999).

Onstage, Bourbon underscored, as many impersonators did, globe-trotting glamor that appealed to diverse audiences in part because it displayed a democratic-capitalist promise of attainable luxury. Yet Rae also gestured toward the structural challenges for individuals attempting such mobility. Bourbon performed across class identities but always included the lowbrow. Throughout career ups and downs, Rae would don a ratty wig and a dirty, cheap dress to comic effect moments after embodying a high-society maven. Bourbon often sang about performing in drag primarily for the money (Bourbon c. mid-1940s, 1956c). In a comic call to unionize queens entitled "We've Got to Have a Union of Our Own," Bourbon utilizes the symbolics of labor solidarity to urge greater queer and transgender collectivity, making explicit the hard work of entertainment labor and a need to respond to systemic discrimination (Bourbon c. late-1940s a).

In addition to regal relationality and the performance of wealth alongside class mobility, Rae bound racial passing within modes of whiteness into claims of imperial privilege. This allowed for an appeal to a vaguely exotic European ancestry. Emma Pérez suggests that, for subaltern women, assimilation into modes of whiteness can figure as interstitial moves, creating possibilities for personal subjecthood within patriarchal structures that refuse such women comfortable or stable identity (Pérez 1999: 81, 87). For queer and gender diverse people, such tactics brought similar opportunities for subversive navigation. In the memoir, Rae proudly represents a comment by a London theater manager in late 1930s that Bourbon has "no Accent that would associate you with America or with England" to signal cosmopolitanism beyond national or racial origins. Bourbon's light skin would have allowed the performer to claim to be Anglo in many contexts.

Rae also sometimes performed a public and private Castilian identity and found comfort in the use of a loose Spanish. In the memoir, Bourbon, in an aside to the reader, writes, "When I'm out of the United States I unknowingly revert too [*sic*] Spanish". In jail in 1970, Bourbon frequently closed letters in Spanish (Bourbon c. 1969–71, 1970a, 1970b, 1970c). In songs such as "Spanish," Bourbon claimed Spanishness proudly, even while mocking Latin culture. Without completely disavowing its hybrid relationship to Mexicanness, Bourbon blended Spanishness and borderland belonging, regal relations with lowbrow associations. In the performance for Franco, Rae awed the audience by joining in a robust flamenco complete with castanets, noting, "I hadn't lived along the Rio Grande for nothing." At the subsequent banquet, Bourbon bragged to the Duchess of Alba about learning to dance at the Molino Rojo. "Franco's daughter laughed," Bourbon recalls, "because Molino rojos are all whorehouses. Leave it too Me to make the Faux-pas of My life" (Bourbon c. 1969–71).[5] Time and again, Bourbon blurred lines even when laboring to draw them. Maneuverability let Rae attach to and detach from racial and national allegiances, exercising the flexibility needed for transgender cosmopolitan citizenship.

Bourbon's transgender and racial hybridity, coupled with a keen sense of cultural nuance surrounding socio-economic and social status markers, made movements through carefully calibrated and contextualized performances useful for survival, prosperity, and self-narration. As tactics, however, modes of passing were threatened by potential "discovery" of the "real." In others' eyes, Bourbon sometimes would "go brown," queer, or trans against the performer's intent. Racial/ethnic ambiguity, like sexual and gender ambiguity, was subject not just to Rae's self-presentation but other people's interpretations of racial, sexual, and gender performance and embodiment. Sometimes that left Bourbon stuck.

In the movies, Bourbon's representational dispersal across time and space allowed movement of queer and transgender possibilities across many eras and locations. Knowing "in the know" showbiz people formed a foundation of contacts through which Rae built a network of possibilities for a lifetime on the go. By the late 1910s, Ramon found transportation routes to Hollywood. Through silent movies and vaudeville circuits, transgender, transracial flexibility was empowering and profitable. Bourbon first got to Hollywood by submitting photos for a competition seeking new screen beauties. As Bob Wright told it, she "[t]urned out to be Ray, this six-foot-one Texan who looked as if he might be a Spanish don with all this luxurious hair." Studio executives said, "We don't want any males who look like you or talk like you." Bourbon replied, "What *do* you want?" They said, "Can you ride a horse?" Rae answered, "I was born on a horse," and got hired as a cross-dressing extra doing actresses' stunts (Wright and Forrest 1999). Bourbon claimed to have been played bit parts in a dozen films from 1919 to 1937, principally with Paramount, where the performer was under contract as a stock player through around 1923.[6] Roles were young and old, male and female, white and nonwhite, spanning across history and around the globe. In *Bella Donna* (1923), Bourbon played a flower vendress and a camel driver. In *Blood and Sand* (1922), Bourbon appears to have played a young bullfighter who dies in Rudolph Valentino's arms and later shows up as a female extra. In *Behind the Rocks* (1922), Rae was an English society woman in the background on a yacht (Bourbon c. 1969–71; Romesburg 2000; Willard 1971: 75).

Bourbon's opportunities to perform racial and gender diversity were furthered by acts that moved transgender queerness globally and transhistorically. Rae later played up this "we are—and I am—everywhere" sensibility in stage routines from the 1940s through the 1960s. Acts placed same-sex action and gender diversity in medieval Europe, colonial North America, and imperial Asia. Famous historical figures such as Ponce de León, Pocahontas, Cleopatra and George Washington became queens, lesbians, and queers (Bourbon c. late 1940s b, 1956b, 1956d). Later routines played off the performer's longevity. In a 1964 Kansas City performance, Bourbon quipped, "I've been around a long time. When the Man said, 'Let there be light,' I'm the bitch that pulled the switch" (Bourbon 1964; Romesburg 2000).

Transgressive camp performance is mobile, refusing fixity. In defiant transtextuality, Bourbon thumbed a nose at immanence. But camp refuses a performer the luxury of autonomy, necessarily soliciting temporary solidarities of double entendre. Such contradictions made Bourbon's self-stylings both nimble and dependent.

Bourbon's movement was driven as much by necessity as yearning for trans-expressivity. Scandal, poverty, and/or illegality dogged Rae whenever success seemed around the corner. In 1923 or 1924, Bourbon's most prolific years of screen work ended after the performer attended a gay party at the house of director Louis Gasiner and Gaston Glass. Police raided the place and Rae hid under dirty laundry to avoid arrest. The next day, Paramount lawyers released all the stock players who had been in attendance from their contracts (Bourbon c. 1969–71; Romesburg 2000; *State of Texas v. Ray Bourbon* 1971: 868).

Transience and Intimacies in Tacit Queer Relations

Queer kinships across the globe enabled Bourbon's life as an exilic traveling subject framed though transgender cosmopolitan citizenship. Complicity between associates was necessary for socio-economic mobility, transnational migration, and survival. Tacitness allowed Bourbon to manage those relations to carve out spaces of navigation. These queer tacit associations started at a young age. In the memoir, Bourbon recalls that Maria, the ranch nanny, affirmed specialness worth protecting in Ramon without naming its source, telling others, "I am the only one who understands his Nature; even his Mother does not understand him." Maria, as characterized by Rae, was *entendida*, someone in the know through whom Ramon could find a generous reflection that could, at the same time, remain vague in its specifics. Like the Latina/o concept of being *de ambiente* (in the life), *entendida* assumes something deeply relational and contextual about identity (Decena 2008; Nesvig 2001). As empowering as an *entendida* tacit subjectivity could be, those who could aid and abet could also harm and abandon. As with the Hollywood party raid, betrayals came on the heels of scandalous public disclosures. Associates could and did turn away, transforming what was tacit into plausible deniability to preserve their own security. When they did, Bourbon got stuck in everything from petty jealousies to criminal immanence. Such dependency and vulnerability contradicted Bourbon's desire to embody the privileged ease of cosmopolitan citizenship. To manage this, Rae characterized queer kin as either accompanists or accomplices.

Accompanists were subordinates upon which Bourbon's well-being, status, material prosperity and mobility depended. In addition to houseboys and chauffeurs during high times, Bourbon frequently had a traveling companion who played piano for the performer's songs and blue patter. These pianists tended to be young, blond, slender, attractive, and male. In the memoir, John "Duke" Kane, who performed with Bourbon on and off from the 1930s through the 1950s, and other accompanists fall in love with Bourbon, a self-testament to Rae's desire to embody importance, maternal and paternal strength, and goodness.

Rae treated employees as if being in the show was a great favor to them. There was some truth to this; Bourbon launched careers for songwriters Bart Howard ("In Other Words (Fly Me to the Moon)") and the team of Robert Wright and Chet Forrest (*Song of Norway*). In 1965, when Bourbon staged *Daddy Was a Lady*, a semi-autobiographical musical, in Cripple Creek, Colorado, the 73-year-old performer made sure that accompanist and lover Pat Lee, an 18-year-old impersonator, had a part (Bourbon c. 1969–71; FBI 1961–62; Romesburg 2000; Strong 1999; Williamson 2009; Wright and Forrest 1999;). These favors, portrayed in the memoir as selfless generosity, were recalled differently by recipients. Through Bourbon, Wright, and Forrest secured an MGM contract, then had to pay Rae $10,000 to buy their way out of the favor. Bourbon even threatened their lives (Bourbon c. 1969–71; Wright and Forrest 1999). When Howard left to work at New York's prestigious Rainbow Room, Bourbon sent management a letter calling him an "untrustworthy degenerate" (Gavin 1992: 52–54). Rae's rage suggests how their success disrupted the hierarchy in Bourbon's transgender cosmopolitan citizenship.

Others, accomplices, were fashioned as if they were equals. Some acted as station agents, arranging papers and services necessary for transportation. Examples included chummy bail bondsmen who sprang the performer when tangled up in anti-cross-dressing and indecency charges and friends who helped Rae travel between gigs. Rae enjoyed femme collaboration with well-placed strong women, too. In the early 1930s, Bourbon booked Singapore and Shanghai runs thanks to club owner "Mrs. Merideth." Through the 1940s, Bourbon palled around with the cranky Marge Finocchio, the tough brains behind San Francisco's popular female impersonation tourist bar. During the 1950s and 1960s, Kaye Elledge, a butch lesbian who had performed in Bourbon's band in the 1940s, hosted Rae at Kaye's Happy Landing in Phoenix, Arizona, one of the state's first gay bars. Lifelong friend Mae West gave Rae prominently billed roles in theatrical touring productions of *Catherine Was Great* (1944–46) and *Diamond Lil* (1948–50) (Bourbon c. 1969–71; Romesburg 2000; "Tucson," *Weekly Observer* 1987).

Celebrities were vital to presentation as a transgender cosmopolitan citizen and instrumental to practical issues of reputation, fame, access, and purpose. Onstage, Bourbon often called out to famous audience members as if they were old friends. As indicated in the memoir and elsewhere, some were, including West, Lana Turner, Lupe Vélez, Rudolph Valentino, Josephine Baker, Martha Raye, Bob Hope, and Robert Mitchum. Such associations gave Bourbon mainstream publicity few impersonators enjoyed, garnering regular mention in bits by Walter Winchell, Hedda Hopper, and other gossip peddlers nationally syndicated in small-town and big-city newspapers.[7]

Bourbon had special acquaintance with officials who facilitated movement across national borders. One story showcases how this enabled transnational movement against nation-states' attempts to police sexual and gender borders. While performing at the Folies Bergère in 1936, Bourbon arranged handsome, blond cast mate Fredric Rey's passage to the U.S. through circuitous means. The U.S. Embassy had rejected Rey on moral perversion suspicions. Bourbon arranged for MGM to advance cash to bring Rey to Hollywood for a screen test. Then, at the Mexican Consulate, Carlos, an old flame from "a very Wealthy Mexican Family" with whom Rae had worked in silent movies and shared a romance *de ambiente*, secured Rey's claim of Mexico as the final destination. Next, a young man at the Cuban Consulate approved the visa after telling Bourbon he had seen the performer in Paris and Miami. Bourbon and Duke sailed to New York and took a train to Miami. An immigration officer whom Rae had met on transportation between Miami and Havana gigs, pledged to get Rey into the U.S. on a six-month visa if arriving from Cuba. Bourbon and Duke took a boat to Havana, meeting Rey and his male companion arriving from Europe. Another Vice Consul stamped the visas after Bourbon pledged to send comedy albums. Fast-tracked through customs, the foursome arrived back in Miami. Bourbon bought a Cadillac from a dealership-owning acquaintance and the group headed to Hollywood. Whatever the story's veracity, it highlights the multiple layers of relationship upon which Bourbon relied to conceptualize and manage transnational cosmopolitan citizenship. Fandom, friendship, *entendida* and tacit relationships, and savvy understanding of the mechanics of transport, allowed Bourbon to work accomplices to manage international travel. Queer sexuality, racial liminality, and gender diversity required interpersonal work-arounds (Bourbon c. 1969–71; S.S. *Lancastria* 1936).

As useful as accomplices proved to Bourbon's longevity and mobility, they con-firmed Bourbon's worst fears of abandonment and immanence in the later years. Those that had enabled Rae's transtextuality and publicity did little when things got dire. While in jail for conspiracy to murder, Bourbon and court-appointed defender William Bell wrote letters to West, California Governor Ronald Reagan, Bob Hope, Gore Vidal, and other Hollywood figures, asking them to testify to Rae's character. None did. Reagan's office sent a terse decline. Hope expressed interest, then never showed. Even West, who called, didn't make the trip. The only person who came from Rae's vast queer kinship network was, ironically, Bob Wright, the partner to 1930s accompanist Chet Forrest that Bourbon had treated with venom long before (Bell 1979, 2000; Romesburg 2000; Wright and Forrest 1999). Bourbon, devastated by these betrayals, on some level understood them. Faced with allegiance to Rae when it meant exposing their own interdependencies with and vulner-abilities to the forces of normativity, nationalism, and the market, most opted for invisibility and passivity. M. Jacqui Alexander suggests that the "meeting place that collapses the enemy, the terrorist, and the sexual pervert is the very one that secures the loyal heterosexual citizen patriot." This place, an orientation within an inter-change of interpersonal relationships, cosmopolitan performance, and the state, clarifies borders, boundaries, and belonging. To navigate, Rae reoriented constantly to new contexts upon which the relationships needed for viability and mobility were conditioned (Alexander 2005: 239).

Perhaps the queerest kinship Bourbon sought to establish was with the U.S. government. Where others made patriotic public stances and associations that allowed cover for transgressive personal lives (paging Roy Cohn and Liberace), Rae lived an openly queer transgender life while seeking private alignment with the nation-state. In September 1960, after reading in newspapers about the Soviet defection of U.S. National Security Agency employees William Martin and Bernon Mitchell, Bourbon contacted the FBI, apparently out of patriotism. Rae explained to agents, who viewed the performer as a "notorious female impersonator," that Martin and Mitchell were homosexuals who had attended a Washington, D.C. party thrown by a mutual friend in the honor of Bourbon (Department of the Army 1960; FBI 1961–62).[8]

The agents turned to the matter of Rae's sex. Bourbon claimed having undergone a "Christine Jorgensen operation," and the report notes that "BOURBON laughingly stated his reason … that he had wanted to save his own life." (Bourbon said it was cancer related.) "Since the operation," it explains, "he has billed himself as RAE BOURBON since actually is now bi-sexual" (male and female). Agents insisted that Bourbon identify "other perverts" in government employ. Rae demurred and refused to meet the agents in person, but continued to phone them for a year. Someone shot the entertainer's windshield, and Bourbon feared an attempted assassination, perhaps by Soviets. The FBI did nothing to aid Bourbon for informing.

Rae had never fit into Americanist gender/sex/sexuality molds either publicly or privately, but by the early 1960s this was truer than ever. Bourbon rejected Cold War cultural logic that presumed a linkage between gender/sex normativity, heterosexuality, and Americanism. Still, Rae believed that communism and the Soviets represented enough of a threat that FBI association was worth risking greater official surveillance by the same legal and administrative system that sought to squash homosexuality and stifle gender diversity in the U.S., at its borders, and beyond.[9] Fear of communist reprisal was the most recent explanation for victimization in a life of being done wrong and let down by intimacies, ranging from the interpersonal to the transnational, that were supposed to provide sustenance and security. By the early 1960s, Rae was turning 70. Bourbon had not regularly made a decent income since touring with Mae West in the 1940s, and had increasingly faced arrest and harassment as a homosexual and/or transsexual performer. Little wonder, then, that Bourbon yearned for freedom, some way to move beyond all of the ugly forces constraining material viability, meaningful embodiment, and intimate belonging on society's margins.

Conclusion: Transgender Talents and the Limits of Freedom

Rae believed that holding together everything that made up livability through transgender cosmopolitan citizenship, from transborder discourses to transtextuality and queer kinships, relied on talent as the fuel that enabled movement across space and time. In the memoir, Bourbon writes, "Talent is the most requisite of all accoutrements One May possess. Your looks are Nothing. Your background is nothing.

Your experience is nothing. If you have TALENT, all else fades into Oblivion. ... With me it is not guess work. ... I have been in Show-Business over FIFTY-Years" (Bourbon c. 1969–71). Harnessing that talent required a lot of work, discipline, and faith.

Bourbon underscored requisite effort and self-control. While others commented on Rae's heavy drinking and an onstage impulsivity that could work against occupational prosperity and security, Bourbon's self-characterization was sober, contemplative, and striving (Bourbon c. 1969–71; Romesburg 2000; Wright and Forrest 1999). Bourbon did not always actualize this, but it reflected what the performer believed was necessary to stay in the game. "Getting to the top in any Profession is an unceasing Struggle; but in Show Business it is even More so," Rae writes in the memoir. "The Competition is unbelievable, the Envy, Deceit, Treachery, and underhanded tricks innumerable. ... Once you have reached the Top, it is twice as hard to Stay There." Being exceptional was not enough, nor was attainment; one had to ceaselessly reenact greatness, watching one's back and adapting. Bourbon's "rules to live by" set out a host of dictums of withholding as self-preservation, such as "Never let People know what you know; if so, then they know twice as much as You—What they know, plus what you know," and, "Never become overly familiar with people; else they may become so with you." Rae relied more and more on "the babies," dozens of stray dogs and cats hauled around in a trailer from town to town, to supply the unconditional affection otherwise lacking. For all of Rae's interdependencies, intimacy with other people was hard to secure.

All of the struggle and loneliness involved in transforming talent into a trade was worth it, though, because the rewards, beyond transgender livability and longevity, were moments of freedom. Sometimes performance allowed for the sublime. Rae could be carried away, spiritually, to a kind of connectivity beyond material embodiment. At times, this could feel liberating, affirming existence in a way that other maneuvers of transgender cosmopolitan citizenship could not. When others truly saw the performer's talent, Rae felt it supplied a deeper, more freeing recognition, one of the few Bourbon could trust as real.

Bourbon believed talent was god-given. One turned away from it to their own detriment, a manifestation of the "Spiritual Blindness of Man that limits Man." In 1929, destitute and sick with jaundice, Rae had discovered Christian Science through a practitioner's office in the transient vice district of downtown Los Angeles. It was transformative and revelatory. Over the years, Rae corresponded with a handful of women, Christian Science practitioners, who pulled the performer back from "false beliefs" and into a "healing" faith. "We are what we think," Bourbon wrote a friend in one letter from jail. Spirituality gave Rae connectivity for the journey and a way to "deny All that" Rae did not "want expressed in the Body" (Bourbon 1970b).

Revelatory talent could also be unnerving, a reminder of the lack and struggle of life. In a Chicago nightclub in 1931, while singing "You're a Million Miles from

Nowhere (When You're One Little Mile from Home)," Bourbon recalls, "I forgot ME, I forgot the Club." Awakened from the state by thunderous applause, Rae was shaken. "There always seems to be one song in every Singers Life, that when they do it they come apart," Bourbon writes. Rae never did the number again (Bourbon c. 1969–71). More than exilic trauma, it was an accidental unveiling of the dependency that said too much.

In the end, Bourbon was caught up in a murder of a Texan pet boarder who, after lack of payment, sold the babies to a laboratory to be used in medical experiments. In the trial, Rae's Texan roots and patriotic anticommunism were downplayed as prosecutors made this queer, racially, and sexually liminal figure into a dangerously mobile drifter and interloping outsider. Tried as a man, Bourbon's gifts for impersonation and transtextuality were recast as capacities for willful deception, pathologies of sexual and gender deviance, and signs of social and economic desperation. Rae's maternal love of pets morphed into a sociopathic, effeminate preference for animals over humans. After a quick deliberation, the jury handed Bourbon a life sentence. Within about a year, on July 20, 1971, Rae died alone under confinement in a small-town Texan hospital.[10] The tools that had sustained a long transgender existence became the means through which to impose brutal immanence.

To what extent should the end of this life come to bear on the rest of it? Literary critic Scott Long suggests that a camp stance exposes "a society that presumes to know what is serious and what is not" as "explicitly inadequate." The loneliness of this position comes from its limits to transform perception more broadly. Camp can only "occupy something like a terrorist's status, conducting intermittent raids on the authoritative centers of ignorance" against "a giant backdrop of defeat" (Long 1993: 79, 89–90). Framing Bourbon's life through the final act obscures remarkable resiliency and innovativeness over many decades within structures and systems inadequate to his/her existence. Still, to ignore the end is to elide the real stakes involved. Marcia Ochoa describes how Venezuelan *transformistas*, often street-walking trans sex workers, engage in a self-fashioning through eyebrow plucking, wardrobe, demeanor, and hormonal self-medication that, "without asking permission," allow them to emerge into being through a perversely precarious citizenship. "People who are not subjects of rights are regularly subject to violations of their integrity as human beings and as citizens," she explains, noting that the *transformistas'* innovation and resiliency do not preclude regular disappearing by police and other forms of violence (Ochoa 2008: 149, 155). Bourbon faced similar indignities, often by transforming them into comedy, shaming and maneuvering around officials. The final arrest changed all that. Rae experienced trauma that could not be recontextualized, stripped of the performative privilege on which claims to transgender cosmopolitan citizenship relied. "I didn't know anything like this could happen in the United States," Rae wrote a friend. "I'd read of such things, but NOW, I was going thru it. The terror, the horror, the face slappings I took. Dear, Dear God. Even to think of it Now the Horror has not lessened one bit" (Bourbon 1970c).

Faced with a precarious existence, Bourbon transformed talent into a long life through transborder discourses, claims of transgender cosmopolitan citizenship, and tenuous but valuable queer kinships. It was a self-fashioning that reiterated a right to personal autonomy and mobility even as it expressed interpersonal, material, performative, and sociopolitical interdependency. But, while performing privilege and entitlement may be like rights, it is not the same as having them. Or freedom. Collaborating with global capital circuits and nation-state paradigms was as obligatory as it was contradictory to Rae's transgression of them. Bourbon never sought to overturn those powerful forces that largely foreclosed upon viability—how, exactly, would that have worked? The spaces Rae was compelled to occupy were not designed to sustain that life.

In closing, a final flight of fancy: Bourbon's maneuvers resonate with Chela Sandoval's methodologies of the oppressed that center on the differential movement of U.S. third world women of color. Rae's uses of transborder, transhistorical camp deconstructed and decolonized signs of culture to create space for multiple possibilities of new consciousness. Claims of imperial privilege and lowbrow democratics appropriated dominant and subcultural forms in potentially transformative ways. Like Sandoval's differential movement, Bourbon's shifting between modes underscore the yearnings for freedom. Rae's persistent mobility calls upon us to recognize one mode of viability for the oppositional citizen-subject. Bourbon's life story gives us, to paraphrase Sandoval, the presence of an obtuse third meaning that shimmers behind all we think we know (Sandoval 2000: 146). The only predictable outcome is transformation itself, and here Bourbon shines. How might Rae's strategies have been different in a world that embraced him/her as a person worthy of support and sustenance? In our neoliberal present, we are encouraged to believe that talent, wealth, celebrity, faith, patriotism, connectivity, and easy transnational movement can protect us from displacements and violence. This old queen might just be a tour guide, for us all.

Acknowledgements

I am indebted to Trystan Cotten, Susan Stryker, Julian Carter, Corrie Decker, and Randy Riddle, as well as attendees of presentations in the Sonoma State University Gendered Intersections and University of California, Davis Women and Gender Studies speaker series.

Notes

1 On sources and method: Prosser (1998) argues for the primacy of self-authorization in transsexual narratives, but as Halberstam (2005) notes, establishing the archive upon which to base it is challenging for transgender subjects living complex lives that render them unable to provide a coherent narrative. While Bourbon left behind ship manifests, arrest records, court documents, print, sound, and motion picture media, personal letters, performances, and even a half-finished jailhouse memoir, it's not clear how to grant authority. Bourbon used sources to multiple effects—arrest images became publicity stills and the memoir became a front-page story in the *Big Springs Daily Herald*

in 1971. Because Bourbon's spotlight-seeking relied on camp's double entendres and unfixed meanings, reading too much earnestness into self-authorized sources would be a disservice. I cross-checked what could be factually ascertained. To get at structures of affect and enabling strategies of self-presentation, I rely on an eccentric subcultural archive of feelings (Cvetkovich 2003), foregrounding Bourbon's performances and personal writings while attentive to more formal historical records and oral histories.

2 For documentation on the various accountings of Bourbon's birth, see Romesburg (2000).

3 For an analysis of Bourbon's relationship to rurality and roadsides, see Romesburg (2007).

4 Evidence makes some of Bourbon's claims plausible. Ship manifestos prove travel to and from London around the time of the purported performance before the king (*City of Hamburg* 1936; S.S. *Lancastria* 1936).

5 In the 1930s, several lavish whorehouses in Mexican border towns that served mostly U.S. patrons were named "Molino Rojo" (Ruiz 1998: 55).

6 Films in which Bourbon claimed to appear: *Behind the Door* (Famous Players-Lasky/ Paramount, 1919); *The Four Horsemen of the Apocalypse* (Metro, 1921); *The Sheik* (Paramount, 1921); *The Young Rajah* (Paramount, 1922); *Blood and Sand* (Paramount, 1922); *Beyond the Rocks* (Paramount, 1922); *Manslaughter* (Paramount, 1922); *Bella Donna* (Famous Players-Lasky/Paramount, 1923); *The Ten Commandments* (Famous Players-Lasky/Paramount, 1923); *Son of Sheik* (United Artists, 1926); *The Volga Boat-man* (DeMille Productions/Producers Distributors Corp., 1926); *Gold Diggers of 1937* (Warner Brothers, 1936); *The Hurricane* (United Artists/Samuel Goldwyn, 1937).

7 For sample syndicated column mentions, see Kilgallen (1955); Sullivan (1946); Winchell (1943, 1968).

8 On dubious claims about Martin's and Mitchell's homosexuality, see Johnson (2004: 144–46).

9 In the memoir, Rae rants about communism in acting schools and claims having seen it in England, Europe, Africa, Mexico, and the U.S. "COMMUNISM IS A DIS-EASE," Rae writes (Bourbon c. 1969–71).

10 For trial analyses, see Romesburg (2000, 2007).

PART IV
Troubling Trans and Queer Theory

8

THE PERSISTENCE OF TRANSGENDER TRAVEL NARRATIVES

Aren Z. Aizura

> Welcome! Transsexual transition is simply a journey. Just like a trip, you decide on
>
> * your destination
> * the time you'll need to get there
> * the money you'll spend
>
> Transsexual Road Map is a travel guide to set priorities and choose your route. It's about making informed purchasing decisions and setting realistic, achievable transition goals.
>
> (http://tsroadmap.com)

The text above sits on the front page of an English language website called tsroadmap.com. Created by Los Angeles-based trans woman Andrea James, TS Roadmap offers free advice, information and resources for transsexual women who are "on the road" to gender transition. Thorough, sensible and clear, the site details every aspect of gender transition for trans women, from book lists to information about standards of therapeutic care, physical and mental transformation, legal issues, sexuality and more. Of course, the process may differ for each individual: "Because of all the variables in transition," James continues:

> your journey will be unlike anyone else's. Some people want to get to their destination in a big hurry on the fastest route they can find, even if it's not the safest and is a steeper climb. Others want a slow, smooth road they can take cautiously. I've tried to discuss as many of these roads as possible. There is no right way or proper path, either. Everyone has a different destination, different timetable, different resources available to get there.
>
> *(http://tsroadmap.com)*

So far, so much like a guide book—for a sprawling country criss-crossed with routes, each promising a different experience for the transsexual in transition. TS Roadmap's journey metaphor works on almost every level: to reassure readers that every individual's journey is different, but also to offer road markers that will shape the aspirations and expectations of those same readers.

TS Roadmap is hardly the first artifact of contemporary American trans culture to frame gender transition as a journey. As the Introduction to this volume makes clear, travel narratives are central to understanding trans experience. From man to woman, from woman to man: the "from" and "to" denote a one-way trajectory across a terrain in which the stuff of sex is divided into male and female territories, divided by the border or no man's land in between. Travel metaphors are, however, more complicated than a simple spatialization of gender, as TS Roadmap illustrates. They also draw on the specificity of particular modes of traveling to make meaning: road trips, overseas vacations, immigrant stories. In turn, different understandings of modes of traveling both condition and shape trans travel narrative conventions. As I elucidate in this chapter, trans travel narratives have material force as discursive ideals, but also as modes of unofficial folklore that equip gender variant subjects with senses of possibility, futurity and community.

The proliferation of trans travel narratives has been remarked upon before now (Crawford 2008; Prosser 1999). Prosser points to transsexual autobiographies of the 1960s and 1970s, beginning with Christine Jorgensen's *A Personal Autobiography* (Jorgensen 1967), in which transsexual women, overwhelmingly, would recount their journeys to Copenhagen, Casablanca or Mexico to find surgeons willing to operate on them. More recently, Lucas Crawford asks why transgender narratives so often mimic that of the "queer pilgrimage to the city," as when *The L Word*'s butch lesbian Moira moves from Skokie, Illinois, to Los Angeles and reinvents himself as trans man Max (Crawford 2008: 127). The one-way trip scenario is obviously not the only metaphor used within trans cultural productions to think about or write about gender variance. But although they both acknowledge non-teleological and non-linear trans narratives, both Crawford and Prosser contend with the *persistence* of a one-way narrative of transgender movement. As Crawford points out, "this model configures gender modification as a safe return rather than a risky exploit or experiment in embodied selfhood" (128).

Drawing on Crawford and Prosser, and my own doctoral research on the metaphoric and material intersections of transgender travel, this chapter seeks to identify why the "safe return" is so persistent in transgender travel narratives. How can we talk of a "one-way" narrative that is also structured as a return? From where does the subject of the transsexual travel narrative issue, and where does she or he go? When and where did this persistent transgender travel story emerge, and how did it shape popular understandings of transsexuality? What does this travel metaphor import from Euro-American geographical narratives about the shaping of the (colonized) world into a center, a here, and a periphery or elsewhere—a destination and a home to which to return? And what does it import from other narratives again, equating geographical peregrination elsewhere with the capacity to become *socially* mobile?

Despite the target of these questions being the ostensibly abstract logics structuring representational metaphors of trans experience, they are of central importance to understanding contemporary trans culture and politics. As trans studies grows, it is becoming more and more evident that the "ideal" subject of most advice columns, days of remembrance, medical standards of care, legislative models, employment policy documents and sundry other things pertinent to or created for trans people is white, affluent, middle-class or aspiring to be middle-class (Roen 2006). This is despite how often trans women of color are the violated bodies in whose name these things are produced: for example, Transgender Day of Remembrance, which in too many cases has been a day organized by and for trans college students, far from the locations where most trans people (the majority of them people of color doing sex work) become the victims of violence (Lamble 2008). Mobility is central to these questions: gender variant people, as a population, are highly mobile. Those trans people subject to their movements being regulated most militantly are often undocumented migrants from the global "south," and who, as sex workers, care workers and/or informal workers, constitute part of the huge racialized economy Pheng Cheah calls the New International Division of Reproductive Labor (Cheah 2007: 89). For these subjects, the "journey" is markedly different. As theorists, we need to remain alert to the circulation of racialized narratives of gender variant experience and how non-white gender variant subjects can access mobility and self-determination. But we also need to trace the historical emergence and circulation of the ideal, as an ideal.

In particular, we need to trace transsexual narratives in relation to broader cultural understandings of life, embodiment and personhood. An impressive body of work in trans theory has established the relationship between standard transsexual narratives and medical discourse: for example, Prosser's observation that transsexual discourse itself is structured by the conventions of recounting one's autobiography, or case history, from the earliest moments of sexological research into, and treatment of, inversion (Prosser 1998: 135); or Spade's observation that an individual's presentation of the correct autobiographical narrative has always been central to an individual's ability to obtain diagnosis as transsexual and gain access to treatment (Spade 2006: 325). But how do standard transsexual narratives draw on other historical forms of narrative, other imaginaries? How do those imaginaries reproduce themselves within what we relate to as a medically inflected discourse? Quoting Teresa de Lauretis (1994), historian Joanne Meyerowitz emphasizes the dynamic transformation of transsexuality "by forms of fantasy both private and public, conscious and unconscious, which are culturally available and historically specific" (Meyerowitz 2002: 35). This historiographical strategy of framing the emergence of transsexuality as a process of imagination and interpellation is instructive in reminding us to attend to popular narratives just as much as medical discourse.

Narrating Transition, Containing Indeterminacy

In February 1953, a beautiful blonde bombshell stepped off an airplane in New York City. Wrapped in a sumptuous fur coat and surrounded by paparazzi, this beautiful woman was none other than Christine Jorgensen, America's first transsexual celebrity. As is well known, Jorgensen had unsuccessfully sought out doctors who would perform gender reassignment surgery on her in the United States in the late 1940s. In 1950 she sailed to Denmark on vacation, resolving to attempt to obtain gender reassignment surgery in Europe. Serendipitously a doctor in Copenhagen, Dr. Christian Hamburger, agreed to arrange her treatment. Jorgensen returned home to New York in 1953 to a flurry of media excitement over her prodigal transformation.

The story of Jorgensen's return home sparked off numerous other stories of transsexuals, most of them trans women, who marked the pivotal moment of gender transition as that moment when they return home after gender reassignment surgery. While I return to a more considered reading of Jorgensen's place in the transsexual canon below, the investigation of what a trans travel narrative does— what its persistence effects—begins with a consideration of this return home. In transsexual autobiographies, films, cultural artifacts, transitioning gender is often framed as a "coming home" to one's new body—the body one also always should have been. The same texts synchronize the metaphorical return to the protagonist's gendered home with an account of their arrival at the protagonist's *literal* home. This necessitates that the protagonist be on a journey to begin with: a vacation, or an overseas trip. As I note above, Prosser refers to this trope as the "journey out and the return home." Journeying away from the scene of the everyday/domestic is often framed as journeying into the exotic, or into space external to the subject's home nation. Christine Jorgensen's real journey to become a woman took her to Copenhagen and back to New York, while in *Conundrum* Jan Morris' final step to becoming woman, her gender reassignment surgery, takes her from her home in the United Kingdom to Casablanca, Morocco, and back. Riffing on both of these early accounts, the movie *Transamerica* dramatizes the journey out and return home when Bree, the transsexual protagonist, flies to New York then drives across the United States. While travel to a different country for gender reassignment surgery (GRS) was necessary for Jorgensen and Morris because no surgeons were practicing GRS in their own countries, this journey out and return home (and the home-elsewhere distinction it depends on) is specific to a particular envisioning of transsexuality. It is also specific to a locatable ideology of gender itself.

In order to illustrate this fully, we need to critically interrogate the context in which the journey out and return home narrative is articulated. One domain in which this narrative clearly becomes recognizable is in the workplace and public life. Public announcements and media coverage of transitioning employees often narrate transition as the declared intention that one will go on vacation and return as a different gender. The cause of the vacation is taken to be self-evident, yet it is consistently noted. A 2007 article about a transitioning journalist in *Fortune* magazine declares, "L.A. Times sportswriter named Mike Penner told his readers that he would take a vacation and return as a woman, Christine Daniels" (*Fortune*, August 27, 2007). Another article in the gay and lesbian lifestyle magazine *The Advocate* echoes this formulation almost verbatim:

> Sarah Blanchette was a computer programmer for Saint Anselm College in Manchester, N.H. In March 2004 she informed her superiors that she would return from a two-week vacation presenting herself as female. St. Anselm College then fired her.
>
> (The Advocate, *July 29, 2006*)

While discrimination against trans people is the article's primary concern, the vacation and return appears here as an incidental aside—which nonetheless serves to render transition intelligible for readers. Advice pamphlets for employees and employers about transition in the workplace often note the necessity of trans employees taking leave of absence for medical reasons (i.e., surgery); others make enigmatic references to trans employees preferring to take a short vacation and assume new pronouns and public gender presentation on their return. A policy document written for transgender employees of University College London outlines the following:

> A very good practice is for the Trans person to take a short holiday before the day of transition (the day s/he will come to work dressed in the clothes of their preferred gender).
>
> (*University College London, n.d.*)

Gender Reassignment: A Guide for Employers, published by the Women and Equality Unit of the British Government, offers similar wisdom:

> At the point of change of gender, it is common for transsexual people to take a short time off work and return in their new name and gender role. This is often used as an opportunity to brief others.
>
> (*UK Government Equalities Office 2005: 14*)

Janis Walworth, writing for the website gendersanity.com, a trans employment resource, offers the same advice to employers dealing with transition in the workplace:

> How much time off does he anticipate needing and when? Some transsexual people want to have some surgical procedures done before they start working in their new role. They may have such procedures several weeks or months before or immediately before assuming their new role. Depending on the

procedure, they may need to take off a few days to a few weeks. In addition, the transsexual employee may want to take off a little time between roles to adjust his appearance and take care of paperwork.

(Walworth 2003)

A different article on the same website opines that transitioning workers "prefer to coordinate their transition with a vacation period to give themselves and their co-workers time to adjust" (Walworth n.d.). Time off between roles benefits the trans person, giving them time to adjust, as Walworth suggests. It also gives co-workers time to adjust in the absence of the trans employee.

What logics govern this narrative? Or more importantly, what is foreclosed by a journey out and a return home? I propose that the journey out and return home narrative works to render transsexuality intelligible within the logic of binary gender, through containing gendered indeterminacy. By this I mean that the possibility of changing sex, or changing gender, opens up a space that threatens the clear conceptual separation of male and female articulated in biological determinism. This argument should not be unfamiliar for readers of trans and queer theory. Judith Butler, for example, argues that gender variance reveals the performativity of gender, while earlier Marjorie Garber argued that gender variance indicates an "epistemological crux that destabilizes comfortable binarity, and displaces the resulting discomfort onto a figure that already inhabits, indeed incarnates, the margin" (Garber 1992: 17).

Both authors have been critiqued from within trans theory for appropriating the transsexual or the cross-dresser as a symbol of transgression, neglecting the real desires of many gender variant subjects to be read as merely male or female.[1] The idea I am advancing here, however, relies on a reading of binary gender as performative, as an "enabling violation" that is destined always to fail precisely because it is never complete in the beginning. However, it is the *idea* of gender variance rather than transsexual or transgendered people themselves that we might theorize as threatening to that dominant order of knowledge. Gendered indeterminacy indexes two interconnected meanings here. One signifies the existence of bodily or psychic identifications that complicate, or venture outside, a correlation between male/masculine and female/feminine. The other is the impossibility of fully determining the correlation between biological sex and gender identity. Gendered indeterminacy includes the surplus of gendered acts, practices, affects, feelings that might take place on what Butler calls the heterosexual matrix: "the production and normalization of masculine and feminine ... along with the interstitial forms of hormonal, chromosomal, psychic, and performative [*sic*] that gender assumes" (Butler 2004: 42). Indeterminacy could also be understood as the specter haunting gender: the frightening possibility that anyone's gender might not be a stable, static equivalence between male and masculine, or female and feminine, endures even as the logic of binary gender dictates that such a thing is impossible. Gendered indeterminacy does not necessarily refer to transsexuality, or gender variance. If we can identify a gendered category of the *unheimlich*, or a form of radical difference that comes to bear on epistemological understandings of gender, then this is what I am referring to as gendered indeterminacy.

The culmination of this line of thought is to understand transsexuality as a concept—constituted both by medicalizing discourses that regulate the material procedures of transition, and the constellation of cultural understandings that circulate in a variety of sites about how transition may proceed, or what transsexuals are like—that domesticates gendered indeterminacy through the application of gender norms in regulating who may access gender reassignment technologies or social recognition as transsexual. This domestication takes place precisely through a geographical displacement of that indeterminacy. Thus, the ideology that gender is biological and determined from birth by one's genitals gives way, provisionally and inconsistently, to a new idea: individuals may change sex—indeed, this process may be a socially permissible act—but only if they conform to particular ideological constraints about what is and is not allowable. Of course, constraints on what is and is not allowable may be subject to discursive tensions, but gender continues to be understood as binary and normative. The logic of gender identity disorder stipulates that to access surgical or hormonal treatment, one must experience persistent discomfort with the sex one is assigned at birth. As Butler points out, the idea of persistent discomfort assumes that an appropriate, or normal, gender identity is always available, and that gender identity disorder (GID) diagnoses permit the individual to find the right one:

> [A GID] diagnosis does not ask whether there is a problem with the gender norms that it takes as fixed and intransigent, whether these norms produce distress and discomfort, whether they impede one's ability to function, or whether they generate sources of suffering for some people or for many people.
>
> *(Butler 2004: 95)*

Or, to follow Spade's Foucauldian analysis of GID, the diagnostic criteria produce a "fiction of natural gender, in which normal, non-transsexual people grow up with minimal to no gender trouble or exploration" (Spade 2006: 321). We could read all of these possibilities—that no-one embodies gender norms in a fixed manner, or that gender is not as stable as it is assumed to be—as parts of what I am calling gendered indeterminacy. In order to be socially legible at all, transsexuality as a discourse must attempt to contain and domesticate that indeterminacy. Transsexuality comes to be socially and culturally tolerable in a limited sense only if it conceals the possibility that gender is not binary and presents transsexuality as a one-way trip from man to woman or woman to man.

The dominant spatial narrative of transsexual transition, the journey out and return home, is central to this domestication. It displaces the gendered indeterminacy that haunts gender everywhere to a spatially contained location: the "elsewhere," or the liminal moment when the trans individual is imagined to cross from one gender to the other. When the employment policy documents I cite above recommend that the transitioning individual absent herself or himself temporarily from the scene of the workplace "to give themselves and their coworkers time to adjust," they formalize the displacement of gendered indeterminacy simultaneously to a contained moment and to a space outside the workplace. Within this idealized narrative, the transsexual person changes pronouns and appearance and returns to the workplace transformed. Ideally, this is a vacational space: it subsists in the "what is hidden" of the private sphere, and it is also potentially located outside the nation-state. It should be clear by now that the idea of the short vacation may not exist for the benefit of the transsexual employee, but rather for others in the workplace, assumed to be non-transsexual, for whom the transsexual person's temporary absence may provide some marker of transition that clearly distinguishes between the past and the future, the old and the new, of the transsexual's gender.

It should already be clear that gender transition in a material, embodied sense does not always follow this idealized temporal template. Indeed, such a template may have no relevance to many gender variant subjects, even if we only consider the prohibitive costs of gender reassignment surgeries, which might make the possibility of a short vacation abroad just to smooth the process of coming out at work rather unlikely. Some of the workplace policy documents I consider above negotiate this contradiction between the commonsense expectation that transition ought to happen all at once, in a conveniently marked fashion, and the far more complex reality, while others neglect complexity in the interests of rendering transsexuality bureaucratically manageable.

However, we can make an easy analogy between those ritualized writing strategies that domesticate otherness through translation, and the ritualized practices that attend and indeed *constitute* the discourse of transsexual transition by instituting a distinction between here and elsewhere in which gendered indeterminacy is what must be rendered intelligible, translated and domesticated. Gender variant people can be permitted to access the medicalized legitimacy of transsexuality only in a way that does not reveal that gender is socially constructed or performative. It is no accident that the epistemological problem of how to contain gendered indeterminacy imbricates racial or geo-cultural difference as well as the mobility of class in its distribution of gendered significations across different spaces.

Situating Transsexuality

Thus far I've identified the geographical narrative structuring transition within employee advice books and media articles about trans people, and have argued that the structuring logics of the journey narrative of gender transition work to contain gendered indeterminacy. But when did this journey narrative emerge? How did it begin to look like common sense? I now reconsider the Christine Jorgensen story, arguing that the process of Jorgensen's transition and what is said about it became the standard transition narrative, animating what would become known as transsexuality. Here, I recall Meyerowitz's historiographical strategy of framing the emergence of transsexuality as a process of imagination and interpellation, reminding us to attend to popular narratives just as much as medical discourse.

In the 1930s and 1940s, the science of endocrinology was developing on both sides of the Atlantic. Endocrinologists had learned to isolate estrogen and testosterone in the 1910s and 1920s, although it wasn't until the late 1940s that pharmaceutical companies began to produce synthetic formulations of the "sex hormones" (Meyerowitz 2002: 28). At this moment, a theory of human bisexuality had become popular in medical circles. Human bisexuality as it was understood then meant the concept that sex was determined not only by gonads but by hormones, and that men and women normally had a combination of both "male" and "female" hormones. Consequently, changing sex was no longer thought to be such a fantastical leap of the imagination. Surgical procedures such as castration and early precursors of gender reassignment surgery had been practiced on those characterized as inverts occasionally since the 1880s: Earl Lind, a "self-proclaimed invert, androgyne, homosexual, and fairy," obtained a castration from a doctor in 1902 (Lind 1918: 196; Meyerowitz 2002: 17). At around the same time, particularly in Germany, sexologists such as Magnus Hirschfeld were developing diagnostic criteria for individuals who, differentiated from those who merely wanted to wear the attire of the "other sex" and homosexuals, desired to *be* the "other sex." Hirschfeld referred to this condition as *Transsexualismus* (Meyerowitz 2002: 19).[2] In the 1930s and 1940s, on both sides of the Atlantic, the popular press ran various accounts of individuals who went through "sex reversals." In Europe, at least three athletes gained notoriety for having transitioned from female to male, the subjects of a "quasi-scientific" pamphlet entitled *Women Who Become Men* (Meyerowitz 2002: 34). At this stage, however, it was not clear what caused these "sex reversals," and neither was it widely known what precise surgical and endocrine technologies doctors were using to assist such individuals. A discourse naming the condition as transsexualism and advocating, or debating the efficacy of, surgical and hormonal reassignment did not emerge until the 1950s in the United States. Medical debates about surgical and hormonal gender reassignment did not, however, catapult "sex change" into the public eye. Rather, it was Christine Jorgensen.

Far more detailed and rigorous accounts of Jorgensen's life can be found than is possible here, but I will briefly offer some essential details.[3] Christine Jorgensen was born in New York and led a rather undirected life working in various industries, including the Hollywood film studios, before beginning to research sex change as a possibility in the late 1940s. Returning to New York, she enrolled in a course to learn about human biochemistry and obtained estradiol from a pharmacist to feminize her body. Gender reassignment surgery was unheard of in the United States at that time, although it had been practiced in Europe for decades. Determined to access surgeries which no American doctor would approve, Jorgensen traveled to Denmark in 1950 to seek out doctors who would treat her. In Copenhagen, she discovered the doctor who would "make history," Dr Christian Hamburger:

> Jorgensen persuaded the endocrinologist Christian Hamburger to use him as a human guinea pig for a program of feminization that included hormones, electrolysis, resocialization and, eventually, genital surgery.
>
> *(Denny 1998: 36)*

The events that surround Jorgensen's return to New York three years later are open to debate. The official story, told in Jorgensen's autobiography, was that a family friend had read correspondence between Christine and her parents and leaked the story to the press. Plagued by telegrams from reporters, Jorgensen negotiated a deal with the *American Weekly* to cover the cost of her return trip from Denmark in exchange for an exclusive. She arrived in New York on February 13, 1953, to reporters, fans and the curious lining up to watch her disembark from her plane, and a storm of newspaper headlines, "descending into a new and alien world" (Jorgensen 1967: 183). *American Weekly* published Jorgensen's own account of her transformation in a five-part series accompanied by numerous photos establishing Jorgensen's new and very feminine embodiment.[4] Since Jorgensen's death, however, new information has emerged. Sources close to Jorgensen have revealed that the leak did not come from a family friend: Jorgensen saw an opportunity to reinvent her life and perhaps earn some income by releasing the story of her transformation to the media herself.[5]

Of course, Jorgensen could not have foreseen the explosion of publicity around the case, or the effect of the public eye might have on her life. Nevertheless, the events of 1953 turned Jorgensen into a legend and role model for others like her. "The media coverage of Christine Jorgensen's story and her own autobiography of 1967 produced a narrative model for many [transsexuals]," observes Prosser; so much so that the phrase "a trip to Denmark" became shorthand for having gender reassignment surgery (Prosser 1998: 124; Prosser 1999: 98). Here, I want to focus on the genealogy and significance of Jorgensen's own narrative. Other transsexuals learned to associate Jorgensen's trip overseas with transsexuality: for instance Mario Martino, a trans man and the author of *Emergence*, recalls his father repeating the pun, "Imagine going abroad and coming back a broad!" (Martino 1977: 40). Meyerowitz's history of transsexuality in the United States details numerous others who recognized themselves in Jorgensen's story (Meyerowitz 1998: 175–76). Numerous other autobiographers cite Jorgensen as the first transsexual they knew of as children, as far from the metropole as the participants in Matzner's collection of first person narratives of Mahu and Hawai'ian trans people: "I very distinctly remember reading in the newspaper when Christine Jorgensen had her sex change. That was such a shock because it meant there was a ray of hope for me," writes one (Mathieu, in Matzner 2001: 230). Jorgensen's experience was made into a B-grade film in 1970, *The Christine Jorgensen Story*, the tagline of which claimed Jorgensen was "the first man to become a woman."[6] Documents, newsreel footage and photographs of Jorgensen are archived on www.christinejorgensen.org, and historians including Susan Stryker have begun to write extensively on the archive of Jorgensen's own photographs and films as well as the large collection of media documents about her (Stryker 2008).

Of course, Jorgensen was not "the first man to become a woman." Despite the fact that Christian Hamburger had never treated a transsexual before, gender reassignment surgery was not unknown in Europe. This was precisely why Jorgensen had traveled there. Meyerowitz's accounts of "sex reversals" indicate that even as Christine Jorgensen was traveling back to New York from her transformative sojourn in Denmark, other gender variant people in Europe, the United Kingdom and even Denmark itself were also undergoing hormone treatment, electrolysis, resocialization and gender reassignment surgeries. However, their stories are not enshrined in mythology quite like Jorgensen's.[7] The reasons Jorgensen's story so resonated with the media and why her story has continued to be regarded within trans history as significant relate to how the facts—the journey overseas, Jorgensen's own transformation on a number of levels—could easily be accommodated within a template relating transsexuality to broader narratives of self-transformation. Those narratives are specific to the geographical and cultural context Jorgensen inhabited and her temporary absence from that context. Elsewhere I contextualize this within an account of the historiographical moves made by historians of gender variance, but here I simply want to alert the reader to how often Christine Jorgensen's case is treated as the moment at which transsexuality enters public awareness.

Mobility's Promise

In this final section I show how this transsexual travel narrative imports tropes both from classical Euro-American travel discourse and discourses foregrounding (upward) social mobility as the key to successful reinvention, which are specific to postwar United States culture. The trope of leaving and returning transformed is, of course, pervasive within Euro-American cultural productions as a whole. If a classical journey narrative involves leaving home and returning transformed, it also often involves the protagonist returning ready to take their proper place in the social field. In classical journey narratives also, the geographical metaphor's meaning relies on a clear distinction between "here" and "elsewhere." The distinction between here and elsewhere can map onto a range of oppositions: familiar/strange; home/away; centre/periphery; West/East; civilization/barbarism; rootedness/traversal; domestic/foreign; same/other. These oppositions refer us to global and transnational histories of colonialism and imperialism, in which the civilized world, or the "West," can only be imagined as a discrete structure through its differentiation from the uncivilized world, or the "East."[8]

Michel De Certeau's work on ethnography in *The Writing of History* is instructive here. De Certeau proposes that the narrative structure of ethnographic writing also makes a distinction between "here" and "there," which works via a trope of journeying out and returning:

> [T]he literary operation that [enables ethnography] has a condition of possibility in a structural difference between an area "over here" and another "over there". ... The separation (between "over here" and "over there") first appears as an oceanic division: it is the Atlantic, a rift between the Old and the New World.
>
> *(De Certeau 1988: 218)*

This structural difference between here and there, Europe and the "New World," effects a textual and spatial operation of return that is central to the narrative's teleology: "the narrative as a whole belabors the division that is located everywhere in order to show that the other returns to the same" (De Certeau 1988: 219). This return domesticates otherness from the alleged unintelligibility of speech and practices (what is studied by the ethnographer) into translatable writing (what is produced by the ethnographer). In the process, it buttresses the identity of both the ethnographer and the "West," the Old World.[9] While it would be reductive to generalize this difference between Old and New worlds in De Certeau's critique of ethnography to the transnational locations represented in the transsexual travel narratives under consideration in this chapter, we can argue that a similar narrative logic takes place. The inevitability of staging gender transition as a return home places an emphasis on retaining the distinction between "home" and "elsewhere." Even if the transsexual subject undergoes an embodied transformation in a location that is not "home," the specific location of that elsewhere is not important. The elsewhere, in this transsexual imaginary, is just a place to be offstage; just a place from which to return transformed. But what if the transsexual subject never returns home? What if she can never leave in the first place?

To fully understand the role that travel plays in transsexual discourse, it must be thought alongside tropes of social mobility, in which self-transformation plays a central part. In order to make this clear, I return once more to Jorgensen's story. Meyerowitz observes that Christine Jorgensen caught the public's attention because she embodied the public desire for stories about individual success and social mobility, making good in the face of obstacles through self-transformation (Meyerowitz 2002: 73). Jorgensen's own autobiography emphasizes her sense of connection to the great American dream of overcoming hardship through reinvention. Narrating how, living in Los Angeles as George in the 1940s, Jorgensen came to seek out hormonal and surgical treatment for her feeling that she was really a woman, she tells the story of a visit to the Hollywood Athletics Club. George encounters an army colonel who tells him the story of losing his fortune in the 1906 San Francisco earthquake. Despite the destruction of his house and business, the undaunted colonel made his way to Hollywood and took up life in the movie business. Jorgensen reflects on the significance of this story for her own life at the time:

> "Why should I accept defeat anymore than the Colonel did?" I thought. ... [H]e didn't settle down in the ashes and moan about it, he sought a solution. It slowly registered in my mind as an object-lesson. ... In my own case, I knew my tragedies were emotional and physical, and though I had earnestly tried to understand these conditions, I had never done anything positive about them. ... I had never sought a cure.
>
> *(Jorgensen 1967: 55–56)*

It is equally significant that Jorgensen presents the key moments in the temporality of her transformation not, as some might expect, when she undergoes vaginoplasty, but when she arrives back in New York from Denmark and must begin a new life as a social and extroverted person. George had been "shy and introverted"; returning home as Christine is attended by a "difficult social adjustment" where Jorgensen learns "a new ability to meet people and to be accepted by them in return" (Jorgensen 1967: 195). This could be attributed as much, we might imagine, to the necessity of lubricating the wheels of the publicity machine as to Jorgensen's new-found confidence as a woman. The *American Weekly* articles, published just after Jorgensen arrived back in New York, riff on this same spirit of self-transformation. Jorgensen remarks that she was so poor during her time in Copenhagen that she taught herself to sew in order to make her own clothes, and yet in photographs of Jorgensen taken during and after her time in Copenhagen, she is always presented as glamorous and ladylike, clad in tailored, expensive-looking gowns and accessories. If the public was going to regard her sympathetically as an example of the classic American Dream narrative, it was important that she appear to have conquered poverty single-handedly with the help of a trusty sewing machine. That we now know Jorgensen herself decided to embark on public life by leaking her own story to the press only serves to enhance the image of her resourcefulness. However, Jorgensen desired public recognition, and public recognition may have demanded that the transformation she accomplished be not only from male to female, but from undistinguished to glamorous, retiring to outgoing. More importantly, Jorgensen's transformation is also narrated as a transformation from a drifting, rather undirected male existence to success as a female: a life with direction and meaning produced through conscious self-work.

This emphasis on direction and meaning, conquering hardship through individual triumph, resonates with the great narratives of American modernity, not just during the postwar period, but throughout the history of democracy in the United States. In the eighteenth century Alexis de Tocqueville pointed to the alleged lack of a class system in the United States as intrinsic to the idea of progress, as well as "the idea of the indefinite perfectability of man [*sic*]":

[As] the classes of society draw together, as manners, customs, and laws vary, because of the tumultuous intercourse of men. ... [a person] infers that man is endowed with an indefinite faculty for improvement.

(De Tocqueville 2004: 514)

Under the terms of free market democracy, infinite perfectibility becomes not only a capacity of the individual, but a responsibility: if each individual is free, then every individual is responsible for regarding herself as a set of capacities to be transformed, improved and worked on. In the early twentieth-century United States, similar attitudes towards self-discovery and a desire for infinite perfectibility intersected. Both discourses took the body as the vehicle for transformation, with the popular emergence of cosmetic surgery as a route to increased success through aesthetic improvement.[10] Alongside "aesthetic" surgeries, gender reassignment surgeries developed as well, the condition for the capacity to prescribe corporeal transformation in what would later become transsexuality.

Here I want to pause for a moment and reflect on the context of legitimation and subjectivation in which these discourses of self-transformation were circulating. Jorgensen, Meyerowitz points out, refused to comply with being labeled as freakish or perverse, despite being represented as such. "She insisted on her place in the mainstream," writes Meyerowitz, and maintained public appeal as a ladylike, respectable specimen of "sex change" even as many popular accounts of her life stressed deviance (Meyerowitz 2002: 73). Jorgensen was not alone: many early public transsexual voices emphasized that they desired to occupy the mainstream of society, rather than its fringes. Historian Dan Irving points to a trans woman quoted in Harry Benjamin's 1966 book *The Transsexual Phenomenon* who wrote, "we prefer the normalcy's [*sic*] of life and want to be accepted in circles of normal society, enjoying the same pursuits and pleasures without calling attention to the fact that we are 'queers' trying to invade the world of normal people" (Benjamin 1966, quoted in Irving 2008: 49). Drawing attention to precisely the same transformation in Jorgensen's living conditions, from poor, shy man to successful woman, Irving reads Jorgensen as parsing her self-image through the "productive potential" of her condition (Irving 2008: 49). The urgency of social recognition, Irving argues, often forces transsexuals to frame their demands for recognition in terms that emphasize their capacity to earn money and behave as exemplary productive citizens. Irving sees this as part of the alienation of capitalist social order, in which minorities are forced to frame a claim to identity premised on the capacity for "productive citizenship."

The need for transsexual subjects to echo dominant discourses of assimilatory desires to be "normal" and to be productive contributes much to my argument that transsexuality itself is already marked by a discourse encouraging self-transformation and emphasizing the productive capacities of the individual. However, society's convocation to engage in self-transformation assumes that one has the cultural and racial capital to become socially mobile in the first place. In order to "reinvent oneself," one had to be bourgeois, wealthy and have the free time and economic resources to devote oneself to self-transformation.

This is precisely why a travel narrative may be so central to the recognition of a founding moment of transsexual culture and recognition. Jorgensen's journey out and return home travel narrative allowed for a containment of the temporal moment of gendered indeterminacy within a spatialized elsewhere. As this had already taken place, her ability to be accommodated within the narrative of American social recognition and legitimacy, premised on individual triumph over the odds, increased.

In grasping the significance of the travel narrative fully—and particularly understanding its relationship to political economy—we cannot forget that mobility requires social resources. Moreover, the mythology of liberal individualism, that anyone can and should transform themselves and acquire social mobility, requires the institution of a fantasy that, within the American nation-state, class does not exist. Mark Simpson suggests that thinking about geographical mobility in an American context is impossible without thinking about political economy, citizenship or democracy, and specifically discourses of social mobility as they inflect all three. Mobility is a primary symptom of "entangled ideologies of national identity and progress," Simpson writes, "serving to bind together two traits supposedly intrinsic to 'the American': the need to move (freedom as geographical expansiveness) and the need to rise (freedom as social mobility)" (Simpson 2005: xxv–vi).

Simpson argues that the myth equating individual movement with the subject's freedom under democracy in the United States institutes a "fantasy of classlessness," concealing and sustaining class difference.

The practice of travel by transsexual people within that fantasy of classnessness comes to signify as a mode of cultural distinction. Jorgensen's story works precisely as a template for that fantasy: that transsexuals must merely gather the resources to get to Denmark (or later, to Casablanca, or wherever a surgeon was available) in order to return triumphantly having accomplished the feat of self-transformation privately. The travel narrative can only be told retrospectively, after recognition has already been won. It is no surprise to find that, although Jorgensen traveled to Denmark in the early 1950s, her autobiography did not appear until 1967, 14 years later.

The Jorgensen story also demonstrates that the travel narrative can double as a narrative of social mobility. Jorgensen's trip to Denmark, traveling first on a ship because she could not afford to fly, and returning on an all-expenses-paid flight to instant celebrity status, institutes a fantasy of transsexual recognition premised on the transsexual subject's capacity for that particular mode of self-transformation: not only from male to female, or from female to male, but from outsider to insider. The origin story of the transsexual is all about autonomy, self-will, self-transformation through heroic acts of will, hardship and heroic publicness, heroic attempts for public recognition. That is the progress narrative: that Christine made it all possible because she was a public heroine. The discontinuities are what makes Christine Jorgensen's story so interesting and important here: the fact that Jorgensen successfully created her own mythology: that she cleverly convinced a pharmacist to supply her with estradiol; that instead of having been an unwilling victim of a malicious leak to the press, Jorgensen approached the media herself, seeing the opportunity for a big story in her own transition and the possibility of a triumphant return from Denmark to the USA as a star. These continuities would have threatened to destabilize the fantasy of spontaneous recognition via self-transformation Jorgensen labored to put into effect, for the subject of the American Dream cannot be seen to "cheat" or be too resourceful in her efforts to gain recognition.

We also need to attend to the geographical specificity (as well as the historical moment) into which a discourse erupts. Here, we begin to understand the precise difference between the American emergence of transsexuality and the instances of gender reassignment taking place in Europe. As Meyerowitz observes, the European cases of the 1920s and 1930s, preceding Jorgensen's trip to Denmark by 20 or 30 years, were marked by a large, if scattered, volume of mass media coverage. This includes the case of Zdenek Koubkov, a Czechoslovakian athlete who was assigned female at birth and competed in the 1932 Olympics as a woman before becoming a man:

> In his early twenties (or in one account, even earlier) "a great light dawned," and [Koubkov] realized he was a man. He consulted a doctor who confirmed his masculinity, and unspecified operations, "the flick of a surgeon's scalpel," followed.
>
> *(Meyerowitz 2002: 34)*

Indeed, Koubkov even visited the United States to perform on Broadway, and, as Meyerowitz further observes, the American press covered his case quite extensively. However Koubkov was not traveling from home to elsewhere in the American imagination; this was not a story that dovetailed quite precisely with the American narrative of liberal self-transformation enough to push it into the realm of mythology. That Jorgensen's story did contain such amenable elements to recuperate it into that narrative is a historical accident. It precisely demonstrates the real contingency of the historical narrative of transsexuality's "progress" across the twentieth century, but also the importance of geographical location in the emergence of transsexuality as an intelligible object worthy of cultural, scientific or popular attention.

In understanding Jorgensen's case to be the moment at which transsexuality comes into being, we may also forget that, in fact, Jorgensen did not think of herself as a transsexual (indeed, the term was only just coming into widespread use by David O. Cauldwell, Benjamin and his cohorts). Jorgensen herself did define her condition with a label, and many in the press described her as a pseudohermaphrodite, a person who exhibited the characteristics of a "true" hermaphrodite, but whose ambiguous sex characteristics could not be located on her body (Meyerowitz 2002: 69–70). From the beginning, Jorgensen's narrative founded a subjectivity premised on a will to public recognition and acceptance. In its capacity to overcome the contradiction that gender reassignment presented through spatially concealing the moment at which man became female (and both were indeterminate) the story of Jorgensen's trip to Denmark installs recognition at home as the greatest investment in transsexual existence. Geographical travel enables recognition *in particular spaces*—in the space of the modern nation—from the beginning. (Not that there is really a beginning: the lesson is, of course, that there is no "transsexuality.")

This chapter began by arguing that the dominant transsexual travel narrative involves a journey out and return home. I suggested that this works to contain the specter of gendered indeterminacy to a temporally brief moment which is recognized to take place outside public space, either in the private sphere, or in an elsewhere that is geographically other. Further, I argued that rendering transsexuality intelligible depends on containing gendered indeterminacy. I examined Christine Jorgensen's trip from the United States to Denmark and back as the instituting moment of that trans travel narrative, and suggested that it is because of the intersection of tropes of self-transformation and social mobility, and the geographical journey away and return that makes Christine Jorgensen's story so powerful as a narrative recognized to "begin" modern transsexuality. Through its historical overview, this chapter has situated the transections of discourse that make it possible for a subject called the transsexual to live in the late twentieth century and early twenty-first century. Though hardly conclusive, it offers a new answer to the question of why travel is so important to transsexuality's historical and critical presence. It is my hope that this will instigate others to explore further questions.

Notes

1 See, for example, Prosser's critique of Butler, Garber and others in chapter one of *Second Skins* (Prosser 1998); and Namaste (2000: 9–23).

2 On the history of Hirschfeld's research into gender variance, see Magnus Hirschfeld's own volume, *Transvestites: The Erotic Drive to Cross-dress* (Hirschfeld 1991); see also Bullough (1975); Fausto-Sterling (2000); and Hekma (1994).

3 See, in particular, Meyerowitz (2002); Denny (1998); Stryker (1999).

4 Images of the *American Weekly* articles are archived on http://www.christinejorgensen. org. Accessed November 21, 2008.

5 Joanne Meyerowitz notes in *How Sex Changed* that, in an interview she conducted with Vern Bullough, a friend of Jorgensen's, Bullough confirmed this suggestion that Jorgensen had informed the press herself. (see Denny 1998: 41–42; Meyerowitz 2002: 62, 300 n32.)

6 *The Christine Jorgensen Story*, directed by Irving Rapper (1970, USA).

7 An exception might be made for Roberta Cowell, an English trans woman who transitioned in around 1954 and who was feted as the first *English* transsexual. See Meyerowitz (2002: 83–84).

8 On this binary structure, see Said (1995: 12).

9 Postcolonial critics have, of course, questioned the assumption of coherence in categorical distinctions made between a *literal* "here and there," when it maps onto (for example) West/East. In the capacity that it can be useful for my analysis here, the here/elsewhere distinction De Certeau draws attention to exists as a fantasy.

10 On the history of cosmetic surgery, see Gilman (1999); Haiken (1997).

9

TRANS/SCRIPTIONS

Homing Desires, (Trans)sexual Citizenship
and Racialized Bodies

Nael Bhanji

> One man's imagined community is another man's political prison.
>
> (Appadurai 1996: 32)

Introduction

The idea for this chapter is born of a deep frustration with the "imagined community" of transsexual belonging. Consumed by questions of belonging, I write in order to understand how our attachments to the perplexing edifice of "home" shape the theoretical routes that we take, the journeys that we embark on and, in the case of transsexuals, the transitions that we make across borders of gender and/or national identity, among others. I write because I am frustrated by transsexual theory's failure to take into account racial and ethnic differences without resorting to imperializing gestures; because I am tired of reading the kind of theory that Susan Stryker ingeniously describes as limiting itself through an "around the world in eighty genders" approach—a narrative smorgasbord of "gender exotics, culled from native cultures around the world" (Stryker 2006: 14). But, above all, I continue to write because of both my deep respect for trans theory, as well as my skepticism towards it, because it is within these zones of ambivalence and contradiction that we might envision a way forward.

With these paradoxes in mind, my questions are as follows: To what "home"[1] does the trajectory of transition, the act of border-crossing, lead the already in-between diasporic, gender liminal subject? Who is the correct and proper citizen that gets to speak in the name of a transsexual subjectivity? How can we engage in a more nuanced understanding of the re-circulation, regulation and re-inscription of the "transsexual empire" in postmodernity? How do we account for the different imaginings of transsexual mobility within a locality? How do we maintain the relationality of trans-identity without slipping into a formless cultural relativism—without rooting ourselves into isolated social and geographical locations? And finally, what are the tacit knowledges that permeate trans scholarship?

The title of this chapter, "Trans/scriptions," borrows loosely from Avtar Brah's introductory chapter in her seminal text *Cartographies of Diaspora*. Brah's ruminations on situated identities in unstable cartographies of intersectionality have provided a solid foundation for my own conceptualization of differential inscriptions of signifiers of belonging on (trans)sexual and racialized bodies across space and time (Brah 1996: 1–10). Most importantly, her analysis of "homing desires"—which she theorizes as distinct from the desire for a "homeland"—is an invaluable framework through which diaspora and transsexuality may be brought into dialogue with each other (Brah 1996: 197). Yet, this chapter seeks to do more than simply highlight the ways in which racial exclusion within trans theory has resulted in an unspoken white privilege. I prefer, instead, to envision this as a theoretical excursion into the turbulent waters of identity politics. Therefore, in the spirit of risky ventures, this journey will be undertaken with neither a map nor a destination; for it is precisely through exploring those stubborn islands of thought—through challenging our own investments in the protective cocoon of homeliness—that we may envision a trans politics that is critical of its (re)turns to "home."

Before moving on, and to make some of my critical allegiances more apparent, this chapter intends to problematize *both* "transsexuality" and "transgender" for their lack of engagement with the imaginary and affective conditions of "trans" belonging.[2] Indeed, several contemporary gender theorists have already argued that the catch-all phrase "transgender" emerges from the Anglo-American gay and lesbian community (Namaste 2000: 2; Sullivan 2003: 99–118; Wilchins 2003: 141–42). But, as this chapter illustrates, "transsexual" carries its own imperialist baggage, achieved through the "imposition of a particular world view and conceptual framework" (Namaste 2000: 103). Within both transsexual and transgender scholarship, trans people continue to be "rhetorically inscribed in the articulation of specifically nationalist political programs" that effectively conceal histories of imperialism and social relations of racism (Namaste 2000: 98). Reduced thus to the purely figural, the deployment of spatial and temporal metaphors can only implicitly and securely locate the (trans)sexual citizen as one marked by the values and norms of the Anglo-American majority.

Ultimately, this chapter calls for a much-needed phenomenology of transsexual consciousness that firmly situates narratives of (dis)embodied dissonance in specific historical and political frameworks. Initially conceptualized as a piece of "homework," my preoccupation with the "homing desires" in trans theory stems from my perception of trans politics from the (dis)embodied location of an East Indian/Arab immigrant in Canada who has spent most of his life in Kenya. So, if I seem overly occupied with my task of transcribing the multi-placedness of "home" in diasporas onto the lived realities of transsexuality it is because, to borrow from Stuart Hall, "all discourse is 'placed', and the heart has its reasons" (Hall 2003: 234).

Transient Trajectories

> Identities are mapped in real and imaginary, material and metaphorical spaces.
>
> (Phillips 1997: 45)

Contemporary American novelist Lars Eighner once wrote, "Home is the natural destination of any homeless person ... A homeless life has no storyline" (Eighner 1993: 97). But what do we mean by *home*? Is it, as Chandra Mohanty asks, "the place where I was born? Where I grew up? Where I live and work as an adult? Where I locate my community—my people? Who are 'my people'? Is home a geographical space, a historical space, an emotional sensory space," or a libidinal space? (Mohanty 1993: 352). Similarly, when Maya Angelou said, "I long, as does every human being, to be at home wherever I find myself," was she referring to a positioning in the domestic, edifice, or landscape? Must a home be manifested physically or can we also locate it within the self? And when it comes to transsexual theory, do we ask these questions of home because we realize that we have lost home, and if so, does this mean that we were once "at home"? Or is home always something to be traveled towards, an ideal that is constantly renegotiated and reimagined? Put simply, what is the work of "home" in transsexual theory?

As a trans-identified person of color living in diaspora, I am deeply aware that the popular saying that "home is where the heart is" has never been as contradictory as it is today. In our increasingly globalized world, a shared experience of profound discontinuity has contributed to the unstable notions of identity and origin. It seems as though "countless people are on the move and even those who have never left their homeland, are moved by this restless epoch" (Papastergiadis 2000: 2). So, although many of us are fortunate enough to live in a house, we often find that every house is not a *home*. Forever in transit, we find ourselves living on the borders of homes, "dwelling," as poet Meena Alexander has described, "at the edge of the world," "unhoused," and "unselved" (Alexander 1988: 44). If home is where the heart is, then some of us are actually out of place. And if to "haunt" is to frequent a place habitually, then home, in a sense, is always already haunted.

When I say that the home is "haunted," obviously I do not mean paranormal activity or supernatural phenomena. Instead, I want to draw attention to the (*un*)*heimlich* specters that continue to haunt the oft-cited metaphorical borderlands of corporeo-psychic uninhabitability in the quest for a liveable space of "familiarity, comfort and seamless belonging" (Fortier 2003: 130). Briefly, Sigmund Freud theorizes that the feeling of being "at home," which he calls the *heimlich*, is more a condition of the heart than a physical space. *Heimlich* refers to things that are familiar, intimate, friendly and "homely" (Freud 1995: 125). But the word "*heimlich*" can also be used to refer to things that are hidden, concealed or shameful: such as the "*heimlich* places (which good manners oblige us to conceal)" or *heimlich* knowledge that should be withheld from others (Freud 1995). In other words, the two sets of definitions, whilst not contradictory, suggest that "home" itself is the source of hidden and dangerous knowledge; a knowledge that remains obscure and inaccessible until it coincides with the *unheimlich*. With roots set deep into the ambivalent soil of the *heim*, the uncanny, as Freud explains, "is in reality nothing new or alien, but something which is familiar and old-established in the mind and which has become alienated from it only through the process of repression" (Freud 1995: 142).

"Home" is a location of dislocation and desire. Often the questions we ask of home lead to other deeper questions, other deeper longings. It is, as Anne-Marie Fortier explains, "a place of disjunction, of unbelonging, of struggles for assimilation/integration, thus a space that *already* harbors desires for hominess" (Fortier 2003: 127). If we consider that the story of home is "a fantasy of incorporation" that is "ambivalent from the very start," homecoming remains impossible because it implies in its subtext a departure and an arrival, a point of coming *from* and arriving *at* (Hall 1996: 3). But because the concept of home is fraught with psychical tensions and conflicts, because it is unhomely to begin with, there is almost never a definite arrival "at" home. Instead, the individual is always just "getting there."

With these paradoxes in mind, I turn to diasporic theories because they offer "critical spaces for thinking about the discordant movements of modernity" without detaching embodied experiences from historical and cultural specificity (Braziel and Mannur 2003: 3). Etymologically derived from the Greek *diasperein* (from *dia-* meaning "across" and *-sperein* meaning "to sow or scatter seeds"), the term "diaspora" has historically referred to "displaced communities of people who have been dislocated from their native homeland through the movements of migration, immigration, or exile" (Braziel and Mannur 2003: 1). Diasporic theories seek to represent and problematize the lived experiences of diverse groups of people whose lives are marked by hybridity and heterogeneity, and to capture the complex trajectories of human experience resulting from forced or voluntary migration. In the introduction to *Theorizing Diaspora: A Reader*, Jana Evans Braziel and Anita Mannur encapsulate the appeal of theorizing diaspora best when they state, "Diaspora forces us to rethink the rubrics of nation and nationalism, while refiguring the relations of citizens and nation-states" (Braziel and Mannur 2003: 7). By emphasizing multilocationality within and across national, cultural and psychic boundaries, a diasporic framework allows us to imagine the ways in which identities are scattered and regrouped into new becomings and belongings. Most importantly, the field of diaspora studies makes "the spatialization of identity problematic and interrupts the ontologization of place," thereby bringing the concepts of "home" and "away" into creative tension with each other (Gilroy 2000: 122).

Avtar Brah theorizes that questions about "home" are "intrinsically linked with the way in which processes of inclusion or exclusion operate and are subjectively experienced under given circumstances. It is centrally about our political and personal struggles over the social regulation of belonging" (Brah 1996: 192). Moreover, there is a crucial difference between "feeling at home" and labeling a space as home, between the desire for home and the homeland itself. Distinct from the desire for a homeland, Brah's conceptualization of "homing desires" accounts for the fact that "not all diasporas retain the ideology of a return" (Brah 1996: 197). Her analysis of "homing desires" provides a theoretical framework through which to interrogate those problematic discourses of transsexual homecomings that privilege sentimentalized spaces of normative belonging.

I am aware that my attempts to analyze the transsexual turn to "home" within a diasporic framework run the risk of homogenizing all differences under the sign of "movement." Certainly, one of the major pitfalls of diaspora studies is its tendency to flatten experiences of migration, immigration, exile and estrangement. The problem with "diaspora" is that "it can be very general and all-embracing," making us forget that all movements are diasporic (Brah 1996: 196). Braziel, too, cautions that the term "diaspora" "risks losing specificity and critical merit if it is deemed to speak for all movements and migrations between nations, within nations, between cities, within cities ad infinitum" (Braziel and Mannur 2003: 7). Since all diasporas are not alike, we must learn how to demarcate them and take into account their "specific agendas and politics" (Grewal and Kaplan 2001: 665). So we cannot ignore how sense of place is intrinsically linked with both ideas of national identity as well as with the hierarchy of nations. The romanticization of cultural citizenship, one which is bound to the memory of a landscape, will only continue to invoke the fantasy of the nation as a "grand genealogical tree," producing cultural citizens who fail to thrive unless rooted in the same nourishing soil of "imagined community" (Mohanram 1999: 5).

But perhaps these conversations about "homes"—discourses that I find myself drawn to again and again—can be rethought through problematizing the neat and tidy borders that they insist upon, borders which often refuse to acknowledge their paradoxical permeability and confinement. Whilst not all trans people of color are diasporic, a diasporic framework certainly helps problematize those unacknowledged "homing desires" within trans theory. In other words, we must pay attention to the different ways in which people (re)imagine and (re)create the edifice of homely belonging; where one's "real" home can only exist as a romanticized cathedral of constancy—like a strongbox of memory kept safe from the siren dance of modernity through spatial and temporal sleights-of-hand that effectively render it, as Canadian poet Dionne Brand would say, "in another place, not here" (Brand 1996). Wary of deploying diaspora as a "catch-all phrase to speak of and for all movements, however privileged, and for all dislocations, even symbolic ones," I have chosen instead to interrogate the social and political implications of "homing desires" within narratives of transsexual "homecomings" (Braziel and Mannur 2003: 3).

In many trans communities, the pressure to pass, to blend into the mainstream, can be intense. The push from pre-op to post-op, from transitioning to transitioned, from transgressive to transfixed, results in the transsexual forever rushing onwards to find the space beyond, "the promise of *home* on the other side" and the possibility of *being at home in one's skin* (Prosser 1998: 489; emphasis mine). In Jay Prosser's *Second Skins*, sex-reassignment surgery is described as a transsexual "homecoming"—the return to one's true home in the body—a sort of "somatic repatriation," if you will (Prosser 1998: 184). Indeed, transsexuality, as Prosser suggests, has always embraced notions of "place, location, and specificity" (Prosser 1998: 488). Contemporary transsexual narratives are often accounts of linear progression: the journey from one location to another—"from fragmentation to integration, from alienation to reconciliation, from loss to restoration"—where one is meant to leave the transgressive space and transition *towards* one's fully embodied identity (Prosser 1998: 80). The transitional journey itself is merely a link between locations—a sort of gendered non-zone between origin and destination—and not a place to call home. Thus the prefix *trans* signifies multiple crossings, but still within a very confined nexus of homecoming and belonging, of borders and centers.

In transsexual or *"body* narratives," as Prosser has coined, skin seduces as a metaphor for homeliness. Prosser writes of the acute sense of gender dysphoria as akin to the feeling of bodily displacement … of living without a skin of one's own. Although *Stone Butch Blues* (Feinberg 1993) is not a transsexual autobiography, Prosser draws on the experiences of Leslie Feinberg's protagonist, Jess Goldberg, in order to illustrate the extent to which her body—that which should be felt as most familiar—can become radically unhomely. Indeed, Jess's sense of bodily displacement is informed at all points by the longing for "home." Like the female-to-male transsexual, Jess "experiences her female body as that which is most *unheimlich* in herself: as with the transsexual the body that should be home is foreign, the familiar felt as most strange" (Prosser 1998: 178).

Indeed, the analogy between the house and the human body has a long iconographic and metaphorical tradition. As Claudia Benthien explains, the house is the "absolute metaphor" of the body, an orientational guide in the world that provides structure and represents "the totality of reality which can never be experienced and never fully grasped" (Benthien 2002: 25). Furthermore, the absolute metaphor of the body-as-house has always referred to only the skin—that marked epidermal periphery through which we literally feel our way through the world. In a similar vein, Sara Ahmed and Jackie Stacey suggest that the skin itself represents a "bodyscape" that is inhabited by, and inhabits, the space of the nation and the landscape (Ahmed and Stacey 2001: 2). In their co-edited collection *Thinking Through the Skin*, Ahmed summarizes the tenuous connections between homeliness, skin and identity:

> We can think of the lived experience of being-at-home in terms of inhabiting a *second skin*, a skin which does not simply contain the homely subject, but which allows the subject to be touched and touch the world that is neither simply in the home or away from home. The home as skin suggests the boundary between the self and home is permeable, but also that the boundary

between home and away is permeable as well. Movement away is also movement within the constitution of home as such. Movement away is always affective; it affects how homely one might feel and fail to feel.

(Ahmed and Stacey 2001: 89; emphasis mine)

Certainly, the trope of the "second skin," that "burdensome outer layer," is a recurring leitmotif in narratives of the unhomely transsexual body (Prosser 1998: 68). For instance, in *Journal of a Transsexual*, Leslie Feinberg writes of her desire for disembodiment in terms of shedding the unhomely body like a skin: "I think how nice it would be to unzip my body from forehead to navel and go on vacation. But there is no escaping it, I'd have to pack myself along" (Feinberg 1980: 20). Encased thus within the baggage of a false, restrictive outer shell, Feinberg's narrative points to the very real work of embodied unhomeliness. But does this mean that a reprieve from this sort of gender dysphoric "home work" is possible only through a disembodied homeliness? In other words, what is the work of "home" in trans theory? How does the trope of homeliness affect different trans bodies? And in an increasingly globalized world, how do these (re)turns to home collude with liberal discourses of social inclusion in order to institute domesticity and normativity as the privileged trajectory of transsexual citizenship? Given the fractured nature of "home," is a transsexual homecoming at all possible?

Ahmed and Stacey write that "skin's memory is burdened with the unconscious" (Ahmed and Stacey 2001: 2). Skin has a phantasmic writerly effect, functioning as "a canvas for what we wish were true—or for what we cannot acknowledge to be true" (Prosser 2001: 52). And transsexual narratives, as Prosser explains in "Skin Memories," "reveal the skin as a site for unconscious investment, a body memory or fantasy that failed to materialize" (Prosser 2001: 52). A nostalgia for the romanticized ideal of home, the body reconstructed through sex-reassignment surgery— the body that is literally re-membered—is a recovery of the sexed contours that *should* have been: "What makes the transsexual able and willing to submit to the knife—the splitting, cutting, removal, and reshaping of organs, tissues, and skin that another might conceive as mutilation—is the desire to get the body *back to what it should have been*" (Prosser 1998: 84; emphasis mine).

But skin is not simply a "present" surface "in so far as it has multiple histories and unimaginable futures, it is worked upon, and indeed, it is worked towards" (Ahmed and Stacey 2001: 2). In other words, skin can be theorized in spatial and temporal dimensions—remembering, through its imperfect traces, our personal journeys through time and space. As with the act of writing, this testimonial function of skin, its "dermographia," "contains the traces of those other contexts in the very living materiality of its forms, even if it cannot be reduced to them" (Ahmed and Stacey 2001: 15). And, as with the inevitable erasures in the process of writing, the skin always leaves traces of a not-so-absent past to bear witness on what has yet to be written.

A porous, breathing surface, skin allows us to think about the unstable borders between bodies that are always already criss-crossed by differences that refuse to be contained on the "inside" or the "outside" of bodies themselves. So rather than fetishize the marked body, by simply reducing it to the least common denominators of difference contained within a singular figure, perhaps we require an approach that is critical of the tacit knowledges themselves which establish the very boundaries that appear to mark out the body. If, as Ahmed and Benthien suggest, skin is always open to being read by others, how can we think about the unstable borders between transsexual bodies that are always already crossed by differences that refuse to be contained on the "inside" or the "outside" of bodies? Reformulating Ahmed's questions, perhaps we can ask: "How do [trans] bodies re-inhabit space?" and "How do spaces re-inhabit [trans]bodies?" (Ahmed 2000: 90).

"Home," as one might imagine in relation to Prosser's model, "is represented as the place in which one finally settles into the comfort of one's true and authentic gender" (Halberstam 1998: 163). Thus, to feel "at home in one's skin" is to be taken in the world for who one feels oneself to be. But how are these somatic transitions spurred and enabled by the narrative promise/premise of homeliness? Arguing that a "politics of home" may provide a "powerful organizing trope" for a new transsexual politics of possibility, Prosser writes:

> This "politics of home" would analyze the persistence of sexual difference for organizing identity categories. It would highlight the costs to the subject of not being clearly locatable in relation to sexual difference. Above all, it would not disavow the value of belonging as the basis for a liveable identity. The practical applications for such a politics of home are immediate, multiple, and, indeed, transformative.
>
> *(Prosser 1998: 204)*

Of course, "home" can easily be a space of exclusion, a space where the nostalgic dream of communal belonging depends on the "invisible labor of migrant border dwellers," and a luxury that belies the realities of those who cannot afford to dream of home (Halberstam 1998: 171). Taking a practical approach to Prosser's "politics of home," Namaste explores benefits of civil code jurisdiction and state-sanctioned transsexual benefits in Quebec. Skeptical of the tacit discourses of citizenship within Prosser's idea of what constitutes a "livable identity," Namaste states:

> … for transsexuals who "transition" and are able to keep their jobs, providing such evidence [of lived experience] is not difficult. But for individuals who do not work in any kind of legal economy, and who do not go to school, the proof of such an identity, established through official documents—pay stubs, school transcripts, credit cards—is less certain.
>
> *(Namaste 2005: 5)*

What I find most striking about Prosser's work is the way in which the journey towards "home" is conceived of as a form of migration: "an appropriate analogical frame for the transsexual's writing of transition as a journey may be that of *immigration*: the subject conceives of transsexuality as a move to a new life in a new land, allowing the making of home, precisely an act of translation" (Prosser 1999: 88; emphasis mine). Akin to the transitory space of an airport terminal, the in-between space of gender transition figures as a site of *future* homely possibility—"the space in which one is almost, but not quite, at home"—where the subject has an itinerary, a destination and a future but has not yet arrived (Ahmed 2000: 78). Thus, in a noteworthy reversal of the diasporic trajectory, the transsexual migrant must leave the space of unhomeliness to arrive at "home."

Like Prosser, I too am interested in the theme of transit, "both as a figure for transsexual transition and as a literal journey undertaken" (Prosser 1999: 88). On the other hand, I am wary of his lack of engagement with the dynamics of race and class. As with his earlier work in "Exceptional Locations," Prosser's *Second Skins* explores the topography of migrational metaphors through a singularly gendered perspective. But he neglects to account for the ways in which power is distributed and wielded across a matrix of overlapping identities at the same time. The ways in which we theorize transsexuality must necessarily address the question of broader/ border traversals. In these contours of citizenship, belonging and migration, how do the borders themselves deterritorialize and reterritorialize us? Certainly, the borders of gender have a lot in common with those of the home: both police "spaces where those who do not 'belong' are separated from those who do" (Aizura 2006: 289). Bathrooms and border crossings are both equally invested in preserving and maintaining boundaries (between male and female, or citizen and stranger) such that, "at the border it is imperative to produce the right papers and look or act as if we belong—even, paradoxically, when we are sure that we do" (Aizura 2006: 289). In other words, the border marks a sphere of normality, of homeliness, that privileges properly gendered and sexed national bodies.

As Halberstam points out, the "idea of the border sets up some notion of territories to be defended, ground to be held or lost, permeability to be defended against" (Halberstam 1998: 163). We turn to these borders in order to separate citizen from stranger, human from alien, insider from outsider, and self from other. Borders allow us to feel safe in the knowledge that, whatever is out there, the unsettling potential of Homi Bhabha's *terrere* (terror), will not be able to contaminate the sacred *terre* (earth/land) of the nation-state (Bhabha 2004: 142). The resulting interpenetration of space and body, and body and psyche, means that if geographical borders cannot be separated from the integrity of home, then, equally, the boundaries between differently gendered bodies raise the specter of not being at home in one's body. So, if home is doubly inflected as the task of finding a home in one's body and being able to call the nation home, then concealed under the surface of this "politics of home" is the urge for normality and the desire "to belong without complication to a normative social sphere" (Aizura 2006: 290). Thus, the privileged space of the transsexual homecoming is a fantasy: "a fantasy, moreover, racially and culturally marked as Anglocentric, heteronormative and capitalist" (Aizura 2006: 290).

Aren Z. Aizura is one of the few contemporary trans theorists to recognize that the submerged nationalisms which undergird transsexual theorizing have contributed to a problematic "politics of transsexual citizenship" that is invested in metaphors of homecomings, borders and boundaries (Aizura 2006: 290). Furthermore, he argues that narratives of transsexual citizenship have perpetuated this discourse in normality by figuring transition as a necessarily transgressive "but momentary lapse on the way to a proper embodied belonging, a proper home and full social inclusion" (Aizura 2006: 290). This hegemonic construction of linear time and space has obvious implications for the gender liminal body; progress becomes a linear narrative that dictates the body's teleological transition *from* one gender *to* another. So, in a sense, the transitional trope is also the definitive property of a civilizing narrative—an articulation of linear progression towards the ultimate goal of belonging. A striking example of this telic structure of metaphoric corporeogeographic navigation can be found in Claudine Griggs's rather schematic chapter titles in *Passage Through Trinidad*: "Decision," "Arrival," "Hospital," "Pain," "Routine," "Visitors," "Progress," "Freedom," "Anticipation," "Release," "West," "Home," "Aftermath" (Griggs 1996: v).

If, as Richard Phillips has argued, "men are made, albeit loosely, in the image of their settings," then these adventure stories of transition, too, appear to accommodate and condition those unavowed investments in citizenship discourses that pave the road to transsexual-becoming (Phillips 1997: 66). In other words, whilst transsexual scholarship appears to romp freely through geographies of liminal adventure, we need to recognize that the fundamental theories under girding narratives of becoming are rooted in hegemonic notions of embodiment in national, and therefore racialized and gendered, space. According to Kathleen Kirby, this externalization and control of space reflects the need to maintain the ideal of stable and rationalized place in order to formulate a safely encapsulated subject. In other words, the mapping of borders and boundaries "is the very hallmark of a larger cultural order premised on cleanly distinguishing between entities in the natural environment, the psychic environment, and, finally, the social environment" (Kirby 1996: 49). Yet, this delimitation of the external environment, one which emphasizes "borders over sites," is part of the European mapping of ownership, of owness, and of property and propriety (Kirby 1996: 46). So perhaps that "desire to belong" conceals another set of discourses that have as yet gone uninterrogated.

The problem is that metaphorical adoptions of migratory narratives "can have the uncanny effect of using postcolonial rhetorics to redeem colonial contexts" and justify further oppression in the name of the transsexual empire (Halberstam 1998: 172). Such rhetorics assume that the proper solution to painfully wrong embodiment is to migrate to the right body—where, as Halberstam insightfully points out, "rightness may easily depend on whiteness or class privilege as it does on being regendered" (Halberstam 1998: 172). So what is needed is a phenomenology of transsexual consciousness that moves away from the notion of "home" as the stasis of being and firmly situates these (dis)embodied dissonances within historical and political frameworks. To quote Ahmed, "the issue is home is not simply about fantasies of belonging but that it is *sentimentalized* as a space of belonging" (Ahmed 2000: 89). Wary about the unidirectional impulse towards a transsexual "home," Judith Halberstam has suggested that it might be fruitful to turn to Chicano/a and post-colonial studies where debates about the politics of migration have resulted in "a careful refusal of the dialectic of home and border" (Halberstam 1998: 170). Heeding Halberstam's statement that "there is little to be gained theoretically or materially from identifying either home or border as the true place of resistance," I explore next the racial implications of territorial metaphors within the corporeo-theoretical cartography of transsexual writing (Halberstam 1998: 170).

Dis.orient.ations

Perhaps it is unsurprising that I find myself troubled by the origin stories and narrative marks of arrival in trans theory. Thus far, my intervention is purely theoretical for, try as I might, I have found few resources that do not isolate race from the discourses of transsexual embodiment; and yet "there is a huge difference between becoming a black man or a man of color and becoming a white man, and these differences are bound to create gulfs within transsexual communities" (Halberstam 1998: 159). I believe that what we require are interlinking maps of knowledge, theoretical grids that do not shy away from venturing into postcolonial or diasporic theorizing; that any discourse about the "fictional unity" of the transgender collective has to "begin from the premise that genders, sexualities, races, classes, nations, and even continents exist not just as hermetically sealed entities but rather as part of a permeable interwoven relationality" (Shohat 2002: 68).

Yet, as I try and articulate the scope of this project, I am all too aware of the theoretical loopholes, blind spots and black holes that I might inadvertently replicate. Like feminist scholarship, trans theory is always beset by the seductive danger of an essentialist universalism which, according to Ella Shohat, "excludes dialogue by making it pointless since within 'I'm OK, you're OK' logic, everything is legitimate and therefore not debatable" (Shohat 2002: 74). A theoretical approach that assumes everything is "OK"—à la multiculturalism—ends up silencing voices of dissent, which unfortunately only further legitimizes its universal appeal. But in order to explain why Shohat's concerns about the ethics of theoretical writing are important, I must turn, very briefly, to a personal narrative that will foreground my own anxieties about this project.

A little over a year ago, I was hired by a government-funded health collective to assist in a large-scale study of access to trans-specific health care. As part of a community engagement team, my role was to facilitate the creation of a groundbreaking questionnaire that would eventually be circulated to trans-identified individuals across Canada. During the course of my congratulatory phone call, I learned that one of the reasons I was hired was because the collective was striving to be more multicultural in its approach. To this end, the committee had recruited three trans-identified people of color in order to assure diversity within the collective. I never really gave the implications of this multicultural approach any serious thought. At that point in time, I was living in a predominantly white town—a town where a seemingly vague, "you know ... the brown kid with the hair," was usually enough to point someone in my direction—where there were only three other trans-identified people that I knew. So just the prospect of being in a room where there might be dozens of trans-identified men and women excited me; that I might actually *meet* other trans-identified people of color, people who were like me, filled me with the kind of joy that was unfamiliar in its giddy intensity.

On the morning of our first meeting, I walked into the boardroom of a local health center and was quite literally swept off my feet by a stunning South Indian woman, Asha. I had barely recovered from this first onslaught of affection before I felt my hand being grasped, and shaken quite enthusiastically, by Liz, the two-spirited woman who effectively completed our "trio of difference." Over the course of the two-day-long meeting, Asha, Liz and I formed strong bonds with each other. But, this was inevitable. Each meeting found the three of us trying again and again to point out the Eurocentric way in which the health questionnaire had been constructed.

We did not dispute the fact that trans people had trouble accessing emergency medical care or finding supportive mental health care. But what we *did* have a problem with was an unacknowledged elision of the social, political and cultural nuances that shaped the health care system as a whole. For instance, my first appointment with a gender specialist was not as much about my gender identity as it was about whether I, an East-Indian/Arab immigrant from Kenya, was simply having trouble integrating into Canadian society.[3] We were also concerned that the academic jargon used in the questionnaire would alienate both the people who didn't subscribe to those "theoretical pyrotechnics" as well as those for whom English was not a first language (Nnaemeka 2004: 364). And, whilst we were working desperately to get these points across, a hand shot up and a voice, which barely concealed the speaker's exasperation, piped up. "What does race have to do with being trans?!"

In the moments of stunned silence that followed, I remember struggling to contain my emotions. It felt as though I had been betrayed ... both by the collective as well as by my own naïveté. But it was the keen sense of loss that surprised me the most. How do you begin to mourn something that never really existed in the first place? Like three exotic bookmarks marking a chapter in the chronicle of a more diverse and increasingly global trans movement, our presence was meant to signify the dawning of a new era: a proudly Canadian, and therefore multicultural, trans community. Yet, we were, for all intents and purposes, a minority within a minority; held in the discursive grip of a "powerful powerless" we had found ourselves silenced by nationalist discourses of transsexual citizenship (Shadmi 2000: 30).

One might wonder why I was so disenchanted by the siren call of multicultural affiliation ... I suppose I should have been grateful, happy even, to have been included in this landmark project. But I felt far removed from the promise of a multicultural trans community. It seemed as though the fragile work of community building elided more elastic, and more complicated, notions of belonging. What it came down to was this: I was unable to pledge allegiance to yet another insulated form of (be)longing whose visions of cultural tolerance inevitably reproduced the very notions of fixed, hegemonic gender identities that the trans movement rebelled against in the first place. By placating us with its call for "respecting difference," not only did this multicultural approach conveniently ignore our autonomy, it also elided the differences *within* our trio of difference. But what, you may wonder, does this story have to do with discourses of nationalism in trans theory?

In her article "Geography Lessons," Himani Bannerji theorizes that the givenness of any nation-state is a "construction, a set of representations, embodying certain types of political and cultural communities and their operations" (Bannerji 1997: 24). With the ideological category of whiteness set as the core of the Canadian ethos, the ascription of "otherness" not only delimits membership within the cozy centers of the nation-state, but also produces whiteness as its discursive effect such that "European-ness as whiteness thus translates into 'Canada' and provides it with its imagined community" (Bannerji 1997: 24). It follows then that narratives of belonging are intimately entwined with indicators of difference. Or, to put it differently, the "affective alliances" which give rise to those feelings of homeliness are rooted within the socially constructed domain of cultural effects and these affects "define a structure and economy of belonging" (Grossberg 1992: 80).

Narratives of belonging are the "effect of inhabitance," as well as the paradoxical affect and effect, of the unfamiliar and uninhabitable (Ahmed 2006: 7). Haunted by the specter of what is unfamiliar, the domestic landscape of the familiar and familial world can only secure itself through a "repetition of gestures" that can never completely eliminate the threat of disappearance and the possibility of psychic displacement (Ahmed 2006: 57). Drawing upon Sara Ahmed, we can understand whiteness as allowing for the linear extension of a properly oriented body through space; and furthermore, these spaces themselves are the discursive effects of properly orientated bodies. Furthermore, orientation is itself oriented by the repetitions of the things that we "do do" such that what we "do do," and what we "can do," are the effects of difference as well as the mechanisms for the production of difference itself (Ahmed 2006: 59).

Despite the occasional, and sometimes abstract, detour into the quirky world of queer tables, Ahmed's *Queer Phenomenology* highlights how moments of (dis)orientation should be used to think productively about how space is dependent on bodily inhabitance. Ahmed literally queers the "orient" in "orientation" by thinking with, and around, the racialized body in cartographic space. She uses phenomenology to single out the "singling out" of objects, to problematize the orientation of orientation and to destabilize the alignment of alignment. So if repetition engenders an orientation towards homeliness, what happens when one is faced with a body that fails to perform? If orientations are "directional metaphor[s]" turned identification, how can we reconceptualize the body that seemingly repudiates the spatial linearity of socio-historical repetition? The queer phenomenological effect in Ahmed's writing occurs in the constructive interpellation of those "oblique or diagonal lines created by bodies out of space"—the bodies that disrupt, or "stop," the linear extension of *whiteness* (Ahmed 2006: 61). Perhaps it would be quite appropriate then to feel our way through possible answers by "queerying" its first sentence: "what does it mean to be [dis] orientated"? (Ahmed 2006: 1). A body that can extend through space to reach objects in place is "a body at home-in-its-world" (Ahmed 2006: 111). In this sense, whiteness functions as an inherited state in which the legacy of colonialism is passed down the family line as a *disembodied* possession, thereby creating a "proper ideal subject ... with property but no body" (Mohanram 1999: 38). On the other hand, a body that is *not* at home in its world is the very object that produces difference even as it is needed to constitute it; its *difference* shapes the centers of home as well as its hostile boundaries. Therefore, by the dint of their visibility, the racialized "body in excess" exists as *embodied* dispossession: the poverty of placelessness "drains [the racialized body] of identity" and "reverts us to being the visible body, as object, without padding, protection, or consciousness" (Mohanram 1999: 37).

Furthermore, Ahmed's critique of the socio-scientific construction of racial inheritance illustrates that the perception of race as "property" only serves to reinforce a discursive space in which to further perpetuate racial discourse as "oriented" in particular spatial and temporal frameworks (Ahmed 2006: 112). It follows then that a reproductive discourse that rests on the laurels of socio-scientific inheritance results in space envisioned as the cartographic property of whiteness; and the idea of whiteness as inherited can only continue to allow the white body to affect the spaces of those who must occupy the space of "not-quite-white[ness]" (Ahmed 2006: 112). What this indicates is that there is no such thing as "home" itself; that the Oriental, or racialized body, jeopardizes the fictive unity of belonging precisely because of its disorienting presence. So by placing a positive spin on "difference," multiculturalist rhetoric simultaneously "establishes Anglo-Canadian culture as the ethnic core culture while 'tolerating' and hierarchically arranging others around it as 'multiculture'" (Bannerji 1997: 35). Within such a framework, the self-congratulatory slogan "unity in diversity" functions as a mere gesture that implies transcendence as a way to overcome the legitimization crisis of Anglo-Canadian culture.

Drawing upon Bannerji's formulation of the "crisis in [Canadian] citizenship," I would like to suggest that the project of imagining a multicultural transsexual community needs to be further problematized by a sustained critique of both the radical inhabitability of "the idea of belonging" and the exclusionary drive towards a "politics of home" in transsexual theory (Bannerji 1997: 24; Prosser 1998: 204). The journey home for the transsexual may come at the expense of a recognition that others are permanently dislocated from home—that they occupy the inhospitable territories in between. ... the uninhabitable "geographies of ambiguity" at, what bell hooks would call, the very "profound edge[s]" of marginality (hooks 1990: 149). Although metaphors of travel and border crossing are inevitable in transsexual discourses, we must recognize that "they are also laden with the histories of other identity negotiations, and they carry the burden of national and colonial discursive histories" (Halberstam 1998: 165).

As Halberstam argues, this insistence on linearity within transsexual theory fails to account for bodies that inhabit a "persistent present or a queer temporality that is at once indefinite and virtual but also forceful, resilient, and undeniable" (Halberstam 2005: 11). Any trans cartography that prefers to think about transgression using metaphors of border crossings and homecomings will ultimately fail to take into account the lived realities of those who have no choice but to inhabit the border-lands of non-recognition: "some bodies are never at home, some bodies cannot simply cross from A to B, some bodies recognize and live with the inherent instability of identity" (Halberstam 1998: 165). Furthermore, "if the borderlands are uninhabitable for some trans-identified people who imagine that home is just across the border, imagine what a challenge they present to those subjects who do not believe that such a home exists, either metaphorically or literally" (Halberstam 1998: 164). Sadly, it seems that the voice that originated from the margins has begun to (re)produce its own marginalized voices.

Of course, these marginal voices can also be produced from the flip side of liberal universalism—cultural relativism—where multicultural cartographies of knowledge tend to be presumed in isolation from the center and from each other. I am all too aware that, in advocating for a race-conscious trans movement, I might end up re-inscribing marginality as the eye of the proverbial storm—a pure state where "they have their culture and we have ours: never the twain shall meet" (Alexander 2005: 188). Indeed, there is plenty of evidence to suggest that this has been the trend within transgender scholarship. Cast as a specific kind of knowledge that can only exist in opposition to "area studies," transgender and transsexual Euro-American academia has often resorted to comparative frameworks that naturalize and repro-duce nationalist discourses of sexuality through fetishizing gestures that map racial difference as spectacle. Within this trajectory of knowledge, it is all too apparent that trans-identified people of color have been, to borrow from Appadurai, meto-nymically frozen in an anthropological taxonomy which, through a spatial and temporal sleight-of-hand, effectively renders them, as Canadian poet Dionne Brand would say, "in another place, not here" (Appadurai 1992: 34). Such anthro-pological[4] narratives whose DNA contains the genetic blueprint of Judeo-Christian culture have tended to produce a fetishistic sexuality that can only be understood within the primitive realm: as a "pre-modern, pre-capitalist construction, which in turn enables whiteness to be located within capitalism as well as modernity" (Mohanram 1999: 22). In other words, these journeys backwards through time— journeys where "geographical difference across *space* is figured as historical difference across *time*"—produce socio-cultural difference as a space for consumption (Clifford 1997: 20).

In contemporary trans scholarship these theoretical journeys seem to allow us to consume a veritable buffet of exotic (trans)sexuality—from male transvestite shamans in northwest Venezuela to the shamans in the Vietnamese countryside, from the priestly shamans of West Africa to the transsexual augurers and diviners of Angola, from the "native peoples of the arctic basin" to India's ubiquitous *hijras* and so forth (Feinberg 1996: 45; Shohat 2002: 69). Like ice popsicles with referential vanilla centers covered in those thin, exotic fruit-flavor-of-the-month shells—a sweet, but ultimately shallow, veneer beneath which first world theories are thought to remain unaffected—these accounts of transsexual embodiment engage in a double move of universalizing transsexual difference whilst (re)producing difference as "the body in excess" that can then be consumed (Mohanram 1999: 49). This "additive approach" to trans scholarship is akin to a "family of nations pageant" in which a rotating chain of marginality tends to be pitted against an unstated, white, Western norm, effectively putting relationships amongst others "on hold" (Shohat 2002: 69). In this sense, the radical difference of racial specificity—a specificity that is seemingly unmarked by the shifts and fluxes of relations of social, political and economic relations over time—inevitably overshadows what could be parallel and productive dialogues of trans embodiment.

As a spatial marker of possibility, the prefix *trans-* does not just signify movement across or beyond a schism. It is also evocative of the *transgressions, transmogrifications* and *transmutations* of established norms. Indeed, one of the functions of *trans-*, as suggested by Song Hwee Lim's article "Is the Trans- in Transnational the Trans- in Transgender," is to destabilize the notion of space as a controlled location (Lim 2007). Furthermore, we cannot theorize about the politics of *space* without engaging with the subjective experience of *place*. Each requires the other to fulfill its potential. Borrowing from John Agnew, the simplest explanation of the relationship between space and place can be summarized as follows: "Space refers to location somewhere and place to the occupation of that location. Space is about having an address and place is about living at that address" (Agnew 2005: 82). So if the prefixes *post* (as in "postcolonial") and *trans* (as in "transsexual") function as temporal and spatial markers, perhaps we should ask what centers and peripheries are necessarily (r)evoked by transsexual theorist Sandy Stone's early formulation of the "posttranssexual empire"?

Written in response to Janice Raymond's anti-transsexual polemic,[5] Stone's "The Empire Strikes Back: A Posttranssexual Manifesto" is still considered to be a monumental call for transsexual self-expression. Drawing upon autobiographical literature, Stone suggests that the transsexual impetus to disappear into "plausible histories"—to become successfully invisible by "passing" as the gender of their choice—forecloses the radical "possibility of a life grounded in the *intertextual* possibilities of the transsexual body" (Stone 2006: 231). For Stone, the narrative of "passing" is one that denies not just individual history, or political agency, but the destabilizing power of transgression itself. Thus, her "posttranssexual manifesto" calls for a reappropriation of the multiple dissonances of transsexual experience through embracing "physicalities of constantly shifting figure[s] and ground[s] that exceed the frame of any possible representation" (Stone 2006: 232).

Nevertheless, I find Stone's call of a "posttranssexual" epoch troubling because the "implied openness of the narrative, paradoxically, reveals its own closedness" (Shohat 2002: 72). By positioning the transsexual experience as something outside of both time and space, the "posttranssexual manifesto" has the uncanny effect of erasing the criss-crossing effects of global and local configurations of hegemonic power. In other words, the only way that Stone can address her "brothers" and "sisters" as transsexual kinfolk is by simultaneously denying the plurality, fragmentation and contingency of identity even as she advocates for it (Stone 2006: 232). Swayed by the gravitational pull of the "theoretical black hole," Stone's posttranssexual narrative suggests a movement which is devoid of the accumulation of meaning; where the "subtle theoretical finesse of infinite multiplicities" has also multiplied the "possibilities for the subject to … disappear up its own theoretical subtleness"; where the "heralding of subject positions 'at the margins' too often neglects the actual marginalization of subjects" (Mitchell 1997: 108, 109). So perhaps it is only fitting that she reiterates Raymond's notion of the transsexual "empire"—for Stone's formulation of posttranssexuality assumes a transsexual cosmopolitan elite whose "willful ignorance" is vital to (re)creating trans theory as a "fortress rich world" (Sharma 2005: 10, 12).

The problem with "empires" is that they are dependent on difference and conquest for self-definition. If the "transsexual empire" is evocative of the messy terrain of modern, civilized whiteness that can only be articulated through uncivilized, primitive bodies steeped in exotic culture, then the *post*transsexual empire—which engages in the simultaneous denial of both historic specificity and the complex dynamics of local and global interactions—produces a muted movement which can only be complicit in recirculating unequal relations of power. To this end, I agree with Lim's suggestion that "the prefix 'trans' … whether in relation to nation or to gender … while indexing a crossing of boundaries, can in effect fix the boundaries even more firmly and in an essentialist manner" (Lim 2007: 47).

My concerns about the "posttranssexual" moment are as follows: How can we even begin to acknowledge the multi-layered complexities of this palimpsestic global, transsexual movement if the movement itself has already "moved on" so that it is beyond the reach of both history and the politics of the local/global? Whilst I do not mean to suggest that we re-center notions of a global modernity, I am advocating for an affective approach to transsexual embodiment—one which pays attention to the political ramifications of a movement rooted in the space-beyond, and which interrogates the desires behind the push for transsexual homeliness. The dizzying, free-floating paradigm engendered by Stone's framework effectively ignores the dynamics of power, or the continued hegemony of the center over the margins, by making everyone "equally different, despite specific histories of oppressing or being oppressed" (Lavie and Swedenburg 1996: 3). The posttranssexual movement signals a new form of global elite and "evokes the sameness of human differentiation across time by collapsing the processes of time into an unchanging, and highly idealized notion, *the same organized body*" (Mohanram 1999: 31; emphasis mine). Certainly, it seems as though the transsexual "empire" is drawing its inspiration from Benedict Anderson's formulation of the nation as "an imagined political community—and imagined as both inherently limited and sovereign" (Anderson 2005: 49).

Thus far, I have attempted to illustrate that trans scholarship may be affected by the same discourses of affective mapping that have drawn solid lines between "subject and land ... and between European white subjects and others"; that theory, too, can function as a psychic tool that re-circulates neo-imperialist notions of the externalization and control of bodies and boundaries (Kirby 1996: 49). In other words, if cartographic tools are "lifelines" that save us from the ravages of the unfamiliar whilst also marking the spaces that are beyond our bodily horizons, and if the act of claiming "empires" is necessarily bound up with the politics of "withness" and "againstness," then transsexual politics, too, are implicated in the game of mastering one's environment without being mastered in return—of ensuring that the "relationship between the knower and the known remains unidirectional" (Ahmed 2004: 17; Kirby 1996: 48). Although these maps allow for spaces of "becoming"—for a continued investment in the inheritance and reproduction of homely spaces—they simultaneously demand a "turning away" from something else. Trans scholarship is haunted by perpetual discursive acts of psychic violence that can be traced to the ideals of Enlightenment individualism and the European mapping of ownership; that the "antagonism that the imaginary whole of the [trans community] aims to disavow or exclude is thus not just the sign of the failure of any whole to be whole ... [rather] it is an ongoing practice of violence" (Kawash 1998: 337). Furthermore, these discursive acts of violence betray the fundamental insecurities in the fictional unity of a transsexual "empire." As such, it is neither "home" per se that is contested within trans theory, nor the mechanisms that shape home as that contested space. Rather, what are at stake are the things that must necessarily be sacrificed, or disavowed, in order to engage in the very act of imagining home.

Notes

1 My interest in the affective conditions of "homework" takes into account landscapes that are both metaphorical and literal. The meanings of "home" shift across a number of discourses: from the notion of a stable identity to a fluid concept, from private to public spheres, between the nation as an "imagined community" to a mythic space of belonging, or simply as a narrative of the self and the "other."

2 Briefly, my use of the word "trans" as a pseudo-umbrella term—albeit a problematic one—to describe both transsexual and transgender identities follows Jason Cromwell, Aren Z. Aizura and Bobby Noble's application of "trans" as an identity category under erasure. Thus, I ask the reader here to read "trans" not just as a form of categorical indeterminacy, but whilst also keeping in mind the differential modalities of (dis)-identification under the sign itself.

3 Gender specialist number two, on the other hand, seemed more willing to talk about the process of transition itself. But, couched in metaphors of migration and assimilation, his navigation of transsexuality still relied upon un/settling narratives of citizenship:

> He said: "You need to think of transitioning as immigrating to a new country."
> Silence.
> I said: "But I've already had to do that once … when I came to Canada."
> He smiled.
> He said: "Then it should be easier."

4 By way of introduction to their co-edited anthology *Displacement, Diaspora, and Geographies of Identity*, Smadar Lavie and Ted Swedenburg state that "The discipline of anthropology has played a significant role in the extraordinarily historical processes by which the world has come to be seen as divided into the world 'Here' (the West) and the world 'Out There' (the non-West), as well as in the processes whereby the dominant U.S.-Eurocenter was hegemonized" (Lavie and Swedenburg 1996: 1). However, relativistic notions of culture based on the inseparability of identity from geography are not particular to the discipline of anthropology but present themselves throughout the humanities and social sciences (as well as in the political institutions of the nation-state that shape discourse).

5 First published in 1979, Janice Raymond's *The Transsexual Empire: The Making of the She-Male*, is widely criticized for its offensive portrayal of transsexual women as power-hungry rapists who have infiltrated the feminist movement: "Rape is a masculinist violation of bodily integrity. All transsexuals rape women's bodies by reducing the female form to an artifact, appropriating this body for themselves … Rape, although it is usually done by force, can also be accomplished by deception" (Raymond 1994: 134).

   Despite the fact that these so-called "rapists" have been chemically or surgically castrated, Raymond asserts that their masculine privilege and history mean that they are, and will always be, men—hence her reference to MTFs as "male-to-*constructed*-female-transsexuals" (Raymond 132).

   FTMs, of course, didn't really deserve any mention because in Raymond's eyes they were all traitors anyway.

CONTRIBUTOR BIOGRAPHIES

Aren Z. Aizura is a Post-Doctoral Fellow in Gender Studies at Indiana University. He completed his PhD at the University of Melbourne, Australia, in 2009. Aizura has published on the topic of transsexuality and travel in journals and anthologies like *Inter-Asia Cultural Studies, Asian Studies Review, Medical Anthropology: Cross-Cultural Understandings of Health and Wellness,* and *Queer Bangkok.*

Nael Bhanji is a Doctoral Candidate in the Department of Women's Studies at York University. His research focuses on affect, transsexual citizenship, and racialized bodies.

Trystan T. Cotten is Associate Professor of Ethnic Studies in the Department of Ethnic and Gender Studies at California State University, Stanislaus, where he teaches courses in ethnic and postcolonial studies, gender and sexuality, and global economics. He has co-edited three anthologies and authored numerous journal articles and book chapters.

Lucas Crawford is a Doctoral Candidate in English and Film Studies at the University of Alberta. Lucas studies transgender, architecture, and twentieth-century fiction, and his writing has appeared in *Women's Studies Quarterly,* the *Seattle Journal for Social Justice,* and *English Studies in Canada.*

Jin Haritaworn is a Postdoctoral Fellow at the Helsinki Collegium for Advanced Studies. He has edited several (forthcoming) collections and journal issues, including the *European Journal of Women's Studies* and *Sexualities.* He is also completing monographs on cultural and biographical representations of Thainess and "mixed race" (for Ashgate publishers), and on homonationalist travels in Europe and transatlantically (contracted as part of the Pluto series of "Decolonial Studies, Post-colonial Horizons").

Eva Hayward is Assistant Professor in the Department of Cinematic Arts and Interdisciplinary Film and Digital Media Program at the University of New Mexico. She lectures and publishes on animal studies, experimental film, and queer embodiment. Currently, she is a Postdoctoral Fellow in Women's Studies at Duke University.

Vek Lewis is Chair of the Department of Spanish and Latin American Studies at the University of Sydney, Australia, where he teaches courses on contemporary Latin American film, literature and popular culture, and Critical Theory. He is the author of *Crossing Sex and Gender in Latin America* (Palgrave Macmillan, 2010). Additionally he has published work in *Chasqui, Portal Journal of International Multi-disciplinary Studies and Sexualities* and in several anthologies. Besides working on cultural representations, Lewis conducts ethnographic field research around questions of migration, cultural identity, legal systems, and sexual minorities in Mexico and Australia.

Quinn Miller is Visiting Professor of Media Culture at Northwestern University's Qatar School of Communication. Miller's articles include "The Bob Cummings Show's 'Artists at 'Work': Gender Transitive Programming and Counterpublicity," and "Masculinity and Male Intimacy in Nineties Sitcoms: Seinfeld and the Ironic Dismissal." His current book project is *Camp TV: Commercial Counterpublics and the Cultural Production of Queer Gender.*

Don Romesburg is Assistant Professor in the Sonoma State University Women's and Gender Studies Department. A historian with interdisciplinary interests in gender/sexuality studies, he has published on early twentieth-century U.S. discourses, social science, and cultures of adolescence, homosexuality, and citizenship, the social history of queer and trans performers, and male intimacy in popular culture. He also curates exhibits for the GLBT Historical Society in San Francisco.

C. Riley Snorton is Mellon Postdoctoral Fellow in the Department of Media Studies at Pomona College. He directed the film, *Men at Work: Transitioning on the Job,* and has published in numerous journals, including the *International Journal of Communication, Hypatia,* and *Soul.* His current book project, *Trapped in the Epistemological Closet: Black Sexuality and the Popular Imagination,* examines the concept of the "down low" in American popular culture.

BIBLIOGRAPHY

Agathangelou, Anna et al. "Intimate Investments: Homonormativity, Global Lockdown and the Seductions of Empire." *Radical History Review* 100 (2008): 120–43.

Aggleton, P., A. Parker, and M. Maluwa. "Stigma, Discrimination and HIV/AIDS in Latin America and the Caribbean." *Inter-American Development Bank Papers Series*, 1–24. Washington, DC: Inter-American Development Bank, 2002.

Agnew, John. "Space:Place." In *Spaces of Geographical Thought*, edited by Paul Cloke and Ron Johnston, 81–96. California: Sage Publications, 2005.

Ahmed, Sara. *Strange Encounters: Embodied Others in Post Coloniality*. London: Routledge, 2000.

———. *The Cultural Politics of Emotions*. Edinburgh: Edinburgh UP, 2004.

———. *Queer Phenomenology*. Durham: Duke UP, 2006.

———. *The Promise of Happiness*. Durham: Duke UP, 2010.

Ahmed, Sara and Jackie Stacey. *Thinking Through the Skin*. New York: Routledge, 2001.

Aizura, Aren Z. "Of Borders and Homes: The Imaginary Community of (Trans)sexual Citizenship." *Inter-Asia Cultural Studies* 7.2 (2006): 289–309.

Alexander, M. Jacqui. *Pedagogies of Crossing: Meditations on Feminism, Sexual Politics, Memory, and the Sacred*. Durham: Duke UP, 2005.

Alexander, Meena. *House of A Thousand Doors*. Washington, DC: Three Continents Press, 1988.

Álvarez, C. "Cero Tolerancia al Aplicar Reglamentos Municipales." *La Voz de la Frontera*. July 21, 2002.

Anderson, Benedict. "Imagined Communities." In *Nations and Nationalisms: A Reader*, edited by Phillip Spencer and Howard Wollman, 48–60. Oxford: Rutgers UP, 2005.

Andrade, Heather Russell. "Revising Critical Judgments of *The Autobiography of an Ex-Colored Man*." *African American Review* 40 (2006): 1–17.

Anzaldúa, G. *Borderlands/La Frontera: The New Mestiza*. San Francisco: Spinsters/Aunt Lute, 1987.

Appadurai, Arjun. "Putting Hierarchy in Its Place." in *Rereading Cultural Anthropology*, edited by George E. Marcus, 34–47. Durham: Duke UP, 1992.

———. *Modernity at Large: Cultural Dimensions of Globalization*. Minneapolis: University of Minnesota Press, 1996.

Arce Aguilar, J.L. "Colonia Segura. Una Experiencia Local." In *Aproximaciones Empíricas al Estudio de la Seguridad*, edited by González Placencia et al. México, DF: Miguel Angel Porrúa, 2007.

Bacchetta, Paola and Jin Haritaworn. "There Are Many Transatlantics." In *Transatlantic Conversations: Feminism as Traveling Theory*, edited by K. Davis and M. Evans. Aldershot: Ashgate (forthcoming).

Bailey, Michael J. *The Man Who Would Be Queen: The Science of Gender-Bending and Transsexualism*. Washington: Joseph Henry Press, 2003.

Bal, Mieke. *Louise Bourgeois' Spider: The Architecture of Art-Writing*. Chicago: University of Chicago Press, 2001.

Bando de Policía y Gobierno para el Municipio de Tecate, Baja California. *Periódico Oficial 115.46*. October 35, (2002). Accessed January 10, 2009. www.tecate.gob.mx/transparencia/pdfs/MarcoJuridico/reglamentos/BANDO%20DE%20POLICIA%20Y%20GOBIERNO.pdf.

Bannerji, Himani. "Geography Lessons: On Being and Insider/Outsider to the Canadian Nation." In *Dangerous Territories: Struggles for Difference and Equality*, edited by L. Roman and L. Eyre, 23–41. New York: Routledge, 1997.

Barale, Michèle Aina et al. *Touching Feeling: Affect, Pedagogy, Performativity*. Durham: Duke UP, 2003.

Barfly. *Barfly*. Los Angeles: Advocate Publications. University of Chicago Special Collections, 1971.

Bassichis, Morgan, Alexander Lee, and Dean Spade. "Building an Abolitionist Trans & Queer Movement with Everything We've Got." In *Captive Genders Anthology*, edited by Nathan Smith and Eric Stanley (forthcoming).

Basu, Feroza. "The Transgendered Individual as Exilic Travelling Subject." In *Cultures of Exile: Images of Displacement*, edited by Wendy Everett and Peter Wagstaff, 125–36. New York: Berghahn Books, 2004.

BBC News Americas. "Mexico's Transvestite Ban Draws Gay Protest." November 5, 2002. Accessed April 13, 2008. http://news.bbc.co.uk/2/hi/americas/2402571.stm.

Beck, Ulrich. "Cosmopolitical Realism: On the Distinction between Cosmopolitanism in Philosophy and the Social Sciences." *Global Networks* 4 (2004): 131–56.

Bell, William W. Interview by Lorenzo Arbeit, January 8, 1979. Randy Riddle private collection, Winston-Salem, North Carolina.

——. Interview by author via telephone. February 17, 2000.

Benedictow, Ole J. *The Black Death 1346–1353: The Complete History*. Rochester: Boydell & Brewer, 2004.

Benjamin, Harry. *The Transsexual Phenomenon*. New York: Julian Press, 1966.

Benjamin, Walter and Asja Lacis. "Naples." In *Reflections*. New York: Harcourt, 1978.

Benson, Melanie. "'Disturbing the Calculation': The Narcissistic Arithmetic of Three Southern Writers. *Mississippi Quarterly* 56.4 (2003): 633–45.

Benston, Kimberly. "Facing Tradition: Revisionary Scenes in African American Literature." *PMLA* 105.1 (1990): 98–109.

Benthien, Claudia. *Skin: On the Cultural Border Between Self and the World*. Trans. Thomas Dunlap. New York: Columbia UP, 2002.

Berlant, Lauren. *The Female Complaint: The Unfinished Business of Sentimentality in American Culture*. Durham: Duke UP, 2008.

Bhabha, Homi. *The Location of Culture*. New York: Routledge, 2004.

Binnie, Jon and Beverly Skeggs. "Cosmopolitan Knowledge and Sexualized Space: Manchester's Gay Village." In *Cosmopolitan Urbanism*, edited by Jon Binnie et al., 220–45. New York: Routledge, 2006.

Blake, P. "BC, primer lugar por muertes de SIDA." *La crónica*, October 31, 2002.

Bolos, S. (coord.). *Mujeres y espacio público. Construcción y ejercicio de la ciudadanía*. México DF: Universidad Iberoamericana, 2008.

Bonfen, Elisabeth. *The Knotted Subject: Hysteria and Its Discontents.* Princeton, NJ: Princeton UP, 1998.

Bornstein, Kate. *Gender Outlaw: On Men, Women, and the Rest of Us.* New York: Vintage Books, 1995.

Bourbon, Rae. *The Bourbon Motif.* New Bourbon 101-A. 78. c. mid-1940s.

———. *We've Got to Have a Union.* New Bourbon 201 B. 78. c. late 1940s a.

———. *Native.* Lasses 2. 78. c. late-1940s b.

———. *A Girl of the Golden West.* UTC 4. LP. 1956a.

———. *Around the World in 80 Ways.* UTC 8. LP. 1956b.

———. *You're Stepping on My Eyelashes.* UTC 2. LP. 1956c.

———. *Hollywood Exposé.* UTC 9. LP. 1956d.

———. *A Trick Ain't Always A Treat.* Jewel Box 3001-A. LP. 1964.

———. Memoir. Randy Riddle private collection, Winston-Salem, North Carolina. c. 1969–71.

———. Letter to Brian. November 29. Randy Riddle private collection, Winston-Salem, North Carolina. 1970a.

———. Letter to Brian. December 10. Randy Riddle private collection, Winston-Salem, North Carolina. 1970b.

———. Letter to Brian. December 18. Randy Riddle private collection, Winston-Salem, North Carolina. 1970c.

Bourdieu, P. *Logic of Practice.* Palo Alto, CA: Stanford UP, 1990.

———. *Language and Symbolic Power.* Trans. Gino Raymond and Matthew Adamson. Cambridge: Polity Press, 1991.

Bozic, Ivo."Das Große Schweigen: Homophobe Türkische Jugendliche und die Angst vor Rassismusvorwürfen." *Jungle World.* June 26, 2008.

Brah, Avtar. *Cartographies of Diaspora: Contesting Identities.* New York: Routledge, 1996.

Braham, William W. "Giedion and the Fascination of the Tub." In *Plumbing: Sounding Modern Architecture,* edited by N. Lahiji and D.S. Friedman, 201–24. Princeton: Princeton Architectural Press, 1997.

Brand, Dionne. *In Another Place, Not Here.* Toronto: Knopf Canada, 1996.

Braziel, Jana Evans and Anita Mannur. "Nation, Migration, Globalization: Points of Contention in Diaspora Studies." In *Theorizing Diaspora,* edited by Jana Evans Braziel and Anita Mannur, 1–23. Malden, MA: Blackwell Publishing, 2003.

Brown, B., W.R. Benedict, and W.V. Wilkinson. "Public Perceptions of the Police in Mexico: A Case Study." *Policing: An International Journal of Police Strategies and Management* 29 (2006): 158–75.

Brown, Wendy. *Regulating Aversion: Tolerance in the Age of Identity and Empire.* Princeton: Princeton University Press, 2005.

Bullough, Vern L. "Transsexualism in History." *Archives of Sexual Behavior* 4 (1975): 561–71.

Bündnis 90/Die Grünen. *Berliner Aktionsplan Gegen die Homophobie.* Berlin Senate, Print matter 16/1966, 1/12/2008, 16th election period.

Burns, Kellie and Cristyn Davies. "Producing Cosmopolitan Sexual Citizens on *The L Word.*" *Journal of Lesbian Studies* 13 (2009): 174–88.

Butler, Judith. *Gender Trouble: Feminism and the Subversion of Identity.* New York: Routledge, 1990.

———. *Bodies That Matter: On the Discursive Limits of "Sex."* New York: Routledge, 1993a.

———. "Critically Queer." *GLQ* 1 (1993b): 17–32.

———. *Undoing Gender.* New York: Routledge, 2004.

Califia, Pat. "San Francisco: Revisiting 'The City of Desire.'" In *Queers in Space: Communities, Public Spaces, Sites of Resistance,* edited by Gordon Brent Ingram, Anne-Marie Bouthillette, and Yolanda Retter, 177–96. Seattle: Bay Press, 1997.

Camp, R.A. *Politics in Mexico: The Democratic Transition.* 5th ed. New York: Oxford UP, 2007.

Campt, Tina. "The Crowded Space of Diaspora: Intercultural Address and the Tensions of Diaporic Relation." *Radical History Review* 83 (2002): 94–113.

Canaday, Margot. *The Straight State: Sexuality and Citizenship in Twentieth-Century America.* Princeton: Princeton UP, 2009.

Canclini, N.G. *Culturas Híbridas. Estrategias para Entrar y Salir de la Modernidad.* Mexico City: Grijalbo, 1989.

Cantú, L. *The Sexuality of Migration: Border Crossings and Mexican Immigrant Men.* New York: New York University Press, 1997.

Castañeda, C. "Historia de la Sexualidad. Investigaciones del Periodo Colonial." In *Sexualidades en México. Algunas aproximaciones desde la perspectiva de las ciencias sociales,* edited by I. Szasz and S. Lerner. México: El Colegio de México, 1998.

Castells, Manuel. "Cultural Identity, *Sexual* Liberation and Urban Structure: The Gay Community in San Francisco." In *The City and the Grassroots,* edited by Manuel Castells, 138–70. London: Edward Arnold, 1983.

Chauncey, George. *Gay New York: Gender, Urban Culture, and the Making of the Gay Male World 1890–1940.* New York: Basic Books, 1994.

Cheah, Pheng. "Biopower and the New International Division of Reproductive Labor." *boundary* 2.34 (2007): 1, 79–113.

Ciao! Ciao!: The World of Gay Travel. New York: QQ Publishing (Parragon). Gerber/Hart Library Special Collections, 1973–79.

City of Hamburg. "Names and Descriptions of Alien Passengers from Baltimore, MD to London, England." October 12, 1936. Accessed July 21, 2009. www.ancestry.com.

Clarke, Cheryl. "Race, Homosocial Desire and 'Mammon' in *Autobiography of an Ex-Colored Man.*" In *Professions of Desire: Lesbian and Gay Studies in Literature,* edited by George E. Haggerty and Bonnie Zimmerman, 84–97. New York: MLA, 1995.

Cleary, M., and S. Stokes. *Democracy and the Culture of Skepticism: Political Trust in Argentina and Mexico.* New York: SAGE, 2006.

Clifford, James. "Travelling Cultures." In *Routes: Travel and Translation in the Late Twentieth Century,* 17–46. Cambridge, MA: Harvard University Press, 1997.

Crawford, Lucas Cassidy. "Transgender Without Organs? Mobilizing a Geo-Affective Theory of Gender Modification." *Women's Studies Quarterly* 36 (2008): 127–43.

Cruz-Malavé, Arnaldo and Martin Manalansan (eds.). *Queer Globalizations: Citizenship and the Afterlife of Colonialism.* New York: New York UP, 2002.

Cvetkovich, Ann. *An Archive of Feelings: Trauma, Sexuality, and Lesbian Public Cultures.* Durham: Duke UP, 2003.

Decena, Carlos Ulises. "Tacit Subjects." *GLQ* 14 (2008): 339–59.

De Certeau, Michel. *The Writing of History.* Trans. Tom Conley. New York: Columbia UP, 1988.

——. "Walking in the City." In *The Cultural Studies Reader,* edited by Simon During, 127–33. New York: Routledge, [1974] 1999.

De Lauretis, Teresa. *The Practice of Love: Lesbian Sexuality and Perverse Desire.* Bloomington: Indiana UP, 1994.

Deleuze, Gilles and Félix Guattari. *A Thousand Plateaus: Capitalism and Schizophrenia.* Trans. Brian Massumi. Minneapolis: University of Minnesota Press, 1987.

——. *What is Philosophy?* London: Verso, 1994.

Denny, Dallas. "White Refrigerators, Black Telephones: Rethinking Christine Jorgensen." In *Current Concepts in Transgender Identity,* edited by Dallas Denny, 35–44. New York: Taylor and Francis, 1998.

Department of the Army. Memorandum for J. Edgar Hoover. ACSI-SIB, November 30, 1960. Retrieved via Freedom of Information Act by author.

De Tocqueville, Alexis. *Democracy in America*. Trans. Olivier Zunz. Washington, DC: Library of America, 2004.

Diawara, Manthia and Silvia Kolbowski. "Homeboy Cosmopolitanism." *October* 83 (1998): 51–70.

Drag Festival. *Info*. 2008a. Accessed June 6, 2009. http://drag-festial.net/drag/?page_id=2.

———. "Homophober Überfall nach Drag-Festival." *Press Release*. 2008b. Accessed June 8, 2008.

Du Bois, W.E.B. *The Souls of Black Folk*. In *Three Negro Classics*, edited by John Hope Franklin. New York: Avon Books, [1903]/1965.

Duggan, Lisa. *The Twilight of Equality? Neoliberalism, Cultural Politics, and the Attack on Democracy*. Boston: Beacon Press, 2003.

Durkheim, E. *The Division of Labor in Society*. Basingstoke: Macmillan, [1893]/1984.

Eighner, Lars. *Travels with Lizbeth: Three Years on the Road and on the Streets*. New York: Ballantine Books, 1993.

El Paso Herald-Post. "Juarez Actor Gets Fortune." July 27, 1931.

———. Article. July 6, 1933.

El-Tayeb, Fatima. "'Gays Who Cannot Properly Be Gay': Queer Muslims in the Neoliberal European City." *European Journal of Women's Studies*. Special issue on feminist and gay metonymies in the "war on terror," edited by J. Haritaworn (forthcoming).

Encyclopedia Britannica Online. Germ Theory. Accessed April 30, 2009. http://www.britannica.com/EBchecked/topic/230610 /germ-theory.

Escoffier, Jeffrey. "The Political Economy of the Closet: Notes toward an Economic History of Gay and Lesbian Life before Stonewall." In *Homo Economics: Capitalism, Community, and Gay Life*, edited by Amy Gluckman and Betsy Reed, 123–34. New York: Routledge, 1997.

Espinoza Valle, V.A. *Alternancia Política y Gestión Pública: el Partido Acción Nacional en el Gobierno de Baja California*. México, DF: Plaza y Valdés, 2000.

Fairclough, N. *Critical Discourse Analysis*. Boston: Addison Wesley, 1995.

Fajardo, Kale Bantigue. "Transportation: Translating Filipino and Filipino American Tomboy Masculinities through Global Migration and Seafaring." *GLQ* 14 (2008): 403–24.

Fausto-Sterling. Anne. *Sexing the Body: Gender Politics and the Construction of Sexuality*. New York: Basic Books, 2000.

Federal Bureau of Investigation. Memorandum on Ray Bourbon. 1961–62. CG 62–5703. Retrieved via Freedom of Information Act by author.

Feinberg, Diane Leslie. *Journal of a Transsexual*. New York: World View, 1980.

Feinberg, Leslie. *Stone Butch Blues*. Ithaca, NY: Firebrand Books, 1993.

———. *Transgender Warriors: Making History from Joan of Arc to RuPaul*. Boston: Beacon Press, 1996.

Fekete, Liz. "Enlightened Fundamentalism? Immigration, Feminism and the Right." *Race and Class* 48.2 (2008): 1–22.

Fernández, J. *Cuerpos Desobedientes: Travestismo e Identidad de Género*. Edhasa, Buenos Aires, 2004.

Fierce. "LGBTQ Youth Fight for a S.P.O.T. on Pier 40." September 15, 2008. Accessed February 19, 2009. http://fiercenyc.org/media/docs/3202_PublicHearingPressRelease. pdf. Florida, Richard. *The Rise of the Creative Class*. New York: Basic Books, 2002.

Foley, Neil. *The White Scourge: Mexicans, Blacks, and Poor Whites in Texas Cotton Culture*. Berkeley: University of California Press, 1997.

Fortier, Anne-Marie. "Making Home: Queer Migrations and Motions of Attachment." *Uprootings/Regroundings: Questions of Home and Migration*, edited by Sara Ahmed et al., 115–30. Oxford: Berg, 2003.

Foucault, M. *Discipline and Punish: The Birth of the Prison*. New York: Random House, 1975.

———. *The History of Sexuality,* Volume I, *An Introduction.* Trans. Robert Hurley. New York: Pantheon, 1978.

———. "Governmentality." In *The Foucault Effect: Studies in Governmentality,* edited by Graham Burchell, Colin Gordon, and Peter Miller, 87–104. Hemel Hempstead: Harvester Wheatsheaf, 1991.

———. *Security, Territory, Population. Lectures at the Collège de France, 1977–78.* New York: Palgrave, 2007.

Frank, Dr. *Health in Our Homes.* Boston: Thayer Publishing Company, 1887.

Freud, Sigmund. "Fragments of an analysis of a Case of Hysteria." In *The Standard Edition of the Complete Psychological Works of Sigmund Freud,* Volume VII, edited by J. Strachey, 1–122. London: Hogarth P, [1905]/1957.

———. "The Uncanny." *Psychological Writings and Letters,* edited by Sander Gilman. Trans. Alix Strachey. New York: Continuum, 1995.

Ganster, P. "Perceptions of Quality of Life in Tecate." In *Tecate, Baja California Realities and Challenges in a Mexican Border Community,* edited by P. Ganster et al., 109–26. San Diego: San Diego State UP, 2002.

Garber, Marjorie. *Vested Interests: Cross-dressing and Cultural Anxiety.* New York: Routledge, 1992.

García, Mario T. "Mexican Americans and the Politics of Citizenship: The Case of El Paso, 1936." *New Mexico Historical Review* 59 (1984): 187–204.

Gavin, James. *Intimate Nights: The Golden Age of New York Cabaret.* New York: Limelight, 1992.

Gilman, Sander. *Making the Body Beautiful: A Cultural History of Aesthetic Surgery.* Princeton: Princeton UP, 1999.

Gilroy, Paul. *Between Camps: Nations, Cultures and the Allure of Race.* London: Allen Lane/ Penguin Press, 2000.

Gluckman, Amy and Betsy Reed (eds.). *Homo Economics: Capitalism, Community, and Lesbian and Gay Life.* New York: Routledge, 1997.

Goellnicht, Donald. "Passing as Autobiography: James Weldon Johnson's 'The Autobiography of an Ex-Colored Man.'" *African American Review.* 30 (1996): 51. Accessed April 6, 2008. http://www.thefreelibrary.com/Passing+as+autobiography%3a+James +Weldon+Johnson's+'The+Autobiography ... -a018372101.

González Pérez, C.O. *Travestidos al Desnudo: Homosexualidad, Identidades y Luchas Territoriales en Colima, México.* México, DF: Miguel Angel Porrúa, 2003.

González Roldán, D.J. "Van Autoridades Contra Travestis de Matamoros." *El siglo de Torreón.* July 9, 2006. Accessed November 7, 2008. http://www.elsiglodetorreon.com. mx/noticia/224051.van-autoridades-contra-travestis-de-matamoros.html.

Grassmann, Philip. "Migrantenkinder gegen Schwule: Homophobes Berlin." *Süddeutsche Zeitung.* September 26, 2007. Accessed February 2, 2010. http://www.sueddeutsche.de/ panorama/migrantenkinder-gegen-schwule-homophobes-berlin-1.335341.

Green, Jamison. *Becoming a Visible Man.* Nashville: Vanderbilt UP, 2004.

Grewal, Inderpal and Caren Kaplan. "Global Identities: Theorizing Transnational Studies of Sexuality." *GLQ* 7 (2001): 663–79.

Griggs, Claudine. *Passage Through Trinidad: Journal of a Surgical Sex Change.* Jefferson, NC: McFarland, 1996.

Grossberg, Lawrence. *We Gotta Get Out of This Place: Popular Conservatism and Postmodern Culture.* New York: Routledge, 1992.

Grosz, Elizabeth. *Architecture from the Outside: Essays on Virtual and Real Space.* Cambridge: MIT Press, 2001.

Grube, John. "'No More Shit': The Struggle for Democratic Gay Space in Toronto." In *Queers in Space: Communities, Public Spaces, and Sites of Resistance,* edited by Anne-Marie Bouthillette, Yolanda Retter, and Gordon Brent Ingram, 127–46. Seattle: Bay Press, 1997.

GSW. *WohnmarktReport 2010.* Accessed 1 April, 2010. http://www.businesslocationcenter. de/imperia/md/content/blc/leben/wmr_dt.pdf.

Gunther, Mark. "'Trans'-forming Corporate America." *Fortune*, August 27, 2007. Accessed June 12, 2008. http://money.cnn.com/2007/07/23/magazines/fortune/transgender_ workplace.fortune/index.htm.

Habermas, Jurgen. *The Theory of Communicative Action*. Boston: Beacon, 1984.

——. *Between Facts and Norms: Contributions to a Discourse Theory of Law and Democracy*. Trans. William Rehg. Cambridge: MIT Press, 1996.

Haiken, Elizabeth. *Venus Envy: A History of Cosmetic Surgery*. Baltimore: Johns Hopkins UP, 1997.

Halberstam, Judith. *Female Masculinity*. Durham and London: Duke UP, 1998.

——. *In A Queer Time and Place: Transgender Bodies, Subcultural Lives*. New York: New York UP, 2005.

Hall, Radclyffe. *The Well of Loneliness*. London: Sundial Press, 1928.

Hall, Stuart. "Encoding/Decoding." In *Culture, Media, Language: Working Papers in Cultural Studies, 1972–79*, edited by S. Hall et al., 128–38. Hutchinson: Centre for Contemporary Cultural Studies, Birmingham, 1980.

——. "Who Needs Identity?" In *Questions of Cultural Identity*, edited by Stuart Hall and Paul Du Gay, 1–17. London: Sage Publications, 1996.

——. "Cultural Identity and Diaspora." In *Theorizing Diaspora*, edited by Jana Evans Braziel and Anita Mannur. Malden, MA: Blackwell, 2003.

Hanhardt, Christina B. "Butterflies, Whistles, and Fists: Gay Safe Streets Patrols and the New Gay Ghetto, 1976–81." *Radical History Review* 100 (2008): 61–85.

Haritaworn, Jin. "Loyal Repetitions of the Nation: Gay Assimilation and the 'War on Terror.'" *DarkMatter* 3 (2008): Special Issue on Postcolonial Sexuality. Accessed January 12, 2008. http://www.darkmatter101.org.

——. "Wounded Subjects: Sexual Exceptionalism and the Moral Panic on 'Migrant Homophobia' in Germany." In *Decolonising European Sociology*, edited by M. Boatcá, S. Costa, and E. Gutiérrez Rodríguez, 135–52. Aldershot: Ashgate, 2010.

——. "Queer Injuries: The Cultural Politics of 'Hate Crime' in Germany." *Social Justice*, Special Issue on Criminalization and Sexuality (forthcoming).

Haritaworn, Jin and Petzen, Jennifer. "Invented Traditions, New Intimate Publics: Tracing the German 'Muslim Homophobia' Discourse" (working title). In *Islam in its International Context: Comparative Perspectives*, edited by Chris Flood and Stephen Hutchings. Cambridge: Cambridge Scholars Press (forthcoming).

Hausman, Bernice. *Changing Sex: Transsexualism, Technology, and the Idea of Gender*. Durham: Duke UP, 1995.

Hayward, Eva. "More Lessons from a Starfish: Prefixial Flesh and Transspeciated Selves." *Women's Studies Quarterly* 36 (2008): 64–85.

——. "FingeryEyes: Impressions of Cup Corals." *Cultural Anthropology* 7 (2010): 576–98.

Hekma, Gert. "A Female Soul in a Male Body: Sexual Inversion as Gender Inversion in Nineteenth-Century Sexology." In *Third Sex, Third Gender: Beyond Sexual Dimorphism in Culture and History*, edited by Gilbert Herdt, 213–40. New York: Zone Books, 1994.

Herman, Joanne. "Transgender? You're Fired!" *The Advocate*, July 29, 2006. Accessed July 1, 2008. http://www.advocate.com/exclusive_detail_ektid34806.asp.

Herzog, L.A. *Where North Meets South: Cities, Space, and Politics on the U.S.-Mexico Border*. Austin, TX: University of Texas Press, 1990.

Heyes, Cressida J. *Self-Transformations: Foucault, Ethics, and Normalized Bodies*. New York: Oxford UP, 2007.

Hirschfeld, Magnus. *Transvestites: The Erotic Drive to Cross-dress*. Trans. Michael Lombardi-Nash. New York: Prometheus Books, 1991.

Holm, Andrej. "Hohe Mieten Machen Kreuzberg Pleite." *Gentrificationblog*. Accessed April 1, 2010. http://gentrificationblog.wordpress.com/2010/03/05/berlin-hohe-mieten-machen-kreuzberg-pleite/.

Homosexuals Intransigent! *Homosexual Renaissance*. Publication of Homosexuals Intransigent! of the City University of New York. Charles Deering McCormick Library of Special Collections, Northwestern University Library, 1969.

hooks, bell. *Yearning: Race, Gender and Cultural Politics*. Boston: South End Press, 1990.

Howard, John. *Men Like That: A Southern Queer History*. Chicago: University of Chicago Press, 1999.

Howe, Cymene, Susanna Zaraysky, and Lois Lorentzen. "Transgender Sex Workers and Sexual Transmigration Between Guadalajara and San Francisco." *Latin American Perspectives* 35 (2008): 31–50.

INCITE! *Color of Violence: The INCITE! Anthology*. Cambridge, MA: South End Press, 2006.

Incognito. *Incognito Guide*. University of Chicago Special Collections, 1972.

Indymedia. "Homophober Angriff in Kreuzberg." June 8, 2008. Accessed August 8, 2008. http://de.indymedia.org/2008/06/219458.shtml.

Ingram, Gordon Brent. "Marginality and the Landscapes of Erotic Alien(n)ations." In *Queers in Space: Communities, Public Spaces, and Sites of Resistance*, edited by Anne-Marie Bouthillette, Yolanda Retter, and Gordon Brent Ingram, 27–54. Seattle: Bay Press, 1997.

"International Guild Guide." Washington, DC: Guild Press. University of Chicago Special Collections, 1965–1976.

"International Lesbian/Gay Freedom Day Parade and Celebration" Program. San Francisco: Charles Deering McCormick Library of Special Collections, Northwestern University Library, 1985.

Irving, Dan. "Normalized Transgressions: Legitimizing the Transexual Body as Productive." *Radical History Review* 100 (2008): 38–59.

Jeffreys, Sheila. *Unpacking Queer Politics: A Lesbian Feminist Perspective*. Cambridge: Polity Press, 2002.

Jiménez Vega, J. "La Familia, Fundamento de las Transformaciones en México." *La Voz de la Frontera*, July 22, 2002.

Johnson, David K. *The Lavender Scare: The Cold War Persecution of Gays and Lesbians in the Federal Government*. Chicago: University of Chicago Press, 2004.

Johnson, James W. *Autobiography of An Ex-Colored Man*. In *Three Negro Classics*, edited by John Hope Franklin. New York: Avon Books, [1912]/1965.

——. *Along This Way: The Autobiography of James Weldon Johnson*. New York: Penguin Books, [1933]/2008.

Jorgensen, Christine. *A Personal Autobiography*. New York: Eriksson, 1967.

Katchadourian, Nina. *Mended Spiderweb*. Accessed August 5, 2010. http://www.ninakatchadourian.com/uninvitedcollaborations/spiderwebs.php.

Kawash, Samira. "The Homeless Body." *Public Culture* 10 (1998): 319–39.

Kent, Kim. "EOS-Guide 70/71." Copenhagen. University of Chicago Special Collections, 1970–71.

Kilgallen, Dorothy. "Voice of Broadway." *Weirton Daily Times*. April 1, 1955.

Kirby, Kathleen. "Re: Mapping Subjectivity: Cartographic Vision and the Limits of Politics." In *Body Space*, edited by Nancy Duncan, 44–45. New York: Routledge, 1996.

Kirk, Sheila. *Feminizing Hormonal Therapy for the Transgendered*. Pittsburgh, PA: Together Lifeworks, 1999.

Klaus, Veronica. http://www.veronicaklaus.com/. Accessed January 15, 2009.

Kostelanetz, Richard. *Politics in the African-American Novel: James Weldon Johnson, W.E.B. Du Bois, Richard Wright, and Ralph Ellison*. New York: Greenwood Press, 1991.

Krenzer, K.L. and M.R. Dana. "Effect of Androgen Deficiency on the Human Meibomian Gland and Ocular Surface." *Journal of Clinical Endocrinology and Metabolism* 85 (2000): 4874–82.

Kuntsman, Adi. *Figurations of Violence and Belonging: Queer Immigrants in Cyberspace and Beyond*. Oxford: Peter Lang, 2009.

Lacan, Jacques. *Ecrits: A Selection.* Trans. A. Sheridan. New York: Routledge, 2001.

La Fountain-Stokes, Lawrence. "Trans/bolero/drag/migration: Music, Cultural Translation, and Diasporic Puerto Rican Theatricalities." *Women's Studies Quarterly* 36 (2008): 190–209.

Lamble, S. "Retelling Racialized Violence, Remaking White Innocence: The Politics of Interlocking Oppressions in Transgender Day of Remembrance." *Sexuality Research and Social Policy: Journal of NSRC* 5 (2008): 24–42.

Lavie, Smadar and Ted Swedenburg (eds.). *Displacement, Diaspora, and Geographies of Identity.* Durham, NC: Duke UP, 1996.

Le Corbusier. *The Decorative Art of Today.* Trans. James I. Dunnett. London: Architectural Press, 1987.

Lefebvre, Henri. *The Production of Space.* Cambridge: Basil Blackwell, 1991.

Lentin, Alana and Gavan Titley. "Crisis of Multiculturalism." *European Journal of Cultural Studies.* Special Issue: Questioning the European (forthcoming).

Lesbian Connection. Gerber/Hart Library, 1974–.

Lewis, V. "Of Lady-Killers and 'Men Dressed as Women': Soap Opera, Scapegoats and the Mexico City Police Department." *PORTAL Journal of Multidisciplinary International Studies* 5 (2008). Accessed October 12, 2008. http://epress.lib.uts.edu.au/ojs/index.php/portal/article/view/480.

Lim, Song Hwee. "Is the Trans- in Transnational the Trans- in Transgender?" *New Cinemas: Journal of Contemporary Film.* 5 (2007): 39–52.

Lind, Earl. *Autobiography of an Androgyne.* New York: Medico-Legal Journal, 1918.

Lingis, Alphonso. *Dangerous Emotions.* Berkeley: University of California Press, 2000.

Linklater, Andrew. "Cosmopolitan Citizenship." *Citizenship Studies* 2 (1998): 23–41.

Lipsitz, George. *The Possessive Investment in Whiteness: How White People Profit from Identity Politics.* Philadelphia: Temple UP, 1998.

Lomas, Clara. "Transborder Discourse: The Articulation of Gender in the Borderlands in the Early Twentieth Century." *Frontiers* 24 (2003): 51–74.

Long, Scott. "The Loneliness of Camp." In *Camp Grounds: Style and Homosexuality,* edited by David Bergman, 78–91. Amherst: University of Massachusetts Press, 1993.

Love, Heather. "Compulsory Happiness and Queer Existence." *New Formations: A Journal of Culture/Theory/Politics* 63 (2008): 52–64.

Luibhéid, Eithne. *Queer/Migration: An Unruly Body of Scholarship.* GLQ 14 (2008): 169–90.

Luibheid, Eithne and Lionel Cantu (eds.). *Queer Migrations: Sexuality, U.S. Citizenship, and Border Crossings.* Minneapolis: University of Minnesota Press, 2005.

Luig, Judith. "Ein Tag als Arag King." *Tageszeitung,* November 6, 2008. Accessed August 20, 2008. http://www.taz.de/1/leben/alltag/artikel/1/und-dann-werden-wir-behaart/?src=SE&cHash=71964b40bc.

Lupton, Ellen and J. Abbott Miller. *The Bathroom and the Kitchen and the Aesthetics of Waste: A Process of Elimination.* Cambridge: MIT Visual Arts Center, 1992.

Lyotard, Jean-François. *Libidinal Economy.* Trans. Ian Hamilton Grant. Bloomington: Indiana UP, 1993.

MacDougall, Carla. "Competing Visions of a Cold War Capital: Urban Renewal and Popular Protest in Berlin, 1963–89." PhD diss., Rutgers University (forthcoming).

Manalansan, Martin F. IV. "Race,Violence, and Neoliberal Spatial Politics in the Global City." *Social Text* 23 (2005): 141–55.

——. "Queer Intersections: Sexuality and Gender in Migration Studies." *International Migration Review* 40 (2006): 224–49.

——. "Queer Love in the Time of War and Shopping." In *A Companion to Lesbian, Gay, Bisexual, Transgender and Queer Studies,* edited by George E. Haggerty and Molly McGarry. Oxford: Blackwell, 2007.

"MAN SCAPE." *Surface* 75 (2009): 46–47.

Martín-Barbero, J. *De los Medios a las Mediaciones.* Barcelona: G. Pili, 1987.

Martínez, O.J. *Border People: Life and Society in the U.S.-Mexico Borderlands.* Tucson: University of Arizona Press, 1994.

Martino, Mario. *Emergence: A Transsexual Autobiography.* London: Crown, 1977.

Marx, Karl. *Das Kapital: Kritik der Politischen Ekonomie.* Hamburg: Meissner, 1867.

———. *On Colonialism and Modernization*, edited by S. Avineri. New York: Doubleday, 1968.

Marx, K. and F. Engels, *Die Deutsche Ideologie.* London: Lawrence & Wishart, [1846]/1965.

Massad, Joseph. *Desiring Arabs.* Chicago: Chicago UP, 2007.

Matzner, Andrew (ed.). *O Au No Keia: Voices from Hawaii's Mahu and Transgender Communities.* Philadelphia: Xlibris, 2001.

Méndez, R.M. "Solo Quiero Limpiar la Ciudad." *Siete Días: Semanario Regional de Baja California.* December 13, 2002. Accessed April 13, 2008. http://websietedias.tripod.com/Ed304/index.htm.

Meyerowitz, Joanne. "Sex Change and the Popular Press: Historical Notes on Transsexuality in the United States, 1930–1955." *GLQ: A Journal of Lesbian and Gay Studies* 4 (1998): 159–87.

———. *How Sex Changed: A History of Transsexuality in the United States.* Cambridge, MA: Harvard UP, 2002.

Millán Dena, R. "Análisis Normativo del Ambito Local en Materia de No Discriminación." Dirección General Adjunta de Estudios, Legislación y Políticas Públicas, Documento de Trabajo No. A-9-2005 CONAPRED.

Millot, Catherine. *Horsexe: An Essay on Transsexuality.* Trans. Kenneth Hylton. Brooklyn: Autonomedia, 1990.

Mitchell, Katharyne. "Transnational Discourse: Bringing Geography Back in." *Antipode* 29 (1997): 101–14.

Mohanram, Radhika. *Black Body: Woman, Colonialism, and Space.* Minnesota: University of Minnesota Press, 1999.

Mohanty, Chandra. "Defining Genealogies: Feminist Reflections on Being South Asian in North America." In *Our Feet Walk the Sky*, edited by Women of South Asian Descent Collective, 51–58. San Francisco: Aunt Lute Books, 1993.

Moloeznik, M.P. "The Challenges to Mexico in Times of Political Change." *Crime, Law, and Social Change* 40 (2003): 7–20.

Montejano, David. *Anglos and Mexicans in the Making of Texas.* Austin: University of Texas Press, 1987.

Moore, E., A. Wisniewski, and A. Dobs. "Endocrine Treatment of Transsexual People: A Review of Treatment Regimens, Outcomes, and Adverse Effects." *Journal of Clinical Endocrinology and Metabolism* 88 (2003): 3467–73.

Namaste, Ki. "Tragic Misreadings: Queer Theory's Erasure of Transgender Subjectivity." In *Queer Studies: A Lesbian, Gay, Bisexual, and Transgender Anthology*, edited by B. Beemyn and M. Eliason, 183–203. New York: New York UP, 1996.

———. *Invisible Lives: The Erasure of Transsexual and Transgendered People.* Chicago: University of Chicago Press, 2000.

———. *Sex Change, Social Change: Reflections on Identity, Institutions, and Imperialism.* Toronto: Women's Press, 2005.

———. "Undoing Theory: The 'Transgender Question' and the Epistemic Violence of Anglo-American Feminist Theory." *Hypatia* 24 (2009): 11–32.

Nealon, Christopher. *Foundlings: Lesbian and Gay Historical Emotion Before Stonewall.* Durham: Duke UP, 2001.

Nesvig, Martin. "The Complicated Terrain of Latin American Homosexuality." *Hispanic American Historical Review* 81 (2001): 724–26.

Niemi-Kiesiläinen J., P. Honkatukia, and M. Ruuskanen. "Legal Texts as Discourses." In *Exploiting the Limits of Law*, edited by A. Gunnarsson et al., 69–87. Burlington, VT: Ashgate, 2007.

Nnaemeka, Obioma. "Nego-Feminism: Theorizing, Practicing, and Pruning Africa's Way." *Signs* 29 (2004): 357–86.

Núñez Noriega, G. *Sexo Entre Varones. Poder y Resistencia en el Campo Sexual,* 2nd ed. México: Universidad Nacional Autónoma de México, M.A. Porrúa, 1999.

Ochoa, Marcia. "Perverse Citizenship: Divas, Marginality, and Participation in *Loca*-lization." *Women's Studies Quarterly* 36 (2008): 146–69.

Orozco Gómez, G. (coord.). *Miradas Latinoamericanas a la Televisión.* México, DF: Universidad Iberoamericana, 1996.

Páez Cárdenas, J. "Juan Vargas: las Minorías no Gobiernan." *El mexicano,* November 29, 2002.

Pallasmaa, Juhani. *The Eyes of the Skin: Architecture and the Senses.* West Sussex: John Wiley & Sons, 2005.

Papastergiadis, Nikos. *The Turbulence of Migration: Globalization, Deterritorialization and Hybridity.* Malden, MA: Polity Press, 2000.

Patton, Cindy and Benigno Sanchez-Eppler (eds.). *Queer Diasporas.* Durham: Duke UP, 2000.

Pérez, Emma. *The Decolonial Imaginary: Writing Chicanas into History.* Bloomington: Indiana UP, 1999.

——. "Queering the Borderlands: The Challenges of Excavating the Invisible and Unheard." *Frontiers* 24 (2003).

Pérez de la Madrid, A. "Cultura Política y Democracia en México." *Así legal: Asistencia legal por los derechos humanos.* August 1, 2008. Accessed July 10, 2009. http://asilegal.org/index.php?option=com_content& task = view& id = 156& Itemid = 2.

Petzen, Jennifer. "Home or Homelike? Turkish Queers Manage Space in Berlin." *Space and Culture* 7 (2005): 20–32.

——. "Gender Politics in the New Europe: 'Civilizing' Muslim Sexualities." PhD thesis, University of Washington, 2008.

Phillips, Richard. *Mapping Men and Empire: A Geography of Adventure.* London: Routledge, 1997.

Philo, C. "De-limiting Human Geography: New Social and Cultural Perspectives." In *New Words, New Worlds: Reconceptualising Social and Cultural Geography,* edited by Chris Philo, 14–27. Lampeter: Social and Cultural Geography Study Group, 1991.

Pisiak, Roxanna. "Irony and Subversion in James Weldon Johnson's *The Autobiography of An Ex-Colored Man.*" In *Critical Essays on James Weldon Johnson,* edited by Kenneth Price and Lawrence Oliver. New York: G.K. Hall, 1997.

Pollock, Griselda. "Maman! Invoking the m/Other in the Web of the Spider." In *Louise Bourgeois Maman,* edited by Marika Wachtmeister, 65–97. Stockholm: Atlantis, 2005.

Potts, Alex. "Louise Bourgeois: Sculptural Confrontations." *Oxford Art Journal* 22 (1999): 39–53.

Price, J.A. (ed.). "Tecate: An Industrial Town on the Mexican Border." Los Angeles: University of California, Los Angeles Ethnographic Field School, 1967.

Prosser, Jay. *Second Skins: the Body Narratives of Transsexuality.* New York: Columbia University Press, 1998.

——. "Exceptional Locations: Transsexual Travelogues." In *Reclaiming Genders: Transsexual Grammars at the Fin de Siècle,* edited by K. More and S. Whittle, 83–114. New York: Continuum International Publishing Group, 1999.

——. "Skin Memories." *Thinking Through the Skin,* edited by S. Ahmed and J. Stacey, 52–68. London and New York: Routledge. 2001.

Puar, Jasbir. *Queer Tourism: Geographies of Globalization.* North Carolina: Duke UP, 2002.

——. *Terrorist Assemblages: Homonationalism in Queer Times.* Durham: Duke UP, 2007.

Quammen, David. "The Face of A Spider." In *The Flight of the Iguana.* New York: Touchstone, 1988. Accessed August 9, 2010. http://www.stanford.edu/~jonahw/AOE-SM06/FaceSpider.html.

Ramos García, J.M. "Seguridad Pública Local: Hacia Nuevos Enfoques de Gestión." In *Elsa Inseguridad, Riesgo y Vulnerabilidad*, edited by Patiño Tovar and Jaime Castillo Palma, 223–42. Red de Investigación Urbana: Universidad Autónoma de Puebla, 2005.

Ramos García, J.M. and V. Sánchez Munguía. "Government and Civil Society." In *Tecate, Baja California: Realities and Challenges in a Mexican Border Community*, edited by P. Ganster et al., 47–63. San Diego: San Diego State UP, 2002.

Raven, Sailor. "Winter (Transition)." In *From the Inside out: Radical Gender Transformation, FTM and beyond*, edited by Morty Diamond, 50–52. San Francisco: Manic D Press, 2004.

Raymond, Janice. *The Transsexual Empire: The Making of the She-Male*. New York: Teacher's College Press: 1994.

Reed, Christopher. "Imminent Domain: Queer Space in the Built Environment." *Art Journal* 55.4 (1996): 64–70.

Reilly, Maura. "The Drive to Describe: An Interview with Catherine Opie." *Art Journal* 60.2 (2001): 82–95.

Rivera, Sylvia. "Queens in Exile: The Forgotten Ones." In *Genderqueer*, edited by J. Nestle, C. Howell, and R. Wilchins, 67–85. Los Angeles: Allyson Books, 2002.

Rodriguez, Juana Maria. *Queer Latinidad: Identity Practices, Discursive Spaces*. New York: New York UP, 2003.

Roen, Katrina. "Transgender Theory and Embodiment: The Risk of Racial Marginalization." In *The Transgender Studies Reader*, edited by Susan Stryker and Stephen Whittle, 656–65. New York: Routledge, 2006.

Romesburg, Don. "Ray Bourbon: A Queer Sort of Biography." MA thesis, University of Colorado (Boulder), 2000.

——. "Camping out with Ray Bourbon: Female Impersonators and Queer Dread of Wide-Open Spaces." *Reconstruction* (2007). Accessed June 15, 2010. http://reconstruction.eserver.org/072/romesburg.shtml.

——. "The Tightrope of Normalcy: Homosexuality, Developmental Citizenship, and American Adolescence." *Historical Sociology* 21 (2008): 417–42.

Rose, Nicolas. *Governing the Soul*. London: Free Association of Books, 1989.

Ross, Marlon. *Manning the Race: Reforming Black Men in the Jim Crow Era*. New York: New York UP, 2004.

Roth, Claudia. "Liebe besucherinnen und besucher des 'Drag Festival' Berlin." *Drag Festival Berlin*, 2008.

Rottenberg, Catherine. "Race and Ethnicity in the Autobiography of An Ex-Colored Man and the Rise of David Levinsky: The Performative Difference." *MELUS* (2004). Accessed April 6, 2008. www.questia.com.

Ruby, Ilka and Andreas Ruby. "Medicine or Cosmetics on the Transformation of the Relationship Between Architecture and Hygiene." In *Bathroom Uunplugged: Architecture and Intimacy*, edited by D. Hebel and J. Stollman, 119–27. Boston: Birkhauser, 2004.

Ruiz, Ramón Eduardo. *On the Rim of Mexico: Encounters of the Rich and Poor*. Boulder: Westview Press, 1998.

Said, Edward. *Orientalism*. London: Penguin, 1995.

Salessi, J. *Médicos Maleantes y Maricas. Higiene, Criminología y Homosexualidad en la Construcción de la Nación Argentina (Buenos Aires, 1871–1914)*. 2nd ed. Argentina: B. Viterbo Editora, 2000.

Salvaggio, Ruth. *The Sounds of Feminist Theory*. New York: SUNY Press, 1999.

Sanders, Joel (ed.) *STUD: Architectures of Masculinity*. Princeton: Princeton Architectural Press, 1998.

Sandoval, Chela. *Methodology of the Oppressed*. Minneapolis: University of Minnesota Press, 2000.

Sears, Clare. "All That Glitters: Trans-ing California's Gold Rush Migrations." *GLQ* 14 (2008): 383–402.

Sedgwick, Eve Kosofsky. *Epistemology of the Closet*. Berkeley: University of California Press, 1990.

Seidman, Steven. "Introduction." In *Queer Theory/Sociology*, edited by Steven Seidman, 1–2. London: Blackwell, 1996.

Sender, Katherine. *Business, Not Politics: The Making of the Gay Market*. New York: Columbia UP, 2004.

Serano, Julia. *Whipping Girl: A Transsexual Woman on Sexism and the Scapegoating of Femininity*. Emeryville: Seal Press, 2007.

Shadmi, Erella. "Between Resistance and Compliance, Feminism and Nationalism: Women in Black in Israel." *Women's Studies International Forum* 23 (2000): 23–34.

Sharma, Nandita. "Canadian Nationalism and the Making of a Global Apartheid." *Women and Environments International Magazine* 68–69 (2005): 9–12.

Sheehy, John. "The Mirror and the Veil: The Passing Novel and the Quest for American Racial Identity." *African American Review* 33 (1999): 56 pars. Accessed April 6, 2008. www.questia.com.

Shohat, Ella. "Area Studies, Gender Studies, and the Cartographies of Knowledge." *Social Text* 72.20 (2002): 67–78.

Silverman, Victor and Susan Stryker. *Screaming Queens: The Riot at Crompton's Cafeteria*. 2005. 57 minutes.

Simon, Bernd. "Einstellungen zur Homosexualität: Ausprägungen und Psychologische Korrelate bei Jugendlichen Mit und Ohne Migrationshintergrund (Ehemalige UdSSR und Türkei)." *Zeitschrift für Entwicklungspsychologie und Pädagogische Psychologie* 40 (2008): 87–99.

Simpson, Mark. *Trafficking Subjects: The Politics of Mobility in Nineteenth-Century America*. Minneapolis: University of Minnesota Press, 2005.

Smith, D.M. *Moral Geographies: Ethics in a World of Difference*. Edinburgh: Edinburgh UP, 2000.

Smith, Neil, Jens Sambale, and Volker Eick. "Neil Smith: Gentrification in Berlin and the Revanchist State." *Policing Crowds: Privatizing Security*. 2007. Accessed April 1, 2010. http://www.policing-crowds.org/news/article/neil-smith-gentrification-in-berlin-and-the-revanchist-state.html.

Smith, Valerie. "Privilege and Evasion in *The Autobiography of An Ex-Colored Man*." In *Critical Essays on James Weldon Johnson*, edited by Kenneth Price and Lawrence Oliver. New York: G.K. Hall, 1997.

Snorton, C. Riley. "A New Hope: The Psychic Life of Passing." *Hypatia* 24 (2009): 77–92.

Sobchack, Vivian. "Simple Grounds: At Home in Experience." In *Post Phenomonology: A Critical Companion to Inde*, edited by Evan Selinger, 13–20. New York: SUNY Press, 2006.

Somerville, Siobhan. *Queering the Color Line: Race and the Invention of Homosexuality in American Culture*. Durham, NC: Duke UP, 2000.

Spade, Dean. "Mutilating Gender." In *The Transgender Studies Reader*, edited by Susan Stryker and Stephen Whittle, 315–32. New York: Routledge, 2006.

——. Remarks at Transecting the Academy Conference, Race and Ethnic Studies Panel. *Make*. Accessed January 7, 2008. http://www.makezine.org/transecting.html.

——. Comments in talk given in panel "Bodies of Law." A Symposium Honoring the Contributions of Professor Judith Butler to the Scholarship and Practice of Gender and Sexuality Law. Columbia School of Law. March 5, 2010. Accessed August 11, 2010. http://media.law.columbia.edu/CGSL/butlersymposium100305pt1flv.html.

Spartacus. Gerber/Hart Library, 1975.

SPD/Die Linke. *Initiative Berlin tritt ein für Selbstbestimmung und Akzeptanz sexueller Vielfalt*. Motion of the Faction of the Social Democrats and the Left Party in the Berlin Parliament, March 1, 2009.

S.S. *Lancastria*. List of United States Citizens from Liverpool, England to Boston, MA. November 29, 1936. Accessed July 21, 2009. www.ancestry.com.

State of Texas v. Ray Bourbon. 8067 Tex. 35d. 1971.

Stehle, Maria. "Narrating the Ghetto, Narrating Europe: From Berlin, Kreuzberg to the *Banlieues* in Paris." *Westminster Papers in Communication and Culture* 3 (2006): 48–70.

Stepto, Robert. *From behind the Veil: A Study of Afro-American Narrative.* Urbana: University of Illinois Press, 1991.

——. "Lost in a Quest: James Weldon Johnson's *The Autobiography of An Ex-Colored Man.*" In *Critical Essays on James Weldon Johnson,* edited by Kenneth Price and Lawrence Oliver. New York: G.K. Hal, 1997.

Stone, Sandy. "The Empire Strikes Back: A Posttranssexual Manifesto." In *The Transgender Studies Reader,* edited by Susan Stryker and Stephen Whittle, 221–35. New York: Routledge, 2006.

Strong, Lester. "L.A. and 'Lily Law': A Talk with David Hanna." *Journal of Gay, Lesbian, and Bisexual Identity* 4 (1999): 179–90.

Stryker, Susan. "Christine Jorgensen's Atom Bomb: Transsexuality and the Emergence of Postmodernity." In *Playing Dolly: Technocultural Formations, Fantasies and Fictions of Assisted Reproduction,* edited by E. Ann Kaplan and Susan Squier, 157–71. New Brunswick: Rutgers UP, 1999.

——. "(De)Subjugated Knowledges: An Introduction to Transgender Studies." In *The Transgender Studies Reader,* edited Susan Stryker and Stephen Whittle, 1–17. New York: Routledge. 2006.

——. "Dungeon Intimacies: The Poetics of Transsexual Sadomasochism." *Parallax* 14 (2008): 36–47.

——. "We Who Are Sexy: Christine Jorgensen's Transsexual Whiteness in the Postcolonial Philippines." *Social Semiotics* 19 (2009): 79–91.

Stryker, Susan, Paisley Currah, and Lisa Jean Moore. "Introduction: Trans-, Trans, or Transgender?" *Women's Studies Quarterly* 36 (2008): 11–22.

Sullivan, Ed. "Little Old New York." *Morning Herald,* March 5, 1946.

Sullivan, Lou. "Transvestite Answers a Feminist." In *The Transgender Studies Reader,* edited by Susan Stryker and Stephen Whittle, 159–64. New York: Routledge, [1973] 2006.

Sullivan, Louis H. "The Tall Office Building Artistically Considered." *Lippincott's Magazine* (1896): pages unknown.

Sullivan, Nikki. *A Critical Introduction to Queer Theory.* New York: New York UP, 2003.

Summers, Martin. *Manliness and Its Discontents: The Black Middle Class and the Transformation of Masculinity, 1900–1930.* Chapel Hill: University of North Carolina Press, 2004.

Szasz, I. "Sins, Abnormalities, and Rights: Gender and Sexuality in Mexican Penal Codes." In *Decoding Gender: Law and Practice in Contemporary Mexico,* edited by Helga Baitenmann, Victoria Chenaut, and Ann Varley, 59–74. New York: Rutgers UP, 2007.

Tattelman, Ira. "The Meaning at the Wall: Tracing the Gay Bathhouse." In *Queers in Space: Communities, Public Spaces, and Sites of Resistance,* edited by Anne-Marie Bouthillette, Yolanda Retter, and Gordon Brent Ingram, 391–406. Seattle: Bay Press, 1997.

Texas Department of Health—Bureau of Vital Statistics. Ray Bourbon Certificate of Death. July 29, 1971. Howard County Court.

Teyssot, Georges. "Cleanliness Takes Command." In *Bathroom Unplugged: Architecture and Intimacy,* edited by D. Hebel and J. Stollman, 74–104. Boston: Birkhauser, 2004.

Thaemlitz, Terre. "Transportation." In *Nobody Passes: Rejecting the Rules of Gender and Conformity,* edited by Matt Bernstein Sycamore, 173–85. San Francisco: Seal Press, 2007.

Thilmann, Pia. "Nach dem Fest Gab es Schläge." *Drag Festival Berlin,* 2008.

Tomes, Nancy. "The Private Side of Public Health: Sanitary Science, Domestic Hygiene, and the Germ Theory: 1870–1900." In *Sickness and Health in America: Readings in the History of Medicine and Public Health,* edited by J. Leavitt and R. Numbers, 506–28. Madison: University of Wisconsin Press, 1997.

Tongson, Karen. "The Light that Never Goes out: Butch Intimacies and Sub-Urban Sociabilities in 'Lesser Los Angeles.'" In *A Companion to Lesbian, Gay, Bisexual,*

Transgender and Queer Studies, edited by George E. Haggerty and Molly McGarry, 355–76. Oxford: Blackwell, 2007.

TOPOS. *Sozialstruktur und Mietentwicklung im Erhaltungsgebiet Luisenstadt (SO 36)*. Berlin: Bezirksamt Friedrichshain-Kreuzberg, 2008.

Tschumi, Bernard. *Architecture and Disjunction*. Cambridge: MIT Press, 1996.

UK Government Equalities Office. *Gender Reassignment: A Guide for Employers*. London: Women and Equality Unit, 2005.

University College London. "Transgender Issues—Guidance Notes on Inclusive and Supportive Practice." Human Resources and Policy Procedure Manual, UCL Online. Accessed September 1, 2008. http://www.ucl.ac.uk/hr/docs/transguidance.php.

Usborne, David. "Gay LA." *Architectural Design* 43 (1973), quoted in Christopher Reed, "Imminent Domain: Queer Space in the Built Environment." *Art Journal* 55.4 (1996): 64–70.

Valentine, D. *Imagining Transgender: An Ethnography of a Category*. Durham: Duke UP, 2007.

Valverde, M. *Law's Dream of A Common Knowledge*. Princeton, NJ: Princeton UP, 2003.

Van, Marcus Rene. "Thoughts on Transcending Stone: The Tale of One Transgendered Man and His Journey to Find Sexuality in His New Skin." In *From the Inside out: Radical Gender Transformation, FTM and beyond*, edited by Morty Diamond, 53–55. San Francisco: Manic D Press, 2004.

Vanden, H. and G. Prevost. "Politics, Power, Institutions and Actors." In *The Politics of Latin America: The Power Game*, 175–235. New York: Oxford University UP, 2005.

Van Dijk, T. A. "The Discourse Knowledge Interface." In *Critical Discourse Analysis: Theory and Interdisciplinarity*, edited by G. Weiss and R. Wodak, 85–109. Houndsmills, UK: Palgrave-Macmillan, 2003.

Vector. San Francisco. Charles Deering McCormick Library of Special Collections, Northwestern University Library, 1964–75.

Vila, P. *Crossing Borders, Reinforcing Borders: Social Categories, Metaphors, and Narrative Identities on the U.S.-Mexico Frontier*. Austin: University of Texas Press, 2000a.

———. "La Teoría de la Frontera Versión Norteamericana: Una Crítica Desde la Etnografia." In *Fronteras, Naciones e Identidades*, edited by Alejandro Grimson, 99–120. *La Periferia Como Centro*, Buenos Aires: CICCUS/La Crujía, 2000b.

Wallace, Maurice. "'Are We Men?' Prince Hall, Martin Delany, and the Masculine Ideal in Black Freemasonry, 1775–1865." *American Literary History* 9 (1997): 396–424.

Walworth, Janis. "Managing Transsexual Transition in the Workplace." (2003) Accessed September 2, 2008. http://www.gendersanity.com/shrm.html.

———. "Gender Sanity Strategies for Managing Transition (Advice for Employers)." Accessed September 2, 2008. http://www.gendersanity.com/strategies.html.

Warner, Michael. "Publics and Counterpublics." *Public Culture* 14 (2002a): 49–90.

———. *Publics and Counterpublics*. New York: Zone Books, 2002b.

Warner, Michael and Lauren Berlant. "Sex in Public." *Critical Inquiry* 24 (1998): 547–66.

Washington, Booker T. *Up from Slavery*. In *Three Negro Classics*, edited by John Hope Franklin. New York: Avon Books, [1907]/1965.

Weber, M. "The Three Types of Legitimate Rule." *Berkeley Publications in Society and Institutions* 4 (1958): 1–11.

Weekly Observer. "Tucson: A Gay History (Part One)." June 17, 1987.

Weeks, J. *Sex, Politics, and Society: The Regulation of Sexuality since 1800*. London; New York: Longman, 1981.

Werther, Ralph. *Autobiography of an Androgyne*. New Brunswick, NJ: Rutgers University Press, [1918]/2008.

Wheels! Leather Archives & Museum, 1968–81.

Wigley, Mark. "Untitled: The Housing of Gender." In *Sexuality and Space*, edited by Beatriz Columina, 327–83. Princeton: Princeton Architectural Press, 1992.

——. *White Walls, Designer Dresses: The Fashioning of Modern Architecture.* Cambridge: MIT Press, 1995.

Wilchins, Riki. "Airport Insecurity?" *The Advocate.* June 25, 2003.

Willard, Avery. *Female Impersonation.* New York: Regiment, 1971.

Williamson, Skip. "Daddy Was a Lady." Accessed July 24, 2009. http://open.salon.com//blog/snappy_sam/2009/04/05/daddy_was_a_lady.

Winchell, Walter. "On Broadway." *Zanesville Signal,* July 21, 1943.

——. "Winchell Everywhere." *Anderson Daily Bulletin,* September 16, 1968.

Wittgenstein, Ludwig. *Philosophical Investigations.* Oxford: Blackwell, 2001.

Wright, Robert (Bob), and George (Chet) Forrest. Interview by author via telephone. July 28, 1999.

Yıldız, Yasemin. "Turkish Girls, Allah's Daughters, and the Contemporary German Subject: Itinerary of a Figure." *German Life and Letters* 62 (2009): 465–81.

Zoé. "We Break the Gender Binary Every Day at Breakfast." Interview with Shuki (Jerusalem Kings) from Israel, 20–22. *Drag Festival Berlin,* 2008a.

——. "Totally Mindblowing: Interview with 'Da Boyz' Drag-Kings from Poland." *Drag Festival Berlin,* 2008b.

INDEX